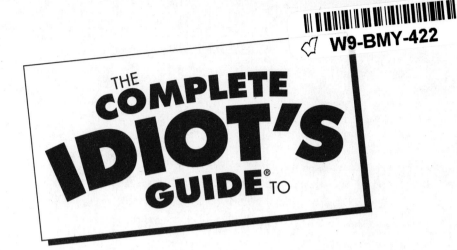

THE COMPLETE IDIOT'S GUIDE® TO

English Literature

by Jay Stevenson, Ph.D.

ALPHA

A member of Penguin Group (USA) Inc.

This book is gratefully dedicated to all my English teachers.

ALPHA BOOKS

Published by the Penguin Group

Penguin Group (USA) Inc., 375 Hudson Street, New York, New York 10014, USA

Penguin Group (Canada), 90 Eglinton Avenue East, Suite 700, Toronto, Ontario M4P 2Y3, Canada (a division of Pearson Penguin Canada Inc.)

Penguin Books Ltd., 80 Strand, London WC2R 0RL, England

Penguin Ireland, 25 St. Stephen's Green, Dublin 2, Ireland (a division of Penguin Books Ltd.)

Penguin Group (Australia), 250 Camberwell Road, Camberwell, Victoria 3124, Australia (a division of Pearson Australia Group Pty. Ltd.)

Penguin Books India Pvt. Ltd., 11 Community Centre, Panchsheel Park, New Delhi—110 017, India

Penguin Group (NZ), 67 Apollo Drive, Rosedale, North Shore, Auckland 1311, New Zealand (a division of Pearson New Zealand Ltd.)

Penguin Books (South Africa) (Pty.) Ltd., 24 Sturdee Avenue, Rosebank, Johannesburg 2196, South Africa

Penguin Books Ltd., Registered Offices: 80 Strand, London WC2R 0RL, England

Copyright © 2007 by Jay Stevenson, Ph.D.

International Standard Book Number: 978-1-59257-656-2
Library of Congress Catalog Card Number: 2006940262

08 07   8 7 6 5 4 3 2 1

Interpretation of the printing code: The rightmost number of the first series of numbers is the year of the book's printing; the rightmost number of the second series of numbers is the number of the book's printing. For example, a printing code of 07-1 shows that the first printing occurred in 2007.

Printed in the United States of America

Note: This publication contains the opinions and ideas of its author. It is intended to provide helpful and informative material on the subject matter covered. It is sold with the understanding that the author and publisher are not engaged in rendering professional services in the book. If the reader requires personal assistance or advice, a competent professional should be consulted.

The author and publisher specifically disclaim any responsibility for any liability, loss, or risk, personal or otherwise, which is incurred as a consequence, directly or indirectly, of the use and application of any of the contents of this book.

Most Alpha books are available at special quantity discounts for bulk purchases for sales promotions, premiums, fund-raising, or educational use. Special books, or book excerpts, can also be created to fit specific needs.

For details, write: Special Markets, Alpha Books, 375 Hudson Street, New York, NY 10014.

Publisher: *Marie Butler-Knight*
Editorial Director: *Mike Sanders*
Managing Editor: *Billy Fields*
Executive Editor: *Randy Ladenheim-Gil*
Production Editor: *Megan Douglass*
Copy Editor: *Krista Hansing*

Cartoonist: *Richard King*
Cover Designer: *Kurt Owens*
Book Designer: *Trina Wurst*
Indexer: *Heather McNeill*
Layout: *Brian Massey*
Proofreader: *John Etchison*

Contents at a Glance

Appendixes

Contents

Appendixes

Introduction

In its narrowest sense, English literature is the literature of England. As national literatures go, English literature is well developed and full of variety. It feeds into and draws on literary traditions from many other countries while reflecting the history and culture of the English people. For centuries now, the English have taken great interest in their literature and have been justifiably proud of it.

More broadly, English literature is literature written in the English language. Because England has been a powerful imperialist nation, and because English-speaking nations have many immigrants, many people all over the world write and speak the English language. While many speakers and writers of English from other countries have strong affinities with English people, many do not.

Of course, literature isn't simply all about political and national concerns. Yet increasingly, politics has come to play an important part in the ways literary scholars think about literature. The fact is, we're all different; we all have different backgrounds, orientations, and beliefs; and as a result, we all respond to literature in different ways.

This book deals, for the most part, with English literature in the narrower sense—the literature of England. This enables a historical and cultural focus that would be difficult to achieve in a book on English-language literature in general. The point is not that we should read and study English literature from England rather than from other places, but to begin to look at literature in its historical and cultural context.

In addition, this book provides guidance for understanding English literature as its own particular kind of expressive project—in understanding what makes it what it is and what makes it different from other kinds of writing.

What's in This Book

Here, in brief, is a map of the English lit terrain covered in this book:

Part 1, "Angles on English," takes on some of the most controversial and problematic topics in literary criticism, including historical and cultural context, the canon, genres, meaning and interpretation, and political criticism.

Part 2, "Fitting Forms," provides an overview of each of the main literary forms: poetry, drama, narrative fiction, and prose.

Part 3, "Way Back When," discusses the literature of ancient times through the eighteenth century, including the Old English, Middle English, Renaissance, and Augustan periods.

Part 4, "These Days," focuses on more recent literature from the nineteenth century to today, including the Romantic, Victorian, modern, and postmodern periods. There's also a concluding chapter on cultural studies.

In the back of the book, you'll find two appendixes. One is a glossary so you can look up any terms you're not sure of. The other starts off with a greatest hits list of English lit. Traditionally, most of these books have made up a big part of the core field of literary study. In addition, for good measure, there's a reading list of American literature and a list of literature written in English in other countries as well.

Extras

Sprinkled throughout are extra tidbits of information on English lit. Here's what to look for:

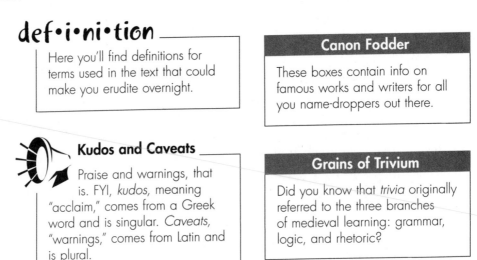

def•i•ni•tion
Here you'll find definitions for terms used in the text that could make you erudite overnight.

Canon Fodder
These boxes contain info on famous works and writers for all you name-droppers out there.

Kudos and Caveats
Praise and warnings, that is. FYI, *kudos*, meaning "acclaim," comes from a Greek word and is singular. *Caveats*, "warnings," comes from Latin and is plural.

Grains of Trivium
Did you know that *trivia* originally referred to the three branches of medieval learning: grammar, logic, and rhetoric?

Trademarks

All terms mentioned in this book that are known to be or are suspected of being trademarks or service marks have been appropriately capitalized. Alpha Books and Penguin Group (USA) Inc. cannot attest to the accuracy of this information. Use of a term in this book should not be regarded as affecting the validity of any trademark or service mark.

Part 1

Angles on English

The field of English literature has been undergoing important changes over the past several decades. Old priorities are getting thrown out as new perspectives make their way in. As a result, things are in a somewhat complicated state of flux. Today English lit is a field fraught with debate and disagreement. It isn't just that literary scholars love to fight, but that the issues are important and there's no clear, simple way to resolve them. It's all part of the challenge of English literature in today's academy. The best way to meet the challenge is to get involved.

Part 1 covers some of the major sticking points at issue in literature study today and helps you make sense of what it means to study English. I provide an overview of English through the ages, a chapter on history and culture, one on the literary canon, and others on genre, meaning, and political criticism.

*"If you read just **some** literature, we'd have something to talk about."*

Lit and Crit

In This Chapter

- Literature and criticism
- Why we read and study literature
- How attitudes toward literature have changed over time
- Why literature and the study of literature are problematic

English literature is a hugely broad subject. It's broad not only because it includes many kinds of writing produced over many centuries, but also because of the many ways and the many reasons people study it. While English scholars are all good at interpreting literature, they differ markedly in how and why they do what they do.

The dazzling variety of literary works and of the things people think about them poses challenges and opportunities at the same time. Because of English lit's enormous scope, the ability to read it allows people to encounter and interpret creativity, culture, language, history, ideology …. In fact, English lit is bigger than all of us. It's so broad and diverse that there isn't much consensus on what we should take away from it or what aspects of it to focus on.

All this diversity can make it tough for anyone trying to get a handle on what it's all about. This chapter provides a way in by covering some big-picture issues that make the field of English literature what it is. In the following pages, we look at a range of different attitudes toward literature that have developed over the centuries, as well as some of the things people look for in lit study today.

The It of Lit

Creativity with language is as old as the linguistic hills. Riddles, puns, and other kinds of word games; songs, stories, and role-playing speeches; and dialogue are apparently produced in every culture. Playful, imaginative use of language is a basic human activity. But the reach, scope, and consequence of literary language are far from basic.

Serious Play

Reading literature is a time-honored leisure activity, something people do in their spare time for mental recreation. It's baseball for your brain; it's dancing between your ears; it's stories and a game of charades by the fireside of civilization. It's hard to imagine life without literature in some form or another. For many people, literature expands their sense of reality and awakens them to new possibilities. It holds out the promise of communication across epochs and cultures, the promise of understanding, in a privileged and intimate way, what life might be like for other people in another time and place. It offers a glimpse—sometimes more—of how life's greatest personal and public challenges might be met and mastered.

Kudos and Caveats

Educators stress the fundamental importance and value of reading to very young children to promote language acquisition and literacy. Reading to them can also increase their attention spans, calm them, and help them bond with others. It also fosters the attitude that reading is an enjoyable, worthwhile activity.

But literature also imposes limits, reinforces boundaries, and defines and determines what can be possibly and properly imagined. It's the "good cop" of culture that almost always does what the "bad cop" of politics wants it to do. None of it is simply for everybody. If it were, we'd all be the same. Literature is too important and too compelling for us not to be concerned about what it might be doing to us and might not be doing for us. That's why we don't simply read it for fun. We also study it.

A Full Plate

Reading literature may often be a personal and private activity, but studying it is a thoroughly social process. You study as part of a community of scholars. This doesn't mean everyone can or should read and think about literature in the same way. It means everyone has the chance to develop a point of view. In the world of literary scholarship, having a point of view counts for quite a lot. A point of view is meaningful only in relation to other points of view. One of the things that makes a literary text especially worth reading is its power to elicit multiple interpretations. Being able to understand multiple perspectives on an issue and, at the same time, know where you stand in relation to it all is a clear sign of literacy at a high level.

If you've read thoughtfully and studied fully enough to develop a point of view, you've arrived at a productive place. You may change your mind, shift your focus, or deepen or broaden your perspective, but once you know what you're looking at and where you're coming from, that "baseball in your brain" becomes a team sport, and you're ready to take the field. More important, you may take your rightful place as a steward of a civilization you can live with. (Such a civilization may not yet exist, so you'd better get going!)

Canon Fodder

These days, many scholars, especially the "radical" and "progressive" ones, regard criticism as a means of working toward an optimal society, or *utopia*. They harbor, on principal, high hopes for the future of humanity and attempt to expose and refute whatever stands in the way of social, political, and cultural improvement.

(*Utopia*, Latin for "no place," is the title of an unusual work of fiction written in 1516 by Sir Thomas More [1478–1535]. The book, written in Latin, describes life on an imaginary island where the people are governed by perfect laws.)

You can have useful exchanges with others, whether in writing or in oral discussions. Scholarly exchanges provide a great opportunity to develop ideas and air differences in constructive ways. Much literary study is extremely process oriented. The point is not simply to gain knowledge, but to gain experience with the sharing and questioning of ideas.

The Worm Turns

English literature has been many different things to many different people at many different times. As a result, it's very difficult to define what it's all about once and for all. It has become what it is today through a long series of historical twists and turns that reflect a slow, ongoing process of cultural change. If literature sometimes looks crazy to you, that's probably a good sign. It means you're paying attention!

Shifting Focus

English lit has deep roots in ancient Greece, Rome, and the Middle East. It also has roots almost as deep in Scandinavia and the lands we now call Germany, Ireland, and Wales. Today it has wide branches spreading and blending with other literatures almost everywhere in the world.

> ### Grains of Trivium
>
> Today the term *English lit* usually refers to any literature written in the English language. Often, however, the term *literatures in English* is used to emphasize and include the growing body of work written in English by non-Anglo writers. Neither of these terms is normally used to refer to literature translated into English from other languages unless the author is Anglo. For example, the Latin poems of the Anglo scholar Alcuin (735–803) and the play *Waiting for Godot* (1955), originally written in French (*En Attendant Godot*, 1952) by Irish playwright Samuel Becket (1906–1989), who translated it himself, are generally considered "English" works. Convenient terms are often imprecise!

All along the course of its development, notions of what constitutes—or should constitute—a literary work have been subject to debate, as have notions about what literature people should read and why they should read it. This is at least as true today as ever. For the most part, something like literary criticism has developed right alongside literature.

Although lit and crit can be seen as a continuous tradition, very little about either has remained constant throughout the ages. Who has written it for whom and for what reasons keep changing. Here's a very broad (exceptions abound), highly selective (a lot is left out) outline of the by-whom, for-whom, and why of English lit through the ages.

The Old English, or the Early Medieval Period (Fifth to Eleventh Centuries)

During the Old English or early medieval period, bards wrote for warriors to foster bravery. Some of the oldest literature written in English includes written versions of works composed by heart and transmitted by word of mouth centuries earlier by harp-toting minstrels who sang at banquets. This oral Old English (Anglo-Saxon) poetry dates from as far back as the fifth century. It was composed by pagan Germanic tribes who relied on war as well as agriculture for their livelihood, and includes heroic stories that glorify prowess and bravery in battle. Most of what we know about this tradition comes from the partly damaged manuscript of the poem *Beowulf*, which was probably transcribed around the tenth century.

The Middle English, or the Late Medieval, Period (Twelfth to Fifteenth Centuries)

During the Middle English, or the late medieval, period, courtiers penned for noblemen to promote chivalric (knightly) ideals that helped stabilize a social hierarchy based on bloodlines. At this time, feudal society was dominated by aristocrats who ruled by military power, owned land, and controlled agricultural production. They based their privileges on the patrilineal inheritance of wealth and status ("*estate*"). Court literature, including chivalric romances such as *Sir Gawain and the Green Knight*, celebrated ideals that served to foster a sense of mutual obligation among the nobility, as well as a respect for bloodlines maintained through the chastity of unmarried noblewomen.

def•i•ni•tion

The term **estate** originally referred to social status as well as land and other possessions, all of which were passed along from father to son. Medieval Anglos belonged to one of three estates: the nobility, the clergy, or the commons.

The Renaissance (1540–1640)

During the English Renaissance, professional playwrights wrote for citizens of the newly consolidated, absolute British state, and public theaters presented plays that celebrated a semifluid social order governed by absolute state power. These dramas portrayed any unchecked social mobility that might threaten state stability as the result of personal evil, corruption, and perversion. Shakespeare's history plays celebrated the "Tudor myth" of divine right kingship, while Marlow's tragedies graphically represented the doom that awaits those who don't rein in their ambitions and submit to the lawful power of Church and state.

The Augustan Period (1670–1790)

During the Augustan period, the literate elite wrote for an emerging middle class. Our modern concept of English "literature" as a particular kind of expressive writing emerged in response to a particular set of historical circumstances. Since the invention of the printing press in the late fifteenth century, printed material of all kinds proliferated. News, political and religious tracts, instructional and moralistic writing, scientific, historical, and philosophical treatises all became widely available thanks to print.

In time, the well-educated elite began to fear that, amid all the new writing, traditional attitudes toward "learning" were in danger of getting lost. By the early eighteenth century, educated gentlemen began to complain that the "ancients" were getting ignored. You might say that people who placed great importance on the study of the classic texts of ancient Greece and Rome felt they were getting spammed by a lot of lowbrow hack writers.

They responded by identifying "literature" as a worthy cultural pursuit capable of reconciling respect for classical learning with the evolving interests and tastes of the educated middle class. They translated, imitated, and elucidated the most respectable ancient and modern authors in an outpouring of learning and literacy. At this time, the first professional writers and critics emerged. Soon afterward, a new literary form known as the novel appeared on the scene, together with a literate middle class.

The Romantic Period (1790–1840)

Following the Augustan period was the Romantic period, when inspired and individualistic poets wrote for an increasingly democratic and industrialized society. In the wake of earth-shaking revolutions in France and America that promised to liberate the democratic individual—and amid a growing industrial economy that threatened to enslave the worker—English poets of the Romantic period turned inward for the inspiration to celebrate the powers of nature and the creative spirit of individualism.

Canon Fodder
Romantic poet Percy Bysshe Shelley (1792–1822) wrote an essay titled *A Defence of Poetry* (1821, published 1840), in which he famously said, "The great instrument of moral good is the imagination."

The Victorian Period (1840–1900)

During the Victorian period, secular "priests" penned for the improvement of godless "Philistines." At this time, God lost his grip on society, and money started to take over. Religious belief was significantly on the wane, and a stodgy, complacent middle class wallowed increasingly in shallow prosperity. Regarding the situation with alarm, writers and scholars who were concerned about "English culture" prescribed liberal doses of "English literature" as a means of restoring higher ideals to a society that appeared to grow increasingly crass.

For the first time in history, English lit became simply (and dubiously) a good thing in its own right, regardless of whatever individual literary works actually had to say. It began to be studied in grade school and, in time, became a major course of study in college. Meanwhile, the concept of English literature came to serve nationalist and imperialist interests, helping cast a pleasingly virtuous light on British imperialism, as well as generating patriotic feeling through the years of the Great War (World War I).

The Modern Period (1900–1945)

During the modern period, amid a flowering of experimental work intended to test the boundaries of literary "art," literary criticism emerged as an academic subject. Scholars studied literature to hone their critical faculties and become budding stewards of civilization.

The phenomenally successful scholarly movement known as New Criticism (1920–1960) ensured the status of English literature as a major academic discipline. It enshrined the literary work as a subtle, sophisticated, complex artifact worthy of close, careful critical attention while holding up literature as a worthy alternative to commercialism and narrow party politics.

The Postmodern Period (1945–Present)

The next—and current—period is the postmodern period. Traditional literature has been found to have been written by "dead white males" to serve the *ideological* aims of a conservative and repressive Anglo *hegemony*. As a result, literature is getting reread "against the grain" as a cautionary lesson in the power of *discourse* by radical socially conscious critics.

def•i•ni•tion

Ideology refers to thought patterns, ideals, attitudes, values, and beliefs that are shaped by political interests. **Hegemony** is cultural power that works alongside overt force (the police, military, etc.) to control people's thoughts and behavior. **Discourse** is a conventional way of thinking, speaking, and writing that defines and limits what can be accepted as meaningful and true. Hegemony, ideology, and discourse help explain how ideals and values enable one group to dominate another.

Meanwhile, emergent voices representing groups that have been marginalized by the same repressive hegemony are constructing alternative discourses for the empowerment of the subjugated and the edification of all. At the same time, literary study is as important as ever for enabling young people to develop the critical skills of reading, writing, and thinking. (Don't worry just now if you don't understand all of this. It's supposed to be hard!)

In an array of reactions against the race, gender, and class biases found to be woven into the tradition of Anglo lit, multicultural writers and political literary theorists have sought to expose, resist, and redress injustices and prejudices. These prejudices are often covert—disguised in literature and other discourses as positive ideals and objective truths—but they slant our sense of reality in favor of power and privilege. Thus, lit study has been rethinking itself in recent decades—drastically and radically.

These days, multiculturalism and political criticism have wrought a transformation in literary studies that, in some more conservative views, threatens to undermine the discipline of "English" itself. Nevertheless, English lit remains a vital and exciting subject. While the traditional canon of recognized literary texts remains in place (and seems to generate more interest and critical attention the more it's denounced), the field of English lit has expanded into the multicultural fields of "literatures in English" and *"cultural studies."* Among cultural studies advocates "literature" loses something of its privileged status as it takes its place among other aspects of culture, including such things as bondage, Bollywood, Barbie dolls, and the blues.

def•i•ni•tion

Cultural studies is an emerging academic discipline that's grown out of the field of English literature. It uses techniques of literary study but applies them to any and all areas of culture.

The More Things Change ...

Amid ongoing changes, literature and literary study remain thoroughly, through-and-through problematic. They're filled with intriguing ideas that don't always hold water and with counterintuitive abstractions that are deliberately tough to grasp. They're subject to doubt and debate. They're vexed and contentious, provisional and contextual, subversive and subvertible.

So Why Study English?

Teachers, scholars, and educational policy makers frequently disagree—among themselves and with others—about why lit is important, what there is to learn from it, and how it should be taught. Most people agree, however, that literature is well worth reading, teaching, and studying. The problem isn't that people can't think of enough good reasons to study lit, but that the reasons they think of tend to be contradictory.

 Kudos and Caveats

In response to a growing crisis in public education in the United States, in 2001, the controversial No Child Left Behind Act was passed to hold schools and teachers responsible for the "adequate yearly progress" of students and to promote "proven methods" of teaching, both of which have resulted in greatly increased emphasis on tests. Critics of the act have argued that education has been supplanted by test preparation—taking time away from qualitative reading and discussion, and redirecting it to quantitative drill and memorization.

See which of these reasons to study English literature make sense to you:

- It helps develop critical intelligence.

- It teaches you to understand alternative points of view.

- It's less boring than math.

- It shows how we're trapped in the ongoing dialectic of freedom and bondage.

- It's the cornerstone of liberal society.

- No, English studies *us!*

Grains of Trivium

The Modern Language Association (MLA), founded in America in 1883 as a forum for scholarly and academic discussion, has more than 30,000 members in 100 countries. It's best known as the publisher of the comprehensive *MLA International Bibliography* of studies in language and literature, and of the prestigious academic journal *PMLA* (*Publication of the MLA*).

- It helps develop perspective on history, culture, and humankind.

- The pleasures of the text hold a singular fascination.

- I'm going to become a great writer!

- It helps you deconstruct your personal mythology.

- You can sublimate your inner turmoil by fetishizing words.

- You can bluff your way through the essay questions.

Holding Your Own

To put it mildly, English lit study today is fraught with squabbles. And why not? The interrelationships between literature and society are multifarious, malleable, and crucially important. They are also imperfectly understood and infinitely debatable. Teachers and scholars disagree with one another like never before. But even if everyone disagrees on what to study and how to study it, everyone agrees that study is worthwhile. If you're a student, this is where you come in.

Don't be put off by the problematic nature of lit study. It's all part of the terrain. Think of the problems as opportunities to explore and reinterpret. There's more to be said precisely because we haven't figured everything out already. And the more insolid and uncertain things have become, the better it is that you're here to help sort things out!

Kudos and Caveats _____

Amid all the academic upheaval and critical debate, English class remains a place where students can read, discuss, and write about interesting texts. If you're a student, this simple truth can guide you through all the controversy, complexity, and change you'll ever encounter in English class. You don't have to know everything. You don't even have to know more than you already know. All you have to do is show up, stay involved, and do your own work.

You can do this by thinking about the texts you read, developing your own point of view, and sharing your ideas with others. In fact, if you don't develop and discuss your own point of view, there is—literally—no point! Whether you like or dislike a work of literature and whether you agree or disagree with a piece of criticism matters very little if you can't think and talk about writing on your own terms.

You certainly can and should learn from others, but you may be selling yourself short if you let others think for you. That's not to say it's easy to think for yourself about challenging works of literature and criticism. It isn't! It takes years of study and practice!

You may feel frustrated and confused at times. Everyone does. But if you hang in there, the challenging process of personal development tends not only to become easier as you go along, but more exciting and rewarding as well. Meanwhile, you'll fit in with the scholarly community as long as you're willing to read, think, write, and discuss.

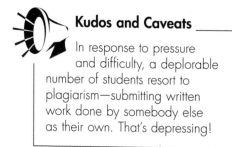

Kudos and Caveats

In response to pressure and difficulty, a deplorable number of students resort to plagiarism—submitting written work done by somebody else as their own. That's depressing!

The remaining chapters in this section talk about important problematic topics—the canon, genres, meaning, politics, history, and culture. Each one is crucial to lit study, and each is subject to more or less heated debate in the academy. Getting acquainted with these issues should help you get your bearings in the field. But first comes a chapter on the bread and butter of literary scholarship: an activity known as close reading.

The Least You Need to Know

- ◆ Literature is a form of mental recreation. It's supposed to be enjoyable.

- ◆ Literature is tremendously important from an educational and cultural point of view. Literary study is a thoroughly social process.

- ◆ Notions of who reads and writes literature and why have changed markedly over the past 1,500 years.

- ◆ Literature and literary study are problematic—subject to doubt and debate.

- ◆ Developing and exercising a point of view is an important goal to have and a necessary process of literary study.

Up Close and Textual

In This Chapter

- ◆ A close look at close reading
- ◆ What to look for when looking closely—semantics, structure, and imagery
- ◆ A brief close reading of a brief Emily Dickinson poem

The single most important skill of a literary scholar is the ability to *close read* a text. Through close reading, scholars demonstrate their understanding of a literary work, display their sensitivity to language, and frame interesting discussions and compelling arguments about just what is going on in the work. More than anything else, close reading is what English lit scholars do. And in just about every college English literature class, students get the chance to practice and develop their close-reading ability. In most classes, close reading makes up an important part of the work students are graded on. If you're a good close reader, chances are you can do well in college-level literature classes.

The vast empire of academic literary scholarship has been built by people who read and reread literary texts with great interest, extreme care, and close attention. As they read and reread, they write about what they find: their interpretations, impressions, responses, hypotheses, and discoveries.

Don't be misled into thinking close reading is just *reading;* writing is an important aspect as well. In fact, writing is a big part of what makes close reading close.

Close Calls

Probably most writing assignments in literature classes are close readings. Students read and find interesting things going on in the text. They raise questions about what they notice and develop interpretations to suggest possible answers to their questions. And they frame arguments to show their interpretations are borne out by textual evidence. In doing so, writers of close readings take their readers through their interpretive process to show just how it works.

Kudos and Caveats

Most literature teachers are skilled close readers of student papers. Much of the teaching they do takes effect through the written exchanges between student and teacher in the process of assigning, drafting, commenting on, revising, and evaluating papers.

Of course, there are all sorts of different things to pick up on in a work of literature. In addition, there are all sorts of ways to develop interpretations. Variety is good. Different people take an interest in different aspects of a text. But in general, a good close reading sheds light on an aspect of a work of literature by showing that it is significant in ways that might not be apparent to most people on a general first read.

Still Critical

The practice of close reading as an academic exercise emerged during the early and middle decades of the twentieth century as part of a scholarly approach known as New Criticism. In focusing attention specifically on the texts of literary works, New Critics helped raise literary study from a mere intellectual pastime to a *bona fide* academic discipline.

Canon Fodder

New Critics tended to see works of literature as constructs that fused and reconciled complex paradoxical elements within an organic pattern. This approach is set forth and deployed in the book *The Well Wrought Urn* (1947) by New Critic Cleanth Brooks (1906–1994).

Of course, so-called New Criticism is no longer new. As you can see in Chapter 3 of this book, much of the thinking behind New Criticism has become outmoded. Even so, close reading continues to play a vital and fundamental part in literary study. The ability to work carefully with written language, to come up with "readings" of literary texts, and to write about them with detailed precision are essential critical skills.

Open and Close

The idea that there can be more than one valid interpretation of a single text may seem difficult to grasp. Many inexperienced students wrongly assume their job is to figure out the "right" answers to their teachers' questions and, more generally, to do some predefined task the teachers "want" them to do.

The purpose of close reading, however, is not to rework a problem someone else has already solved once and for all. Instead, the point is for the person doing the close reading to make his or her own decisions on what's worth saying about a text and to put his or her observations together into an interesting and persuasive piece of writing.

In effect, when you do a close reading, you place yourself on the same level as the author of the text you're writing about. You're exercising authority. You're showing that you understand language well and can use it for your own purposes in thinking about someone else's work. Few things impress English teachers more than student papers that focus on specific details within a literary text and show clearly how those details contribute to the student's understanding of the work.

Cutting Both Ways

Close reading may involve picking up on some of the more subtle details an author incorporates into a literary work and showing how they contribute to the work's significance. This kind of close reading may suggest something about the literary skill of the author or the complexities of literary language itself. The point is not simply to appreciate how great the author is, but to show why the work is interesting.

On the other hand, close reading may involve identifying assumptions or biases at work in the author's thinking that raise issues the author may not directly address. This kind of reading is sometimes called *reading against the grain*. It takes a critical approach toward the work, perhaps by questioning the values it appears to endorse or exposing unintentional ambiguities, paradoxes, or other logical gaps.

> **Kudos and Caveats**
>
> One of the most accomplished close readers of our time is the French philosopher Jacques Derrida (1930–), the founder of a critical approach known as *deconstruction* (see Chapter 5). You might say deconstruction is the process of reading language itself against the grain, showing how writing always generates ambiguities, contradictions, and other unintended results.

Reading Actively

Obviously, studying literature is not the same as reading to acquire information or reading for passive entertainment. These things usually mean taking what an author says at face value and accepting that the author knows what's important and what he or she is talking about. In contrast, literary study involves *active reading,* through which the reader continually measures what's in the writing against what he or she already thinks.

Back and Forth

Active reading is like having a conversation with a text. You ask questions as you read and look for answers. You recognize that the writer of the text makes choices about what to say and how to say it, and you think about the significance of those choices. You get involved with the writer's project in writing the text and, if you go on to write a close reading, develop a project of your own.

Kudos and Caveats

Tips to aid in active reading include taking notes, reading aloud, looking up unfamiliar words in a dictionary, and marking the text (if you own it, not if you don't!). If you mark your copy of a text, limit your marks to point out especially important and interesting details. Highlighting whole big sections of text doesn't really help.

def•i•ni•tion

Semantics is the branch of linguistics (the study of language) concerned with meaning.

Of course, there's nothing wrong with simply reading for information or for entertainment. But it's important to see that there's more to get out of language than the most clear and obvious things. Even so, what's most clear and obvious can be a good place to start, especially if you have difficulty understanding what you read the first time through. It takes a certain amount of practice and experience just to follow the plot of a narrative or identify the main points of a poem or essay.

But assuming you have a good basic comprehension of a text, and assuming you follow it and get the main ideas, what then? The next section offers some suggestions of what to look for when doing a close reading. These suggestions have to do with paying attention to *semantics*—what words mean—and paying attention to structure—how language is organized. Looking at either or both of these areas can provide a good way to dig beneath the surface of a text.

The Ways of Words

Meaning is a slippery thing. When you write down words, the language holds still, but not the meaning. Words can mean different things to different people at different times. And they can mean what they mean in different ways, depending on how you use and interpret them. The meanings of words often get slanted or shaded one way or another, depending on their context.

Writers often use words in subtle ways to convey their ideas and impressions. For example, if a scarf falls into a mud puddle, you could say it gets *soiled* or *dirty* or even *filthy*. The word you choose to describe the scarf suggests something about your attitude toward it. *Soiled* isn't a bad thing, whereas *filth* certainly is.

Both words can be used to refer to what gets on the scarf. They have a similar *denotation*. The denotation of a word is its accepted meaning—its dictionary definition. In contrast, these words have different *connotations*. The connotation of a word is the significance it acquires through association with other things. *Soil* is associated with growing plants. *Filth* is associated with decay and corruption. *Soil* has a neutral or positive connotation, whereas *filth* has a negative one. So a writer who said the scarf got *soiled* would have a different attitude than one who said it was *filthy*.

If you look carefully at a writer's choices, you may be able to detect a pattern in the kinds of words chosen. Literary scholars use the term *diction* to refer to word choice within a text or utterance. A writer's diction can offer important subtle clues about his or her attitude, character, or assumptions regarding the topic at hand. Formal, flowery, crude, casual, blunt, polite—diction can help you get a read on an author's feelings for his or her subject matter.

A close reading of an author's diction can supply evidence about the mood or *tone* with which a text is written. The tone may be earnest, grave, light, impassioned, or detached. It may be sincere, ironic, or even sarcastic. It may change over the course of a work. It isn't always easy to tell, but you may notice words and phrases that suggest a significant emotion—or a peculiar lack of feeling—toward whatever is getting described.

Kudos and Caveats

When you're writing an explication of a text, be sure to quote key words from the text within your own original sentences. Quoting another writer's words within your writing is a great way to bridge the gap between minds.

Let's break for some definitions:

denotation   The literal significance of a word; the dictionary definition considered apart from associations the word may evoke.

connotation   The secondary significance a word acquires through association that goes beyond its literal meaning; the implied meaning, as opposed to the dictionary definition.

diction   The choice of words used in a text or utterance. A writer's diction may indicate something about his or her values or attitude.

tone   The mood or emotional attitude evoked or reflected in a written work.

Reading by Design

The structure and organization of a text—either of the work as a whole or of individual lines and sentences—may also be worth examining. Again, keep in mind that the way a text is organized usually reflects the author's choices, so it might tell you something about how he or she thinks and what he or she feels is important.

Grains of Trivium

New Jersey high school students Gary Graham and Jeffrey Maiden made a discovery regarding the poem "The Mouse's Tale" by Lewis Carroll (1832–1898). The poem appears in the novel *Alice in Wonderland* (1865) and is printed in such a way that the words take the shape of a winding, narrowing mouse's tail. They found that when the poem is written out in rhymed stanzas, each stanza concludes with what is known as a *tail rhyme* and concluded that Carroll knowingly inserted this implicit pun into his poem. They published a paper on their discovery together with their English teacher, Nancy Fox, in issue #72 (1989) of the British literary journal the *Carrollian*.

Structural clues need to be interpreted together with semantic ones (meaning, that is). Sentences, paragraphs, and chapters in prose, as well as lines, stanzas, and cantos in poetry, may emphasize and round off certain ideas and gloss over and interrupt others. Grammatical shifts and shifts in tone, point of view, and subject matter may also be worth examining. Patterns of any kind are good things to notice, especially if they're less than obvious.

Seeing Is Believing

Another fruitful focus for a close reading of a literary work is its *imagery*. Imagery is a key feature of literary language. It enables writers to show events, suggest relationships, and evoke feelings in vivid pictures rather than with the dry, dull terms of expository prose.

Worth a Thousand Words

Imagery is conveyed by words for *concrete* things, as opposed to *abstractions*. Images may be *literal* or *figurative*. These distinctions—abstract versus concrete and literal versus figurative—can be extremely useful when doing a close reading of a literary work. Here are some definitions, with examples to help show what these things are (it's a longish list because imagery is such a crucial and complicated aspect of literary language):

imagery   Any tangible thing named in a piece of writing, regardless of whether that thing is literal or figurative. In the statement "the penny shone like the sun," both *penny* and *sun* are images. *Penny* is literal, while *sun* is figurative. In the statement "the idea shone like the sun," *idea* is not an image, but an abstraction.

Kudos and Caveats

Some words may be either abstract or concrete, depending on how they're used. A foundation of a building is concrete. The foundation of a religion is abstract.

concrete term   A term for anything tangible; an image. Examples include *rose*, *smoke*, *fluff*, *chimpanzees*, *water*, and *tile grout*.

abstraction   A term for anything that isn't tangible. Abstract words—including *power*, *sleep*, *humor*, *pettiness*, and *comfort*—do not convey imagery.

literal language   Language that can be taken at face value to mean what it says.

figurative language   Language that's intended to mean something other than what it literally says.

metaphor   An image used figuratively to represent something it isn't. A metaphor is based on a comparison between two things, known as the *tenor* and the *vehicle*. The tenor is the literal thing, and the vehicle is the figurative, metaphorical thing. For example, in the statement "His mind was a beehive of activity," *mind* is the tenor, while *beehive* is the vehicle.

simile   A metaphor in which the figurative comparison is made explicitly, often by use of *like* or *as*. The statement "Her words were like hot coals" is a simile.

Beyond Compare

These rather technical academic terms are intended to explain how certain kinds of literary effects work, including some unusual and creative uses for language. Metaphors, in particular, can be quite subtle and complicated. It may take considerable thought to understand and explain just how a metaphor works, but the effort is often worthwhile. The task is sometimes referred to as *unpacking a metaphor.*

A metaphor makes a comparison between two different things. The comparison depends on a point or points of similarity between them. Thus, unpacking metaphors involves identifying the things compared as well as examining what they might have in common.

> **Grains of Trivium**
>
> Many metaphors have become so common in ordinary language that their figurative status has all but disappeared. These are known as *dead metaphors.* For example, we commonly use the word *see* to mean *understand.*

For example, if you say the shopping mall was an obstacle course, you're comparing two places that are difficult to get through. You may also be suggesting that you or the other mallgoers were trying to accomplish your shopping as quickly as possible and that you may be motivated in part by a feeling of competition with one another.

Descent from the Mountain

Now let's try to put some of these ideas together in a sample close reading of a short untitled poem by American poet Emily Dickinson (1830–1886), published 1890. First, here's the poem:

> **Canon Fodder**
>
> Dickinson wrote 1,775 poems. Only a few were published during her lifetime, anonymously, and so she was virtually unknown as a poet upon her death. Today she is considered a major American poet.

The Mountain sat upon the Plain
In his tremendous Chair—
His observation omnifold,
His inquest, everywhere—
The Seasons played around his knees
Like Children round a sire—
Grandfather of the Days is He
Of Dawn the Ancestor—

The poem describes the mountain metaphorically as if it were an important, powerful person such as a ruler or leading government official. "The Mountain sat ... In his tremendous Chair" as though on a throne or seat of office. The enormous size of the mountain suggests power greater than any real, human person with limited human abilities could possibly have. He sees everything ("His observation omnifold") and finds out what's going on all around ("His inquest, everywhere").

Playful *irony* is at work in this impressive-sounding description of the mountain's power—after all, a literal mountain just sits there and does nothing. The heightened diction of the terms *tremendous, omnifold,* and *inquest* thus suggest the mountain may be a rather pompous and pretentious sort of official who tries to convey his importance through his appearance and station rather than his actions.

In other words, to unpack the metaphor, the mountain is the tenor, and a pompous ruler or official is the implied vehicle. The mountain resembles the ruler, in that both have an imposing, impressive presence. The mountain is great in stature, and a ruler is great in status.

def•i•ni•tion

Irony is the use of words to convey the opposite of their literal meaning.

Playing with God

Yet while the mountain, amusingly, has qualities of a pompous official, it also appears, mysteriously, rather godlike. Like God, the mountain sees everything and seems capable of making judgments about what he sees. As the poem continues, the mountain is described as having another godlike characteristic: he is the procreator of the "Seasons," "Days," and "Dawn."

Why would Dickinson choose to represent the mountain as a pompous sort of official and, at the same time, as a sort of paternal deity? Possibly she sensed problems with the ways God was commonly understood and represented during her time and wanted to work through these problems in this poem. The mountain does not simply represent God, but may provide the author with a way to rethink traditional representations of God—God the father, God the judge—and unify these with an alternative concept of God that was gaining acceptance during her lifetime: God the remote, detached, unknowable creator of the universe.

In any case, the size, mass, imagined power, and actual inertia of the mountain all contrast with the "Seasons," represented through the simile of "Children" who "played around his knees." It's easy to imagine the seasons moving and changing in succession around their motionless "sire" (king or father), the immovable mountain. Their activity is playful in contrast to his pompous and mysterious immovable grandeur.

Grains of Trivium

An early nineteenth-century edition of Dickinson's poem reads: "The seasons prayed around his knees," substituting *prayed* for *played*. Apparently, the editor misread Dickinson's handwriting. In fact, Dickinson's spelling and punctuation are quite erratic. Early editions of her poetry introduced many editorial changes intended to standardize her language. The poem printed in this chapter is a modern edition intended to preserve Dickinson's original spelling and punctuation.

Up to this point, the poem unfolds in the past tense. "The Mountain *sat*." "The Seasons *played*." As the poem shifts to the present tense in the final two lines, it suggests that we have been looking at the mountain from a temporal as well as a physical distance. Whereas the seasons are the mountain's children, the days are grandchildren and the dawn is a still more distant descendant. Interestingly, as this lineal descent takes us further and further from the mountain, the divisions of time—seasons, days, and dawn—get smaller and smaller.

In fact, the poem traces a progression down from the mountain that occurs on a number of levels simultaneously. It moves from ancestor to descendant, from past to present, from large to small, and from the solid, motionless concrete object that is the mountain to the ambient, transitory, insubstantial event that is dawn. The ancient, ponderous, permanent materiality of the mountain thus serves to offset dawn's new beginning.

Hall of Famer

In general, Dickinson's poetry makes for good close reading. She is quite inventive with her use of diction, imagery, and semantic structure. As a result, you can't really capture the sense of her poetry merely by paraphrasing it. It requires careful explanation. Because her poems tend to be quite short, it's easy to look at them carefully and read them again and again.

Today Dickinson remains a well-known, canonized American literary figure. To find out what it means to be a canonical writer—and to find out about recent squabbles surrounding the literary canon, take a look at the following chapter.

The Least You Need to Know

- Close reading is an essential feature of English literary scholarship.
- Close readings pick up on subtleties of diction, structure, imagery, and more.
- Emily Dickinson made inventive use of language to produce poetic effects.

3

Canon Fighting

In This Chapter

- ◆ The ongoing spat over the literary canon
- ◆ How and why the canon came to be
- ◆ Critiquing the canon—and shooting your discipline in the foot?
- ◆ Defending the canon—and going down with a sinking ship?

The *canon* of English literature is an unofficial grouping of works by authors whose importance has become generally recognized by lit scholars. It represents a traditional focus for literary study. You might say it's the greatest hits of the who's who in English lit. To many, the canon embodies a standard of literary achievement. To others, it embodies the patriarchal, ethnocentric, and elitist values of white male privilege. Some say "Keep it the way it is," while others say, "Revise it and expand it." Others try to ignore it completely. It doesn't appear, however, that the canon is going to disappear.

In essence, debates about the canon are debates about what works of literature teachers should teach and students should study. Issues debated include how and whether politics should or does guide the choices and what role aesthetics and literary tradition should play in the English lit curriculum.

Gone but Not Forgotten

The notion of literary fame developed gradually and emerged during the late Middle Ages as an important rationale to justify secular literature in a religious world. Worldly ambition as such flew in the face of Christian teachings that stressed the importance of the afterlife as opposed to earthly existence. This meant that the desire of a poet to become a great literary figure had to be squared with religious ideals that were essentially otherworldly.

Not Fade Away

Fame came to be regarded as a sort of secular afterlife. Thus, poetic ambition, like religious devotion, could be seen as a pious commitment to an eternal existence. Renaissance poets defended their desire for fame in moral terms as a spiritual virtue. And they pointed to the famous poets of the past as proof of the moral value of poetry.

A convention common in Renaissance lyric poetry is the eternizing conceit—the suggestion that a poem will confer immortality on its subject and on the poet. Shakespeare's "Sonnet 55," addressed to a young gentleman, is a famous example:

> Not marble, nor the gilded monuments
> Of princes shall outlive this powerful rhyme,
> But you shall shine more bright in these contents
> Than unswept stone, besmeared with sluttish time.
> When wasteful war shall statues overturn,
> And broils root out the work of masonry,
> Nor Mars his sword nor war's quick fire shall burn
> The living record of your memory.
> 'Gainst death and all oblivious enmity
> shall you pace forth; your praise shall still find room,
> Even in the eyes of all posterity
> That wear this world out to the ending doom.
> So til the judgment that yourself arise,
> You live in this and dwell in lovers' eyes.

Famous Renaissance poet Edmund Spenser pointed to ancient Roman poet Virgil and to medieval English poet Chaucer, as if to say, "These guys were good and worthy of fame; I want to be like them." This move helped solidify the reputations of all three.

Writers have been making similar moves ever since. "Remember me, too; I'm like these others we remember."

It just so happened that Chaucer was buried in a now-famous section of Westminster Abbey, the church where kings and queens of England are crowned. This was not because he was a poet, but because he was a civil servant. Spenser was buried near him because he, like Chaucer, was an important English poet.

Canon Fodder

The part of Westminster Abbey where Chaucer and Spenser are buried has come to be known as Poet's Corner. Through the years, more poets, and later novelists, have been buried there or have had monuments placed there. Today it's crowded with many memorials to literary figures. Who decides who gets a memorial in Poet's Corner? In general, it seems that literary fan clubs raise money for monuments and rally support for their authors. As recently as 2002, the Fanny Burney Society succeeded in having a monument placed in honor of the eighteenth-century novelist.

Making the Cut

In the eighteenth century, people began to use the term *canon* to refer informally to famous writers as a group. The word comes from a Greek word meaning "rule" or "standard." The term was originally used in the early Middle Ages to refer to religious scriptures that were officially recognized as part of the Christian Bible, in contrast to the biblical *Apocrypha*—scriptures not considered to be divinely inspired.

The term is also used in a religious sense to refer to the list of Christian saints. The Church "canonizes" saints through an official process that determines whether candidates for sainthood are worthy to intercede for, and receive prayers from, Christian believers.

Kudos and Caveats

Some lit scholars say it's no big deal that the term *canon* has official religious significance. Others say it reflects an unhealthy conservative attitude that literature should be endorsed by the academy and closed off to newcomers.

In contrast to the biblical canon and the canon of saints, the literary canon was never an official list of officially recognized writers. Even so, *canon* came to be used to refer to authors on college and university reading lists. For a while—into the 1960s—most of these lists were made up exclusively of white writers who were almost exclusively male.

Well before that time, academic learning and nationalist thinking combined to foster study and appreciation of "great" British writers. Literacy, aesthetic value, and cultural pride became indiscriminately blended within literary study. Great lit was good for students and for society.

Canon to the Right of Them

Since the 1960s, the canon has come under attack from a number of quarters. In general, the assailants have been academics who practice political criticism. These lit and cultural studies scholars say that the canon promotes conservative white male Anglo ideals, that the canon represents the limited and biased values of privileged white males. Although this is a sweeping judgment of a large and long-standing literary tradition, it makes sense insofar as literature tends to accommodate the status quo—whether the aristocratic social order that predominated through the eighteenth century or the capitalist social order that has prevailed ever since.

Annie Get Your Canon

Feminist scholars have criticized the canon, pointing out a persistent male bias at work in traditional canon formation. Women writers tended to get left off the list of important literary figures. Part of the problem stemmed from male-centered criticism that passed over deserving works by women writers. Another part of the problem stemmed from patriarchal attitudes that, for centuries, tended to deny women education and a voice in society, and served to prevent many from pursuing literary careers.

Although female literary figures exist from the Middle Ages on, they are comparatively few and far between. Not until the twentieth century have women writers come into their own in large numbers. Today, of course, women writers occupy an important place on college reading lists.

Canon Fodder

Margery Kempe, an illiterate medieval housewife and mother of 14 children, caused tensions in her family and controversy in the Church when she claimed to have experienced visions in which Jesus Christ and the Virgin Mary instructed her to do pious acts against the wishes of her husband. Her religious visions were eventually recognized by Church authorities, and she dictated her spiritual biography to scribes. That's one way to get published!

Canon Cannot

Today writers from practically every race and ethnicity make their way into both high school and college curricula. These developments indicate changing attitudes on many fronts. But some things stay the same.

Opponents of the canon have argued rightly that the canon was formed in response to particular institutional, cultural, political, and economic interests. This can be said of the expanding multicultural canon as well, which serves the economic interests of the publishing industry. The literary success and canonical recognition of writers who belong to ethnic minorities depends on their acceptance by the academy and by affluent readers. And it depends heavily on the ability of the publishing industry to market their works.

What's more, ethnic writers don't necessarily represent or endorse cultural values shared by everyone in "their" culture. The literary success in America of a radical Jamaican writer doesn't necessarily help impoverished people in Jamaica or necessarily communicate a message all impoverished Jamaicans would want Americans to hear.

Disarming the Canon

Critiques of the canon have prompted a number of efforts to defend it. Defenders of the received canon include those who argue its importance on aesthetic, as opposed to political, grounds. They suggest that politicizing the canon erodes the integrity of literary scholarship and devalues the literary achievements of the great writers of the Anglo tradition.

In Defense of the Canon

Among those who have seen the traditional canon as an important embodiment of aesthetic and literary achievement are former chairs of the National Endowment for the Humanities. During the 1980s, warning against a decline in academic standards and a growing failure to appreciate the lasting ideals of Western civilization, these officials recommended a return to the study of "great," canonical writers. They have also complained of the political bent of the attacks on the canon, saying that they compromise the credibility of literary study. This position has been echoed by conservative journalists who have denounced academic radicals and the threat they pose to Western culture.

A more famous and thoughtful defense of the canon is put forward by literary scholar Harold Bloom in his best-selling book *The Western Canon* (1994): Bloom not only defends the canon on aesthetic grounds, but argues that canon formation takes place as great writers respond in their writing to the work of their predecessors. For Bloom, literary study involves looking at writers through history in relation to one another.

> ### Grains of Trivium
>
> In a study titled *The Anxiety of Influence,* Harold Bloom argues that great poets write poetry in competition with their predecessors and attempt to make the work of their predecessors look like inferior prototypes of their own.

Bloom dismisses political criticism as what he calls "the school of resentment" and insists on the pleasure to be derived from reading. In many ways, Bloom takes on the canon with grandstanding quirkiness. For example, he sees Austrian psychologist Sigmund Freud as a direct literary descendent of Shakespeare. According to Bloom, Freud's ideas about the subconscious were made possible by the "inwardness" of Shakespeare's characters. And he includes Sir Walter Raleigh (talented courtier, not much of a poet) and leaves out Aphra Behn?

Loaded Canon

Various attacks on political criticism have not diminished its importance in today's academy. Political criticism continues to play a major—even a leading—role in literary scholarship. Political critics have offered a number of responses to those who have defended the canon on aesthetic grounds.

Political critics say that political concerns come inevitably into play whenever values are at issue. In other words, everyone is always trying to put a spin on things, no matter what. In this view, politics enters into the equation even when political issues are ignored or denied. So when a traditional literary critic claims to be concerned with aesthetics rather than politics, a political critic would say that the traditional critic is using aesthetics to disguise, idealize, and *mystify* political concerns.

def•i•ni•tion

> **Mystification** is the process of denying or disguising political values by misrepresenting them as natural, universal, or transcendent ideals.

According to political critics, the claim that the canon is not political is itself a political claim. The denial of the canon's political significance attempts to suggest that what is good for privileged white males is good for everybody. In effect, it sweeps under the rug the historical and cultural conflicts that have taken place between Anglos and others, and also overlooks political tensions evident in canonical literature itself. Thus, political critics don't think they are politicizing something that is essentially aesthetic, but rather are exposing the political thrust of writing that aesthetic criticism covers up.

Parting Shots

Critiques of the canon by political critics are not the only cause of canonical shake-ups in the academy. Other factors contribute to a general sense of the declining importance of canonical works, including the argument that there's too much other stuff to read these days. Academic interest in popular culture and cultural studies diverts attention from the traditional canon. And outside the academy, the cultural importance of literacy itself is challenged by video, the Internet, and other developments in communications technology—as well as by a growing sense that reading a lot of literature won't necessarily help you succeed in business.

But despite disagreement, uncertainty, and changing circumstances, the traditional canon remains essentially intact as an important focus of academic study. Today it shares the literary limelight with newer arrivals on the scene, both from within and outside the Anglo tradition, so it gets only a divided share of the academic attention it formerly received. Even so, it appears to be alive and well.

> **Grains of Trivium**
>
> St. Johns College in Annapolis, Maryland, bases its entire curriculum on "great books." Since 1937, all students take the same classes and follow the same program based on established great books (no textbooks are used) in all disciplines, including and especially literature.

The reasons to focus on canonical works when teaching and studying literature are many. Some have as much to do with convenience as with aesthetics or politics. Works that are already widely familiar tend be easier to acquire, easier to teach, and easier to talk about with more people. And because they are already widely recognized, they attract ongoing attention. People want to know more about works and writers with a reputation for greatness.

Canonical works are often taken as representative of their time. One of the reasons a particular writer may become canonized is because his or her work exhibits characteristics associated with important cultural and historical developments. This makes canonical writing important to the study of literary and cultural history.

Similarly, while political critics seek to expose and demystify the political aims behind canon formation and the political significance of canonical works, they don't generally call for canonical works to be banned from the curriculum. Instead, many find the canon and canonical works to provide interesting subject matter for political criticism. In fact, for all these reasons, this book tends to focus on canonical works.

The Least You Need to Know

- ◆ The canon is a hotly contested issue in literature studies.
- ◆ The canon has been attacked on political grounds as an expression of white male privilege.
- ◆ Defenders of the canon say it represents the greatest literary achievements of the Western world.
- ◆ Canon formation responds to political, economic, cultural, and institutional interests.

Chapter 4

It Takes All Kinds

In This Chapter

- ◆ Classifying mutants: literary genres
- ◆ Wrestling with generic instability
- ◆ Coming to terms with generic change
- ◆ An example: the winding journey of the ode

Literature gets written in dizzying, dazzling variety. While each work of literature is unique, all works have features in common with others. Based on common features, works get grouped together into categories called *genres*.

Some genres are defined by their form, some by their content, and some by their style. In fact, genres are purely conventional. They result from patterns that crop up in the way people write that reflect the things they're trying to accomplish. The names of genres identify different sorts of patterns. In practice, a work may have the features of more than one genre. Some works can even introduce changes in how a genre is understood and lead to shifts in genres over time.

This doesn't mean that genres don't tell us important things about literature; they do. But what they tell us is contingent and contextual—it all depends on the interplay of many traditional elements, historical developments, cultural attitudes, and political interests. Good thing lit scholars like to study tradition, history, culture, and politics!

Assigning Labels

Have I mentioned that a work of literature can be difficult to understand? This is especially so if you have no idea what to expect before you start reading it. Literary genres can indicate a great deal about the works that belong to them. Genres have been clueing readers in on what there is to read since ancient times. They identify basic features of what an author is up to within any given work of lit.

Knowing Ahead of Time

If you begin reading a poem you think is an *aubade*, or dawn song (a poem about the joy lovers feel when they wake up together or about the sadness they feel when they part in the morning), but it turns out to be an *epithalamium* (a poem that celebrates a couple's wedding night), you're likely to get confused. Knowing which is which not only helps in understanding the poem, but also makes it easier to compare it to other poems of the same genre. Thus, generic concepts help critics talk about what various works have in common and about significant differences between similar works.

But generic categories aren't written in stone. Old genres fall out of use and new ones spring into being all the time. Writers keep playing around with genres in different ways, and critics keep redefining them. Generic terms don't always do justice to the constant flux and variety of literary activity.

def•i•ni•tion

An **aubade**, or dawn song, is a lyric form stemming from the Middle Ages that treats the subject of two lovers waking up together. It may deal with the joy of being together or with the sorrow of having to part. An **epithalamium** is a poem about a couple's wedding night.

Hard to Pin Down

Some generic terms are invented to describe trends in writing long after these trends first got their start. The moment of generic identification often brings about a new attitude—the acceptance and recognition of practices that were formerly experimental, unpopular, or otherwise considered weird. These terms may then be used retrospectively to refer to the earlier works as though there was never anything weird about them.

So it's possible to talk about a "romance," a "novel," or an "essay" that dates from a period well before any of these terms were first used. These familiar terms cover over the problematic history of the genres themselves. Is a prenovelistic protonovel really a novel, or is it something else?

Generic distinctions are purely conventional and not always universally accepted and agreed upon. Yet genres are indispensable descriptive literary categories. They reflect a shared sense of what lit is and does, and, like everything else in life and literature, they are shaped by history, culture, and politics.

> ### Grains of Trivium
>
> The novel got its name because it was a "new" form, but since this form was first recognized and described, many old "novels" have been identified as well.

Even the most broad and easy-to-recognize categories are defined by convention as much as by inherent qualities of the works they refer to. Or, to be more accurate, the inherent qualities they refer to are themselves conventional rather than timeless and universal. Poetry, drama, prose fiction, and prose nonfiction are porous categories that occasionally let the literary works they aim to describe leak through.

Poking Holes

Here are some critical tidbits that poke holes in the generic distinctions commonly made among poetry, drama, prose fiction, and nonfiction:

- Ancient Greek philosopher Aristotle apparently recognized drama as a subcategory of poetry rather than as a separate category unto itself.

> ### Grains of Trivium
>
> Aristotle divided poetry into four subdivisions: tragedy, comedy, epic, and lyric.

- Well into the seventeenth century, most drama was poetic drama. Since then, poetic drama has all but disappeared, surviving into the twentieth century only as an experimental form.

- The distinction between prose fiction and prose nonfiction didn't become clearly and generally recognized until the eighteenth century, with the rise of the novel.

- Some more recent authors have written so-called "nonfiction novels," notably Truman Capote's *In Cold Blood* (1965).

- Other authors have written "prose poems," notably Charles Baudelaire (French, 1821–1867), Gertrude Stein (1874–1946), and Robert Bly (1926–).

- The novel is traditionally defined as a longer work of prose fiction. However, novels have been written in verse.

Family Resemblance

Even the word *genre* is somewhat misleading. It comes from the same root as words having to do with biological reproduction, such as *gender, engender, gene,* and *generation.* This might suggest that literary genres are like families or species of literary works that can be grouped according to natural, inherent, organic qualities. In some ways, generic categories of literature do resemble classifications used to describe plants and animals. But significant differences reflect the differences between language and living things.

Generic Makeup

In the mid-eighteenth century, Swedish botanist Carl Linnaeus devised a system of classification used to categorize plants. Later in the century, his system was revised to show how different species were related to each other and expanded to include animals. Scientists have since developed a comprehensive taxonomy for all living things. The system even works for now-extinct plants and animals.

Nothing this stable and scientific can be done for literary genres, though. Whereas a living species is, by definition, made up of creatures that can mate with each other to produce live offspring, almost any literary genre can merge indiscriminately with any other. There aren't enough necessary restrictions on what genres are or on how they relate to one another to allow for a stable system of classification.

Generic Mutation

You could say that literary genres are like categories for living things in a world in which any one living thing could be genetically engineered, cloned, and cross-bred with any other. Rats and rutabagas, hippos and butterflies could, in theory, be combined into new forms. Whether these new forms could survive would depend on prevailing circumstances. The scientists in this world would still use categories to talk about living things, but the categories, like the things themselves, would be conventionally determined by any number of factors, including politics.

Scientists in this world would have to learn to think like literary critics. Whether the latest mutation of a so-called rat-abaga would be considered the same sort of critter might be a judgment call, or might simply depend on accepted naming practices. The point is that, even though genre categories for literature are necessary, they run the risk of misleading people who might think they are more definitive and determinate than is actually possible.

Grains of Trivium

Go into any bookstore and you'll find sections devoted to various genres of pulp fiction: sci fi, romance, horror, mystery, manga, western, etc. These genres became genres fairly recently, largely as a result of attempts by the publishing industry to identify and market books readers are likely to buy. Generic categories help commodify pulp fiction—help publishers show what they're selling, help readers see what they're buying, and guide, if not prescribe, the efforts of fiction writers to produce work that will sell.

Genre terms tend to flatten literary history, making individual works seem more natural, obvious, and ordinary than they are. They make it easy to take works of literature for granted by covering their oddness and ignoring the struggles involved in writing them and in the way they reflect the conflicts of their times. They help solidify the slippery nature of the works they refer to, but they themselves are made of the same slippery stuff: language.

Good "Ode" Times

It might help to look in detail at a particular genre—the ode—to see how genres can form, change, and disappear over time. The ode is a time-honored genre that has been defined, at various moments, in terms of style, form, and subject matter. The form stems from ancient Greece through ancient Rome into the Middle Ages and on through the nineteenth century. Then, although the form didn't exactly disappear, the term *ode* fell largely out of use. The term pretty much disappeared, but the poetic features the term refers to have remained an integral part of serious lyric.

You might say the ode dissolved into the essential characteristics of modern lyric poetry itself. Few poets have referred to their poems as odes since the nineteenth century, but the ode sits at the heart of most serious poetry of our time—formal, meditative, and intense.

Song and Dance

The ode originated in ancient Greece around the time of the rise of ancient Greek drama. In fact, many of the first odes were choric songs sung as part of dramatic performances. The chorus would sing a verse called the *strophe* as they marched together across the stage. Then they sang a verse called the *antistrophe* as they marched in the other direction. Then they would stand still and sing a verse called the *epode*.

def•i•ni•tion

The three sections of the Greek dramatic chorus (and the Pindaric ode—coming up in a minute) are the **strophe, antistrophe,** and the **epode.** These forms may be repeated in sequence within a single ode.

This might sound something like the song and dance of a Broadway show tune, but many choral odes were actually very solemn, with words that commented or expounded on the plot of a tragedy. Typically, the strophe and antistrophe had the same verse form, while the epode was different. This three-part structure helped define the ode in ancient Greece.

This structure was also used in odes written by the famous Greek poet Pindar (518–442 B.C.E.), who became an important model for subsequent poets. Pindar was a professional poet who wrote odes in honor of the winners of games and contests. His odes celebrated victory and offered simplistic moral advice: "be humble even though you're great." Pindar's odes are known for their intricate formal variety and their inspired, ecstatic tone. These qualities helped define the form in the minds of Pindar's English imitators.

The Other Ode

Writing in Latin centuries later, the Roman poet Horace (65–8 B.C.E.) wrote a number of influential poems he called odes. Horace modeled his odes not simply after Pindar, but after poems by older Greek poets as well, including Sappho and Alcaeus (both c. 600 B.C.E.).

Horace's odes differed from those of Pindar, in that they consisted entirely of uniform strophes or stanzas, were more restrained and calm in tone, and were more personal. Often reflective, they dealt with such themes as love, friendship, and the peace and simplicity of life in the country. Horace was not a professional poet in quite the same way Pindar was, but he did succeed in making a living by his poetry, thanks to the patronage of the Roman statesman Maecenas.

Like Pindar, Horace served as a model for English poets of the Renaissance, who recognized a distinction between the restrained, sensible tone of the "Horatian ode" and the inspired "Pindaric ode." They also recognized a thematic distinction. The Pindaric ode dealt with worldly achievement and glory, while the Horatian ode dealt with retirement from public life.

Kudos and Caveats

Sappho is reputed to have been one of the great lyric poets of ancient Greece. She ran a school for girls on the island of Lesbos and wrote love poetry to her favorite pupils. Although she produced a considerable body of work, very little of it has survived.

"Ode" English

The ode was one of several lyric genres explored and developed during the High Renaissance, or Elizabethan, period, but it was not the most popular. Poetry was not regarded as a suitable profession for a Renaissance gentleman, so most lyric poets of the time were confirmed amateurs. Poets who hoped to make money through their work wrote for the stage.

As a result, rather than deal directly and straightforwardly with worldly achievement in the Pindaric manner or with retirement in the Horatian manner, gentleman amateur poets of the Renaissance preferred to disguise and idealize ambition and retreat through the conventional poetic voices of the poet-lover in sonnets and song-like poems, and of the poet-shepherd in pastoral elegies and eclogues. Thus, much Renaissance lyric poetry engaged in a kind of make-believe ("pretend we're shepherds," "pretend we're in love") that was not well suited to the more serious ode.

Ben Jonson (1572–1637) was apparently the first English poet to write poems he called odes. A one-time bricklayer and former soldier, Jonson was unusually frank for his time about his ambitions as a professional poet. He was the first English poet to publish his own poetry, and he benefited greatly from noble, and even royal, patronage for his work. He wrote not only drama for the stage, but also *panegyrics* in praise of noble patrons and masques and other works for the royal court.

def•i•ni•tion

A **panegyric** is a poem praising someone for their achievements. It stems from ancient Greece.

Jonson wrote odes in both the Horatian and the Pindaric veins, and he exerted a profound influence on the succeeding generation of cavalier poets, often referred to as "the tribe of Ben." Some of these wrote odes as well.

The Ode Looks Inward

Minor poet Abraham Cowley (1618–1667) wrote several Pindaric odes with irregular stanzas that tapped into the idea of poetic ecstasy and inspiration. Cowley's poems helped detach the idea of the Pindaric ode from the formal structure of strophe, antistrophe, and epode. Cowley's odes got a mixed reception during his time but helped launch a vogue for Pindaric odes among women poets of the late seventeenth and early eighteenth centuries.

The notion of Pindaric inspiration proved useful to women who wanted to write poetry. Generally not as well educated as men and less situated to write about public affairs, women took advantage of the Pindaric vein to suggest they were specially inspired from within to write verse. Among other themes, women writers explored and played with emerging philosophical ideas concerned with the mental and emotional faculties, including wit, fancy, and sympathy.

In so doing, they helped detach the concept of Pindaric inspiration from the traditional Pindaric concern with public achievement on male-oriented terms. For women at the time, simply writing with the possibility of getting published was a daringly public and ambitious undertaking. As a result, they didn't need the public themes of a male-dominated society to write Pindaric odes. These Pindaric women never became famous, but they laid the foundations for a time when a work of poetic inspiration would come to be widely considered as sufficient public achievement in its own right.

The Ode Comes of Age

The ode came into its own as a major genre of poetic expression starting in the mid-eighteenth century. At this time, a number of male poets started to draw on ideas about the ode developed, in part, by the earlier female Pindaric poets. These men, including William Collins (1721–1759) and Thomas Gray (1716–1771), are among those known as the Poets of Sensibility and are widely regarded as important precursors of the Romantic movement in England.

During the eighteenth century, *sensibility* meant sensitivity or susceptibility to powerful feelings. The Poets of Sensibility were interested in "feeling" as a source of poetic inspiration. Many of their most famous and important lyric poems were odes—many of which were concerned with sensibility itself as a theme. Others exhibited sensibility toward various themes such as nature, art, childhood, and death.

A Well-Urned Retirement

The ode remained an important form during the Romantic period of the early decades of the nineteenth century. Most of the major poets of the period wrote odes, which include some of their most important works. The reputation of John Keats (1795–1821) owes almost entirely to his odes. Two of these, "Ode to a Nightingale" and "Ode on a Grecian Urn," are among the most famous lyric poems ever written in English.

A common figure of speech used in Keats's odes, and in many other Romantic odes as well as in odes of sensibility, is the *apostrophe*. An apostrophe is a direct address to an imaginary person, place, abstraction, or inanimate object as though it were capable of hearing and responding. For example, Keats speaks directly to the Grecian urn:

def•i•ni•tion

An **apostrophe** is a figure of speech that consists of an address to an absent person, nonexistent person, inanimate object, or abstraction as if that person or thing could hear and understand.

> Thou still unravished bride of quietness,
> Thou foster-child of silence and slow time,
> Sylvan historian, who canst thus express
> A flowery tale more sweetly than our rhyme!
> What leaf-fringed legend haunts about thy shape …?
> (1–5)

The poem relates the urn's "shape" to the ode form in two ways, both through their common origins in ancient Greece and through their common status as artifacts that are simultaneously aesthetic and expressive. At the same time, the poem contrasts the urn with the poet's work ("our rhyme") by stressing its wordlessness, its silence. Because the urn signifies without speaking, you might say it makes sense to imagine that it could hear without listening. Therefore, the apostrophe seems appropriate somehow.

The poet (obviously and conventionally a poet—who else would talk in this way to a vase?) identifies the urn as a member of a family of abstractions: a virgin ("unravished") bride of "quietness" and an adopted daughter of "time." These relationships appear inevitable insofar as the urn makes no noise and exists in time.

Yet they are artificial relationships, too. The marriage to quietness is never consummated, and the filial relation to time is adoptive. In other words, the things that make the urn-ode form belong to the present as well as the past with its "Sylvan" history are conventional rather than natural relationships.

Forgotten, but Not Gone

Since the Romantic period, not many poets have chosen to call their lyrics odes. But the reflective, inspired, and serious characteristics that define the ode form don't disappear from lyric poetry. To the contrary, they become standard, salient, conventional features of lyric in general.

Previously, the generic term *ode* served largely to position the poet as a serious and socially detached (professional, sponsored, retiring, or inspired) speaker. The term fell into disuse at a time in history when lyric conventions coalesced to a point at which poets no longer needed to position themselves with respect to their readers. Instead, poems became generally recognized and accepted as specially unpositioned utterances. This recognition may seem natural today, but it didn't happen by accident.

The modern lyric is a voice that comes from inside and speaks to something that hears without listening. In a way it's nothing new, and in a way it is new. What's new about it is that it's finally old enough to be taken for granted. It finally makes general sense of a huge, long-standing tradition recast as a brief, contemporary expression.

The Least You Need to Know

- Genres are slippery, unstable categories based on convention and subject to change over time.

- Genres tend to flatten out history, obscuring historical differences among the works ascribed to them.

- The ode is an ancient form that has been adapted to new uses from the Renaissance through the Romantic period. Since then, its characteristics have largely dissolved into those of lyric poetry in general.

Chapter 5

Between the Lines

In This Chapter

- ◆ Making sense of theories of meaning
- ◆ Does the meaning of words fit together?—structuralism
- ◆ Or fall apart?—poststructuralism and deconstruction
- ◆ Does the reader have a say?

Meaning is just about the slipperiest thing you ever thought you understood. For centuries, the greatest literary and theoretical minds have been struggling to pin down the meaning of words so we could all stop arguing. Now, finally, at last … many literary theorists have pretty much given up! Meaning is not going to hold still, no matter what.

This is not an entirely bad thing, but it means that literary criticism is not likely to lead to any resounding consensus about what works of literature finally, definitely mean anytime soon. Instead, critics have to face the fact that their interpretations are only as good as the work and creativity that goes into them.

Coming to terms with meaning is no easy task. The difficulty has to do with the ways meaning connects to everything else: literature, culture, language, writing, the mind, the body, and the world. Drawing on highly sophisticated ideas about society and language, literary theory has given rise to some powerful critical approaches, including and especially a radical critique of meaning itself known as *deconstruction*.

Structure and Beyond

Deconstruction is a major thrust of a broader critical movement known as *poststructuralism* because of the ways it builds on—and moves beyond—an approach to language and culture known as *structuralism*. Structuralism got its start with the work of the founder of structural linguistics, Ferdinand de Saussure (1857–1915). Structuralism laid the slippery foundation for poststructuralism by identifying meaning not in terms of the relationship between words and the things they refer to, but in terms of the relationship between words and other words.

def•i•ni•tion

Structuralism is a theoretical approach, originally to linguistics and later to anthropology. Structuralists regard their field, whether language or culture, as a structure that's organized internally rather than from without. **Poststructuralism** is a major, influential thrust of postmodern theory. The term refers to the insight that the structure apparent in language and culture (described by the structuralists) is unstable, both internally and in relation to whatever's outside it.

The Shape We're In

Structural linguistics sees language as a structure that's organized internally rather than in relation to external reality. Words become meaningful largely as a result of interrelationships among words themselves rather than through a simple reflection of reality—the definition of a word is marked off by other words. Language is a system of signs in which each *signifier* is shaped by its opposition to other signifiers in the system.

def•i•ni•tion

A **signifier** is a term that refers to something else, a *signified*. Words are signifiers, but so are other things that express meaning within a culture. Cultural signification was identified as a focus of study by structural theorists and continues to provide a focus for poststructural theory.

The word *book*, for example, is meaningful in relation to all the words for things like books that are different from books: *pamphlet, magazine, unpublished manuscript, lecture notes, clay tablet,* etc. How we understand *book* depends on all the things a book might be but is not. Thus, *book* fits into a structure of signification, and this structure gives it its meaning.

Meaning Turned Inside Out

Structural linguists see all terms as structurally related to one another. Through their similarities and oppositions to other words, all words take their place in a system of signification. This was a radical, revolutionary notion that changed the way people thought about meaning—not as the truth or falsehood of statements about the world, but as the effect of interrelated elements in a closed system.

Structural linguistics laid the foundation for a new way to study culture, known as *structural anthropology*, strongly associated with the work of French anthropologist Claude Levi-Strauss (1908–2006). Levi-Strauss said that the structure of language is reflected in culture itself and is, in turn, a reflection of the structure of the human mind. In Levi-Strauss's view, a culture's language reflects a culture's thought.

Taking Talk Apart

Current thinking about language owes a great deal to the tremendously influential French philosopher Jacques Derrida (1930–2004), who developed the critical approach known as *deconstruction*. The basic idea behind deconstruction is that language is unstable. Meaning is elusive and indeterminate. As a result, the critical search for the timeless, reliable truth of a piece of writing is futile. The search for truth leads only to more slippery, unstable language.

Coming Up Empty

As a philosopher, Derrida is interested in the ways other philosophers have attempted to express ideas about reality through language. According to Derrida, there's always a gap between language and reality. Deconstruction developed out of Derrida's attempt to show how this gap undermines philosophical claims about reality. In his efforts, he revises the radical ideas behind structuralism in ways that make them even more radical.

 Kudos and Caveats

Derrida has characterized deconstruction as an experience rather than a theory—the experience of reading the instability of language. In its broad historical context, deconstruction is a critique of Enlightenment thinking, the eighteenth-century belief that "reason" can grasp objective truth.

Derrida was intrigued by the notion that language is a structure, but he questioned its stability. Unlike Levi-Strauss, Derrida did not believe that the human mind was somehow present in language. The gap he saw between language and reality also separated language from the mind. According to Derrida, it's impossible for something to be both outside language (such as the mind or reality) and inside it, or "present," at the same time. As a result, there's nothing in the "structure" of language to give it stability.

What's more, while signifiers refer to one another, they don't occupy a fixed place in relation to one another. They aren't solidly detached from other signifiers. They bleed into one another all the time.

Pulling the Rug of Language Out from Under Us

What is a book? When does it become one? Is it set apart from other books by the words it contains? By what its readers think those words mean? By what its author thinks? But doesn't the book exist to render moot all these questions about what people think? Isn't the important thing not what anyone thinks, but what the book actually says? Does the book reflect the difference between saying and thinking? What *is* the difference?

Deconstruction has to do with the insight that language and meaning are two different things, yet one and the same thing. Language/meaning is different from itself. That's how it works, and that's why it never works the way it's supposed to. When people use language, they typically assume that language is capable of conveying truths about reality. Deconstructive analysis of language proves these assumptions wrong.

Deconstructionists are good at discovering things language does without anyone's intending it to. They find accidents waiting to happen and use them to show that there's much more—and much less—to language than what people want it to mean.

Disassembly Required

Thanks to deconstruction, poststructuralist literary critics have a number of interesting concepts in their critical arsenal to draw on when dealing with (deconstructing) texts. Here are some of them:

trace   In referring to things they stand for, signifiers evoke things they do not stand for. These are traces—things that are absent from, yet suggested by, a text.

différance   This French term suggests that signifiers differ from what they signify and defer their significance to other signifiers. In other words, due to the gap between language and reality, and due to the interconnectedness of signifiers, you can't locate a fixed, stable meaning in any one place.

aporia   This is indeterminacy produced by absence of meaning and by multiplicity of possible meanings.

presence   This is the delusory belief or assumption that stable meaning is located within a text. The idea of presence ignores the fact that meaning depends on what it is not.

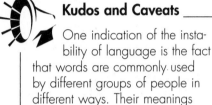

Kudos and Caveats

One indication of the instability of language is the fact that words are commonly used by different groups of people in different ways. Their meanings vary from person to person.

In literary criticism, deconstruction offers a fruitful reminder that there's no single correct way to interpret a text, together with the humbling insight that all interpretations, including one's own, are deconstructable. In fact, deconstructive criticism often seems to provide lessons in the deconstruction of texts rather than interpretations. That is to say, the interpretive process involves working toward an awareness of how a text fails to hold together without gaps, evasions, and self-contradictions.

The Human Element

If language is such a slippery, unreliable world of smoke and mirrors, you might wonder how anyone could ever take writing seriously. Even though language doesn't simply contain and convey the truth, people respond to it as though it did. People meet language more than halfway in order to make it serve their purposes. This involves being selectively receptive to certain ideas that can be milked out of it and blind to others they can't see or don't want to acknowledge. This is the case both when people discuss current events and when they interpret works of literature.

Key Players

You might get the idea from all this that interpreting literature is a highly subjective and scattershot undertaking. If people make language mean what they want it to, and if any interpretation is inherently partial and limited, who's to say what a work of literature means? The answer is you, the reader.

> **Grains of Trivium**
>
> In a famous experiment, literature scholar and theorist Stanley Fish walked into a class he was teaching and found that the previous instructor in that classroom had left written assignments on the board. Rather than erase them, Fish informed his class that they were poems and invited the class to interpret them. They did a brilliant job with what they had to work with! They found that, in fact, the writing on the board yielded an abundance of poetic meaning. Fish's point is that readers are guided by their assumptions when interpreting texts as much as by the texts themselves.

There's no single, correct interpretation of any literary text. Literature can be—and is—read in different ways by different people. Even so, not all interpretations are equally cogent and powerful. To construct a cogent interpretation takes thought and work. You have to identify things that are important, develop a perspective, come to terms with other perspectives, and gather evidence that supports your position.

Meeting the Challenge

Interpreting literary texts is hard, especially if you haven't done a lot of it already. And the challenges can be hard to see. Because the possibilities are so numerous, some students are inclined to assume that the interpretive process is merely subjective or arbitrary and comes down, finally, to so much baloney. They don't appreciate the knowledge and skill that goes into interpretation.

Some students believe that the secret to success in class is to learn and repeat the teacher's take on the material, whatever it might be. In fact, because lit study has become highly politicized in recent years, many students may think that they are being indoctrinated in some kind of weird political outlook. They may also think that their grade depends on how readily they seem to accept a particular dogma.

But that's not how it is. Teachers want to teach classes in which their students can learn. And students learn the most by the work they do, especially when they do work on challenging texts, issues, and ideas. As a result, lots of English class discussions are about stuff that's hard to understand. By working with it, interpreting it, talking about it, and writing about it, students gain knowledge and experience working with texts.

The Point Is How Powerfully You Miss the Point

On a basic level, by interpreting a text, you are simply saying what it means. But it's part of the nature of literary texts that they never simply mean one thing. What they mean depends on how you look at them. When you look at a text in different ways, different things become important. And what's important to you might not be what's important to the person who wrote the text you're interpreting. That's okay.

Noted literature critic Harold Bloom has suggested that many of the most compelling literary interpretations are *strong misreadings*. A strong misreading is an interpretation that works closely with the text but takes it over and interprets it in ways the author never intended. Others have gone further to say that all interpretations are misreadings.

The idea is not to nail down the truth once and for all, but to put together supporting evidence for a way of looking at something. The payoff may not be complete or immediate. Even so, it's good practice that can often yield unexpected pleasures and benefits that are both social and intellectual. And when they're good, literary discussions are fascinating.

def•i•ni•tion

A **strong misreading** is a cogent interpretation of a text to mean things its author never intended. The concept has been used by lit critic Harold Bloom in explaining, for example, how early Christians "misread" the Hebrew Bible in writing the gospels.

The Least You Need to Know

◆ Structuralism gave rise to the radical idea that words get their meanings in relation to other words.

◆ Poststructuralism, especially deconstruction, gave rise to the even more radical idea that the structure of language is unstable and that meaning is necessarily indeterminate.

◆ Interpretations may be cogent and powerful, even if they are inconsistent with the author's intentions.

Chapter 6

P.C. (Political Criticism)

In This Chapter

- Jumping on the bandwagon of political criticism
- Who's in control? Subjects, ideology, and power
- The past has a future thanks to new historicism
- A theory of their own: feminism
- Rethinking foreign affairs with postcolonialism
- Queer theory comes out

The expression *P.C.* usually means "politically correct," a point of view that is aware of and sensitive to cultural differences within society. The notion of political correctness, however, reflects a rather simplistic view of social relations. In fact, there's no single "correct" position. Once you recognize the problem of social injustice reflected in speech and behavior, the questions of where it comes from, how far it goes, and what to do about it remain. These questions get explored by a different sort of "P.C."—political criticism.

Political criticism has emerged on the academic scene gradually over the past 50 years or so and changed things a lot. Political criticism has undermined the traditional rationales for studying literature by exposing cultural biases at work, not only within the old academy, but within the Anglo literary tradition itself.

Theoretically, political criticism is radical, striking at the guilty heart of humanism with a profound, thorough, and inexhaustibly insightful critique of discursive power—the pervasive, invisible pull of language that yanks all our chains. Now we know that the indescribable beauties of literature once celebrated by critics of yore have covered many highly describable uglinesses, including unreasonable and self-serving prejudices of every stripe. But we still can't all agree on what to do about it!

Folks in Focus

The relationship between society and language is an important focus for political criticism. Common thinking holds that language is a tool societies use for communication. A harder concept to grasp is that language shapes people into social individuals. Our behavior and our sense of self are thoroughly guided and shaped by language, which tells us from a young age about the world and our place in it.

Made-Up Selves

Without realizing it, people buy into values, beliefs, and ideals expressed in language. Whenever we communicate, we establish priorities and come to agreements. We evoke shared values. These values are not shared universally across cultures, but they often seem necessary, absolute, and unavoidable to the people who hold them.

What shapes these values? In a word, power. The workings of power are more subtle than you might imagine. Power can influence people indirectly by establishing discourses that organize the ways people think and behave, and who they are inso far as they link people together in society.

def•i•ni•tion

Subjects are individuals to the extent that they're shaped and delineated by discourse. In this view, we become who we are, for all practical and observable purposes, in response to cultural influences acting, by means of power, through discourse.

This may seem counterintuitive. We tend to think that we control language, not the other way around. We can make choices, decisions, and plans concerning our lives. But the choices available to us are defined and limited by society operating through discourse. So are the reasons we have for making them. And so are we.

Our "selves" are actually formed and defined through the process of acquiring—with the help of language, or discourse—our position in society and our points of view on the world. Discourse makes people what they are. Theorists refer to this process as *subject* formation.

The Power of the Powerful

People have no choice but to buy into the power interests that shape society. People often identify with powerful people in various ways, even if they're not powerful themselves. For example, people are likely to think that the way powerful people think is right because of the ability powerful people have to fill the world with things and ideas that serve their own interests and support their point of view. If people are opposed to power interest, their opposition necessarily rests on competing power interests.

The powerful pass laws, build monuments to themselves, and patronize poets to write works of literature. All these things powerfully express the values of the powerful, often making them seem right and true to the whole society. Values change as power relations change and new ideas fall into place in support of new power interests. Patterns of thought internalized as values and organized along the lines of power are called *ideologies*.

def•i•ni•tion

Ideology is made up of the ideas, beliefs, and values shared by members of a society. Ideology serves power interests in ways we might not recognize. For example, by embracing a shared value like freedom, we become less inclined to question all the things in society that make us not free. In its most radical sense, developed by the French theorist Louis Althusser (1918–), ideology includes all ideas, beliefs, and values that are ideological—that is, they are structured by power interests.

Even without the critical concept of ideology, it's clear that power exerts force on society. State power and Church power, for example, are not exactly historical secrets. But throughout most of history, notions of power have been more or less hard to separate from notions of right and wrong and true and false. The concept of ideology adds an important critical wrinkle.

The Legs We Stand On

Any notion of right and wrong and *any* notion of true or false is ideological (even scientific truths, to the degree that they hold significance for society). There's no universal truth or universal goodness. There's only any number of competing ideologies.

We can still believe in what's good for us, and we can work to reach agreements and compromises with others who see things differently, but any claim to universal moral rightness for everyone is itself an ideological ploy.

Power tends to be expressed and reinforced by ideology, but power isn't monolithic—it isn't one big single thing looming over all society. Instead, people are always tweaking it, trying to find new spaces within it, minimize the pressure it puts on them, as well as shift the benefits of power in their favor. Literature provides a fascinating record of this ongoing process.

A work of literature, or any other aspect of culture, can reflect power interests in various ways. It can assert them, glorify them, disguise them, question them, refute them, or reify them (make them the same concretely or essentially real or true, as opposed to provisional or "all made up"). And these interests themselves may be difficult to classify.

For example, power interests can be religious, nationalist, domestic, ethnic, class based, or professional. Power can inhabit many spheres simultaneously. Regardless of which sphere is concerned, theorists tend to think of all power interests as political. In other words, *politics* refers not only to party politics within government, but to family politics, racial politics, etc. Power interests are always political, even when they disguise their political nature. Thus, for example, the widespread eighteenth-century notion that "children should be seen and not heard" is a political ideal, even though no one was necessarily "campaigning" for it through recognized political channels.

 Kudos and Caveats

Is there a school of political criticism that aims to expose and resist the systematic disempowerment of children by means of an age-centric adult hegemony that subjects them and denies them a voice in society? Sorry, kid. "Infantilism" has yet to be recognized as a radical program to subvert the domination of the no-longer-new. Instead, new people's speech is politically contained and culturally marginalized as an unauthorized and supposedly "underdeveloped" discourse—as a "cute" or "precocious" attempt to mimic "maturity" or as a "puerile" inability to "grow up." *Waaaaaa!*

Strange Bedfellows

Political criticism exists in many strains, including new historicism, postcolonialism, feminism, and queer theory. All are generally concerned with power relations, subjectivity, and discourse, and each focuses on a different set of political concerns.

New Historicism: It's All in the Timing

New historicism focuses on the ways literature expresses—and sometimes disguises—power relations at work in the social context in which the literature was produced. Often this involves making connections between a literary work and other kinds of texts. Literature is often shown to "negotiate" conflicting power interests.

New historicism has made its biggest mark on literary studies of the Renaissance and Romantic periods and has revised notions of literature as privileged, apolitical writing. Much new historicism focuses on the *marginalization* of subjects such as those identified as witches, the insane, heretics, vagabonds, and political prisoners.

def•i•ni•tion

Marginalization is the complex social process that pushes certain people outside (to the margins of) mainstream society, usually because they are perceived as a threat to shared values.

Feminism: Angel Killers

Feminism predates the rise of political literary criticism and is especially wide-ranging, including several different movements concerned with correcting the imbalance of power and status between men and women, and exposing the patterns of thought that represent women in an inferior light. These movements have focused on culture in general, literature in particular, and politics per se.

Novelist and essayist Virginia Woolf (1882–1941) offered an early and important critique of male biases at work in literature. Woolf identified a number of obstacles that prevented women from succeeding professionally, especially as professional writers. One was the sentimental and debilitating ideal of the pure, demure, and selfless Victorian wife constructed by men and epitomized in the image of the "angel in the house," who exists solely to make men happy.

Woolf says that to become a writer herself, she had to "kill" the angel in the house. She had to reject the ideal and free herself from its power over her. But this is easier said than done. Years later, Sandra Gilbert and Susan Gubar, in a study of nineteenth-century women writers, identified a disturbing image that characterizes women who "killed" the angel in the house in order to write: the "madwoman in the attic."

The starkly opposed pair of images of angel and madwoman suggest that women who reject the male ideal of femininity risk being seen as crazy, not only by men, but even by themselves. Either way, women are confined to the domestic sphere, where they hold virtually no influence on society. Nineteenth-century literature is full of female characters who resemble one of these types.

Essence Is Optional

Feminism is overtly political, but not all feminists embrace the same political positions or focus on the same critical issues. Strains of feminism are inflected in various ways by other political issues, including class, race, nationality, and sexual preference. Some feminists focus on literary texts, others look to culture, and many are predominantly concerned with theory.

def•i•ni•tion

Essentialism, when applied to gender, is the view that differences between men and women are inherent rather than socially constructed.

Much feminist scholarship is highly theoretical, aiming, for example, to account for perceived gender differences in cultural and discursive terms rather than simply biological terms. In so doing, it radically challenges *essentialist* thinking that sees gender difference as absolute and inherent rather than as a cultural construct. While no one disputes the fact of biological difference between the sexes, how and what this difference may signify is profoundly open to question.

Postcolonialism: Who's "We," White Man?

Postcolonialism is concerned with the ways colonial power constructs itself and the native peoples it subjugates through the discourse of institutions. Such institutions include Western governments, trading companies and industrial corporations, the military, religious missions, and the Western media. Colonial discourse has been markedly reflected in English literature since the Victorian novel, although many postcolonial theorists are concerned with colonial thinking into the present time.

Thus, the *post* in *postcolonial* doesn't necessarily mean that colonial issues have been resolved.

Kudos and Caveats

During the final year of his life, Said spoke out against the Iraq war and deplored the roles of the Pentagon, large corporations, and mainstream media in deceiving the American people into acquiescing to it.

A groundbreaking and foundational postcolonial study is *Orientalism* (1978), by Edward Said (1935–2003). This work describes the ways people of the East and, in particular, Palestine are represented in Western discourse as inferior and incapable of governing themselves. Said finds this tendency at work in the way Westerners have represented others for centuries.

Radicals: Left Out and Taken Over

A continual issue for postcolonialism and for political criticism as a whole is the tendency for radical political stances that call for the empowerment of marginalized peoples who get taken over by the wealthy elite. Many writers from non-Western cultures, including some who have spoken out against Western exploitation, have been embraced and celebrated by the Western media as hip and stylish. As a result, these writers may get rich and famous, but exploitation of the poor and marginalized continues as usual!

The same thing happens with radical writers and other countercultural figures within Western society. Radical politics and radical positions are often turned into hip cultural trends. Novelist and essayist Tom Wolfe (1931–) has referred to the appropriation of radical style by cultural hipsters as *radical chic*. Wolfe coined this term to describe American culture and politics in the 1960s; it has been widely used since to talk about multiculturalism.

Meanwhile, plenty of non-Westerners eagerly embrace Western ways and values in the hope of finding economic opportunities. Global corporate capitalism divides rich and poor, but not along racial, ethnic, or national lines.

def•i•ni•tion

Radical chic is the hip, trendy appropriation by the cultural elite of the style that goes along with a radical political stance. Radical chic makes radical politics more visible as style, but less effective as a means of political change.

Queer Theory: Same Difference

Queer theory has much in common with a good deal of theoretical feminism. Queer theorists are interested in exposing and resisting sexual prejudice in literature and society, as well as in developing subversive, alternate discourses about sexuality. They're also interested in the question of what sexual preference is and how it relates to politics, personal identity, and, more broadly, discourse. Can sexuality exist prior to or outside discourse? If so, how can we talk about it? If not, how do we interpret discourse about sexuality?

These questions are crucial within poststructuralism because sexuality is such a powerful aspect of subject formation. As with other strains of political criticism, queer theory includes a range of different critical positions that are important both as theory and as politics.

Of course, debate abounds within political criticism as well as between political critics and their detractors. As a result, the trendy notion of "political correctness" that suggests there's some basic principle we should all agree to is somewhat simplistic and misleading. While political critics have brought to light many political problems and pitfalls readers must face, they haven't provided solutions that everyone accepts.

The Least You Need to Know

- ◆ Political criticism is concerned with the power of discourse to shape subjects and societies.

- ◆ Political criticism includes new historicism, feminism, postcolonialism, and queer theory.

- ◆ While political criticism articulates a coherent critique of power, debates abound about how to empower those who are disadvantaged by it.

Chapter 7

Time and Tide

In This Chapter

- History, society, and changing trends in literary criticism
- Critiquing New Criticism
- Culture wars and political criticism
- What should be taught in high school?

You might think a poem or a story stands on its own as an independent, self-sufficient entity. You read it for what it is and leave the rest of the world out of it. This, in fact, is pretty much how literature has been read and studied for most of the twentieth century. It has been viewed as its own special, privileged thing.

These days, however, literature doesn't appear to be quite so self-sufficient. It doesn't exist in a vacuum. Nor does it rise above ordinary human reality and human conflict into a transcendent sphere of meaning all its own. It's part—an important part—of political, social, and cultural debates. Because of these debates, people have come to see literature in a new light: the light of history and culture.

History and *culture* are useful terms, but different people understand them in different ways. History and culture are complicated abstractions that can take a fair amount of study to understand. After all, they are challenging subjects in their own right, as anyone who has studied history or sociology can tell you. The good news is that studying literature turns out to be a very good way to study history and culture, too.

It Is Written

Just what we do when we study literature has shifted drastically in many ways in recent decades. Even so, certain key notions have remained much the same. Amid widespread debate about just about everything else, most literary scholars agree on at least one thing: it's a good idea to read carefully, to pay close attention to the text of whatever work or works may be under discussion.

Close Encounters of the Literary Kind

Many of today's college English professors and high school teachers have been strongly influenced, as both teachers and scholars, by a literary approach known as New Criticism. New Criticism developed during the first half of the twentieth century and was instrumental in making English literature a thriving, vital academic subject. It offered both practical guidelines and a compelling rationale for literary study that still carry weight with lit scholars today.

An important rationale for the whole big, scholarly enterprise has to do with the value of critical intelligence. The idea is that if you can analyze and interpret a literary text, you can become intellectually equipped to deal with life's complexities, too, not only on a personal level, but on a social level as well. You stand to make a positive difference in an increasingly complex and confusing world.

 Kudos and Caveats _____

Amid uncertainty regarding the question of how much practical value there is in a college English degree, advocates of the English major often point to the "transferable skills" English majors acquire. These are skills developed in the context of literary study that can be used to further a career outside of teaching and scholarship. There's little doubt that English majors do develop critical skills that could prove useful in the private sector and other nonacademic careers. However …

The interpretive guidelines New Criticism supplies call for paying careful attention to the words on the page. Through a process called "close reading," described in

Chapter 2, you identify what a work of literature actually does, above and beyond aesthetic considerations. You figure out, in detail, what the work says and why it says it that way. You gain a sense of what intellectual conflicts the work deals with and how it resolves them. You discover tensions and ambiguities in the tone, structure, and logic of the work. And you ground your interpretation in the words on the page.

Kudos and Caveats

It's not clear whether prospective employers are likely to favor English majors' "transferable skills" over specific knowledge and pertinent experience. It's also not clear whether prospective employers are likely to be put off by an English major's demonstrated interest in what is, for most people, a leisure-time activity or by an English major's possible indoctrination in theoretical perspectives that are critical of corporate capitalism.

New and Newer

Literature scholars still perform close readings and continue to prize critical intelligence, but New Criticism has become old hat in certain other important respects. In focusing on the written words of a literary work, New Critics tended not to think much about what scholars today call the historical and cultural context of literature. The meaning of a work of literature interrelates with whatever is going on around it. The literary work is infused with historical and cultural considerations that shed light on what the piece says. But New Critics tend to disregard these considerations.

And when New Critics do draw on historical and cultural contexts in their interpretations, they tend to not see them as problematic. They assume that neither history nor culture requires much interpretation. They restrict their interpretive focus to the text. To them, literary works form the central focus of study, whereas contexts are largely inessential to literary criticism.

In contrast, scholars today regard not only the text, but the context as well, as an important critical challenge. History and culture can be interpreted in many different ways, depending on your point of view. And your point of view on history and culture can deepen and enhance your understanding of the text. Scholars of

Grains of Trivium

A notion that proved highly influential within New Criticism but that few scholars accept today is the "intentional fallacy" idea, which says that it's a mistake to interpret a text in light of what you suppose the author intended to do in writing it. The idea is that the literary text is its own objective thing that exists independently of merely personal concerns.

today still need to read closely and think critically. But they can take context much more fully into consideration.

These days, much criticism, especially theoretical criticism, may focus as much or more on context as on an individual work. As a result, there's a great deal more for lit scholars to interpret than there used to be. The field has become much bigger and more complex since the heyday of New Criticism. This can make it much harder to see the big literary picture.

Pride and Prejudice

Traditionally, lit and lit study tended to promote a number of interrelated ideals that have come into question in recent years:

Kudos and Caveats

A leading proponent of the idea that great literature has a positive cultural influence on people is Victorian poet and critic Matthew Arnold (1822–1888), who suggested that literature could replace religion in fostering moral values and holding society together.

◆ Great literature transcends politics.

◆ Great literature is the work of individual genius.

◆ Great literature reflects and speaks to human universals.

◆ We become better, more humanized people when we read and appreciate great literature.

Many have found these ideals appealing. In fact, they've been making lots of people happy for generations. They suggest that there is an abundance of goodness and beauty in the world and that we can all find it and share in it as readers of great literature.

The "Great" Tradition

It's certainly possible to point to evidence that supports these statements. Much literature—and much English literature, in particular—attempts to be "great" in precisely these ways. These ideals are part of a large, evolving cultural program that much literature has been involved in.

It's no secret that English literature has been a source of national pride for the English and a source of cultural pride for Anglos all over the world. This pride has fostered literature and encouraged Anglo writers for centuries. Yet there's a degree to which this pride tends to disguise itself—and disguise English lit, too. People who hold these ideals don't always see them as rooted in cultural pride or see a cultural bias in the way they read literature.

English lit, however—even lit specifically written by Anglos—is too big and diverse to speak with a single voice or send a single unified message about Anglo culture or anything else. For Anglo teachers and scholars to say, as many have done, that "English literature is ours," they have had to ignore significant historical and political differences between themselves and other Anglos. In so doing, they disregard much of what "their" literature has to say.

Canon Fodder

One of England's greatest cultural heroes is the legendary King Arthur, who embodies wisdom and beneficence in the form of an "English" king. Ironically, Arthurian legend appears to be based on a historical sixth-century Welsh (Celtic) chieftain who fought *against* invading Anglo-Saxons. The earliest legends traveled from Wales to France before returning to England in the wake of the Norman invasion (1066). Since that time, Arthur has been embraced by Anglos as *their* English king.

Literature is permeated with traces of cultural, ethical, and political conflict. To say that it rises above these conflicts is to miss out on how it engages them. To study works of literature but ignore the conflicts they address, and often disguise, is to fool yourself—and others, too, if you're a teacher or critic.

Time Warps

Elizabethan (late sixteenth century) poet and playwright Ben Jonson famously said of another Elizabethan poet and playwright, William Shakespeare, that he was "not of an age, but for all time." Jonson apparently meant that Shakespeare's work was so great that people in future times would continue to enjoy it. Literary fame has long been an important concept that is woven into both literature and criticism.

But fame requires more than just the memorable deeds of an important individual. It also takes a society of people who think the individual and the deeds are important and memorable. And their reasons for thinking so have a lot to do with cultural pride and politics.

Actually, Shakespeare did not think the way people think today. In his works, such things as individualism, democracy, and social mobility—capitalist values most people hold today—appear in a consistently negative light as threats to an idealized social order. In contrast, he often represents a repressive absolute monarchy and the inherited social status of the elite as not simply good, but naturally, even divinely, good. He wouldn't have succeeded as an Elizabethan poet and playwright if he hadn't.

The reasons Shakespeare was famous in his own time are different from the reasons he has been famous ever since. In celebrating a great English poet, people tend to focus on certain things and ignore certain others—and to a degree, re-create the poet in their own image. Doing so has been an ongoing cultural project since the Renaissance.

def•i•ni•tion

Reception history is the study of the ways events and artifacts are interpreted at different moments in history. Both literary scholars and historians recognize this concept.

In fact, many modern scholars are interested in the *reception history* of Shakespeare and other writers. Reception history is the study of how an artifact (literary or otherwise) or event is read or "received" at different moments in time. Studies in reception history might look at what people during the Victorian period thought of Shakespeare and discuss why they thought as they did. Such a study might involve looking at critical assessments of Shakespeare written at the time, published editions of his works, allusions to his work in new works of literature, accounts of performances of his plays, and other sources of evidence.

For literature scholars, reception history depends on the recognition that readers at various stages in history have a cultural stake in the literature of the past. They may be looking for something in literature that scholars of today are no longer looking *for*, but are looking *at* in a more critical way. You might say it involves developing a point of view on other points of view.

Bursting Bubbles

A heightened awareness of cultural self-interest and political conflict in literature has helped spark a boom in political criticism that tries to show how literary works are implicated in the power relations of society. Many of these studies aim to expose the duplicity and injustice of such ideological evils as patriarchal thinking, anglocentrism, colonialism, capitalism, racism, and homophobia. (You can read more about political criticism in Chapter 5.)

Many of today's English lit academicians are interested in showing how traditional social ideals, endorsed in historic literary works (say, "chastity" during the Renaissance, or "freedom" in the nineteenth century) tend to cover up, disguise, or deny injustices committed by the privileged and powerful. Double standards, faulty reasoning, and emotional appeals all serve to influence social attitudes in systematic ways that portray self-interested social ideals as somehow "true," "right," and "real," whereas actually they are all "made up" cultural beliefs that stack the political deck in favor of the privileged and powerful.

Bridging the Gaps

Lit scholars of today face interpretive challenges every time they turn around. There's the text, the context, the relationship between the two, and the relationship of both to the scholar and the critical context. Even the significance of the project of scholarship is subject to debate. Any and all may be more or less important as a focus of interpretation.

Levels of Difficulty

Literature can be inherently difficult to understand. One reason for this is that language is a very big, very complicated thing. Learning to use language well—whether reading, writing, or speaking—is a never-ending process that builds on what you already know. Whenever most people read, they find unfamiliar words, ideas, and points of view that pose interpretive challenges. The more you work at figuring out what writing means, the better a reader you become. This is true even with regard to everyday, nonliterary language.

Works of literature use language in special ways, often with the purpose of creating subtle or unusual effects, meaningful ambiguities, and alternative ways of seeing things. So with literature, the interpretive challenges can be heightened. You have to interpret the peculiar things the language *does* in addition to what it *says*.

On top of this, quite a lot of literature poses further challenges. Two major factors that can make language especially hard to understand are *historical* and *cultural differences*. Whoever we may be, we are different from people who lived in the past. And so are people who have cultural backgrounds that differ from ours. These differences make anything such people write inherently difficult to interpret. Interpretation involves seeing things in unfamiliar ways.

It's good to recognize these interpretive problems. If you're willing to work to solve them, you have the makings of a good literary critic. Much literature is written by people who assume they share a great deal of common ground with their readers.

Increasingly, this sort of common ground can't be taken for granted. As a reader, it can be extremely helpful to recognize a writer's assumptions about who and what is important and why, especially if these assumptions differ from what you might think is important.

def•i•ni•tion

Historical difference refers to the radical discontinuity between people who lived in the past and those alive today. **Cultural difference** refers to a similar discontinuity between cultures. Differences in thinking, behavior, and the use of language are everywhere. But those who aren't looking for the differences often overlook them, especially considering this involves the recognition that knowledge is a cultural construct rather than something that is "true for everyone."

Lines in the Sand

Literature can say a lot about the culture that produces it. Lots of literature is written with particular cultural issues more or less explicitly in mind. Often lit is embedded in culture in subtler ways, revealing—without necessarily intending to reveal—values, ideals, and attitudes shared or contested by whole groups of people.

To think about literature in terms of culture doesn't exactly simplify the topic. If anything, culture is even more complex and multifaceted than literature. Culture and literature interrelate in different ways. Literature is shaped by culture. It also makes up an important aspect of culture in its own right. Literature also helps transmit culture from place to place and from generation to generation.

Studying literature can serve as a way to acquire culture as well as study it. As a result, people have always worried about whether given works of literature send the "right" message. And recently, teachers have worried about which cultures the literature they teach should come from. More and more work written in English comes from outside, or at the margins of, Anglo culture—as well it should in a world with so many non-Anglo English speakers.

Grains of Trivium

According to noted scholar and critic Raymond Williams (1921–1988), "culture is one of the two or three most complicated words in the English language" (*Key Words*, 1983) because of its long and varied history and its importance as a concept in a variety of different fields.

Dead White Man's Burden

For over a century now, English (and American) literature has been taught partly to make people feel good about English (and American) culture and society. Shakespeare's comedies show us the wit, harmony, and humanity of jolly old England, while Frank Norris and the muckrakers show us that in this great country of ours, evil and injustice always lose in the end. In today's multicultural climate, such readings seem not only culturally biased, but also simplistic.

Rigorous in some ways as New Criticism was in its approach to the text, it did little to prevent biases and erroneous assumptions about Western culture and history from creeping in. Time was (and in some schools, still is) when a big reason to teach and study lit was to celebrate Western civilization and instill humanistic values in budding young minds. Increasingly, however, scholars have been coming to see literature as a potent channel of cultural biases that serve interests not everyone shares. What represents civilized humanity to one scholar can appear to another as a delivery system for, say, imperialist and sexist ideology.

Multiculturalism

While it's useful to recognize historical difference when reading the literature of bygone days, cultural difference comes strongly into play in the literature of our time. Our society is increasingly multicultural, and the proliferation of non-Anglo literature written in English reflects this.

Multiculturalism is everything that has to do with the presence of diverse cultures within society. It often implies the liberal attitude that even though we may not all share common values, it's nice to be respectful of diversity. It has had a huge impact on literature studies in recent decades, all the way from grade-school English classes to rarified academic circles—but in very different ways for each.

def•i•ni•tion

Multiculturalism is, on one hand, the fact of diverse cultures within society and, on the other hand, an array of debates over how to understand and respond to this fact.

Different Sides of the Story

For academic scholars, multicultural awareness ties in with political criticism. The issues are complex, and the points of view under consideration include perspectives from all over the world. Of particular concern are the legacies of colonialism and imperialism.

Colonialism and imperialism are closely related. Colonialism is the military and political process of expanding into new territory and expelling, annihilating, or subjugating the people who live there. Imperialism is the military and economic process of conquering other countries, exploiting foreign labor and natural resources, and creating new markets abroad for consumer goods. Disturbingly, Anglos have done quite a lot of both, as have the peoples of many European countries.

In the process, the English language has spread to many countries and cultures. Many non-Anglo writers have written in English about the colonial and imperial experience and its legacy, exploring issues related to what happens when two cultures merge on unequal footing, including the efforts of these cultures to understand one another. These texts make up an important part of a growing body of multicultural literature.

Multiculturalism in the Classroom

Meanwhile, many schoolteachers have become increasingly aware of cultural diversity and more and more are promoting it in their classrooms. They are concerned that, by teaching a preponderance of literature written by Anglos, they might be stacking the deck in favor of their Anglo students at the expense of the others. After all, it's easier for students to learn about their own cultures than about someone else's.

> **Grains of Trivium**
>
> Multicultural reform of the U.S. public school curriculum began during the 1980s and focused on teaching new perspectives in literature, history, and social studies.

How people think and feel about literature often depends on where they stand in relation to the culture the literature speaks from—especially as younger students. Whether a particular poem or story gives you a lump in your throat, an itch in your brow, or a knot in your stomach may have a lot to do with whether you think the person who wrote it is essentially like you or largely different from you—or even antagonistic toward you.

Many English teachers these days have students read literary works written by people of all racial and ethnic groups. This way, hopefully, everyone gets a chance to identify strongly with at least some of the class reading, and everyone also faces the challenge of trying to understand unfamiliar perspectives. As a result of multiculturalism, many school students are reading less "English literature," per se, and more works of "literatures written in English."

Finding a Place

Because everyone interprets literature differently, context and perspective are crucial in lit study. There is no single correct meaning of any literary work or literary context. One of the exciting challenges of lit study is learning to think about, and work with, multiple points of view as you develop your own.

Even though English class and, more broadly, the academy represent a place set apart from the world and devoted to study, that study doesn't take place in theoretical isolation from everything else that goes on in life. In fact, literary study, like literature itself, is permeated by culture, shaped by history, and driven by politics.

The Least You Need to Know

- ◆ New Criticism is an important critical movement that took hold in the early decades of the twentieth century. It stresses the importance of paying close attention to the literary text as a way to develop critical intelligence.

- ◆ New Criticism tended to disregard the historical and cultural contexts of literature, in contrast to more recent critical approaches gaining acceptance today.

- ◆ Historical and cultural difference refer to the radical discontinuity between different cultures and different time periods. This discontinuity makes understanding the literatures of remote times and places quite challenging.

- ◆ The notion of "great" literature is a cultural project shaped by political interests.

- ◆ Multiculturalism has incited considerable debate and change at every level of literary study.

Part 2

Fitting Forms

Part 2 includes chapters on four broad subdivisions of literature—poetry, drama, narrative fiction, and prose—and discusses the formal characteristics and briefly sketches the historical development of each. Although, like practically everything else in lit study, these categories are historically and culturally contingent, they seem reassuringly stable. Even though they can be—and frequently are—blended into hybrids, they each have definitive elements that have remained in place through the ages.

So if you're looking for the nitty-gritty, unproblematic basics of English literature, including terminology and subject matter that most lit scholars can accept, check out this part. You'll get a very broad historic overview as well as a sense of the possibility and variety within each form.

"Did Dickens write any poems?"

8

The Best and the Verse

In This Chapter

- ◆ An introduction to poetry
- ◆ Understanding what poetry does and how
- ◆ Examining poetic imagery
- ◆ A look at prosody

Compared with drama and prose fiction, many students find poetry difficult to understand and appreciate. Its difficulty, however, makes it especially worth studying. Often, word for word, more care goes into writing a poem than a play or a novel, so it makes sense that more care be devoted to reading poetry.

It's convenient that many poems are relatively short. The fact that they take less time to read leaves more time for thinking about them. And good poems give their readers a lot to think about, as we'll see in this chapter.

Speaking Strangely

Poets use language in special ways to make poetry. Poetic language is special because of the way it sounds, the ways it generates meaning, and the kinds of meaning it brings to the reader. In particular, poetry tends to produce what you might call poetic insight.

Poetic insight happens when the poet conveys a distinctive sense of how things are or of how we might think and feel about things. It often involves language that resonates in such a way as to make it seem as though different sets of concepts or ideas are dovetailing into one. It often involves a sense that complexities are getting resolved and that seemingly disparate things belong together in a coherent whole.

Kudos and Caveats

Ancient Greek philosopher Plato was wary of poetic inspiration as a potentially dangerous source of delusive notions. He cautions against it in several of his dialogues, contrasting it to philosophy which, of course, he prefers.

However, those special ways poets use language can also make poetry difficult to understand. In fact, it takes study and practice to learn to read poetry well. Only by reading it, thinking about it, and talking about it do you become receptive to all poetic language can do.

Questions and Answers

Let's look at a poem to really see what poetic language is and does. Here's a poem titled "Destiny" by Matthew Arnold (1822–1888):

> Why each is striving, from of old,
> To love more deeply than he can?
> Still would be true, yet still grows cold?
> —Ask of the Powers that sport with man!
>
> They yok'd in him, for endless strife,
> A heart of ice, a soul of fire;
> And hurl'd him on the Field of Life,
> An aimless unallayed Desire.

What's going on here? The poem asks some questions that it proceeds not to answer, at least, not directly. To interpret the poem, we need to figure out what the questions mean and how they get resolved (if they do) or why they don't get resolved (if they don't). To do this, it'll be useful to know what sort of person is asking the questions and to whom and about whom they are being asked.

Talking a Good Game

Often poetry can be understood to be, quite simply, the words of the poet, so the words you're reading are his words, his thoughts. At other times, however, part or all of a poem might imply a *persona*—a made-up character, like a character in a play—who is doing the talking. In other words, the poet may be pretending to be someone else.

Regardless of whether the poet is speaking in his or her own voice or in the voice of a persona, the term for whoever is doing the talking is the *speaker*. One of the most common kinds of speaker in poetry is called the

def•i•ni•tion

> A **persona** is an assumed character such as a character in a play. A **speaker** does the talking in a poem, whether a persona or the poet's actual voice. The **lyrical I** is a conventional poetic speaker in much lyric poetry.

lyrical I. The lyrical I is a conventional poetic speaker for poems that aren't necessarily either the personal words of the poet or the words of a particular persona. You might say the lyrical I is what poets use when the speaker is set to default mode.

Poetic speakers tend to be more or less contemplative and more or less dramatic. Contemplative speakers notice and think about things and might express passionate feeling as well, but they usually do so from the detached perspective of the lyrical I. Dramatic speakers are involved in interpersonal situations. Their personas are reflected in how they deal with their situations both as speakers and as participants.

Less Clear, More Meaningful

"Destiny," our previous poetic example, isn't explicitly clear about who the speaker is, who the hearer or hearers may be, or just who the beings mentioned in the poem are (the "each" mentioned in the first line and the "Powers" mentioned in the fourth). This vagueness makes the poem difficult to interpret.

The vagueness isn't the result of bad, muddy writing, however, but is intentional because the problem of who does what is an aspect of the problem the speaker is concerned with. In other words, the speaker is dramatically wrestling with the very problem he's trying to describe. He's not only describing the problem, but he's having it and exhibiting symptoms. Can you tell what the problem is? (*Hint:* Lots and lots of lyric poetry is concerned with this topic.)

It's love trouble. It's kind of hard to see right away that this is a love poem. In fact, the reason it's hard to see has a lot to do with the difficulty the lovers are having with one another. "Each" refers to the lovers. "Each [of us] is striving to love," "still would be true [always tries to be faithful]," and "still grows cold." The poem expresses this love trouble in a dramatic yet strangely impersonal way by blaming the problem on those mysterious "Powers."

Kudos and Caveats

Poets often use strange grammatical constructions for heightened affect. In "Destiny," the construction "Why each is striving, ... Ask of the Powers ..." is an example. Ordinarily, we'd say "Ask the Powers ... why each of us is striving ...." Poets also might use words you aren't familiar with or use familiar words in unfamiliar ways. "From of old" (since a long time ago), "sport with" (toy with), and "unallayed" (not eased of discomfort) might seem difficult to understand. If you're having trouble understanding a poem, work on figuring out the grammar and vocabulary first, and then move on to getting a handle on the speaker and hearer, subject matter, and figurative language.

These "Powers" seem like malevolent pagan gods who deliberately burden "man" with "a heart of ice, a soul of fire" so they can "sport" (toy) with him. ("Man" is not just the speaker, but everyone, even women. Arnold's Victorian readers would have understood "man" as a generic term for "human." At the same time, even Victorians would have sensed as oddly impersonal the use of "man" to refer to one's [presumably female] lover.) This generic "man" is "hurl'd" on "the Field of Life, / An aimless unallayed Desire."

Spitting Imagery

If this sounds like an unusual way to talk about love trouble, it is. Arnold is using *imagery* to convey abstract feelings and ideas in a *concrete* manner. He does so by using *figurative language*, including *metaphor* and *metonymy*. We talked about imagery and related terms in Chapter 2. Here's a refresher course that applies these concepts to Arnold's poem:

Canon Fodder

A Latin phrase from the ancient Roman poet Horace's *Ars Poetica* ("Art of Poetry") suggests the importance of poetic imagery: *ut pictura poesis* ("poetry is like painting").

imagery Any tangible thing named in a piece of writing, regardless of whether that thing is literal or figurative. In "Destiny," "man" is a literal image, while "ice," "fire," and "field" are figurative images.

abstraction A term for anything that isn't tangible. In "Destiny," "love" and "strife" are abstractions. "Desire" is an abstraction, too, but it's used in a rather concrete way as a metonym for "man."

concrete term A term for anything tangible; an image. Poetry often makes abstractions vivid by representing them in concrete terms.

figurative language   Language that's intended to mean something other than what it literally says. Metaphor, similes, metonymy, and irony are all figurative language.

metaphor   An image used figuratively to represent something it isn't. In "Destiny," "heart of ice," "soul of fire," and "Field of Life" are metaphoric expressions. (Life isn't literally lived on a playing field.)

metonym   A figure of speech that uses an attribute or portion of a thing to stand for the thing itself, such as "wheels" for a car or "printed page" for books in general. "Destiny" ends with a striking metonym, "Desire" for "man."

So the speaker of "Destiny" is a frustrated would-be lover addressing his would-be love, but doing so in an impersonal way that reflects his exasperation and frustration. In effect, he says, "Don't ask *me* what our problem is; I'm just one big 'unallay'd desire,' just like you and everyone else!" The speaker is passionate, but he can't seem to express his passion *for* his lover. Instead, his "desire" appears to be a general, unallayable passion with no particular object. That's the reason for—and expression of—his problem. Such is his "Destiny."

Hearing Things

In addition to speakers, implied hearers, and images, poems have sound patterns. Sometimes the sound of language and its meaning are closely associated. For example, words like *buzz*, *ring*, *rat-a-tat-tat*, and *clang* are words that represent sounds similar to the sounds of the words themselves. This kind of sound representation is called *onomatopoeia*.

Arguably, the sound of many words is related to their meanings. In general, however, the relationship between the sound and the sense of a word is arbitrary, and you won't get far interpreting the meaning of a poem just by the way it sounds. Of course, the sound of a poem is important and adds a lot to the pleasure of reading it, but for the purposes of interpretation, it's generally a good idea to regard sound and meaning as separate issues.

def•i•ni•tion

Onomatopoeia is the use of words that sound like the things they mean. *Onomatopoeia* comes from a Greek word that means "name making." *Poeia*, or "making," is the Greek root for *poetry*.

Sound Off

Even so, many poems have generic features based on sound. These are features that pertain to *versification*, or *prosody*—the *meter, line length, stanza structure,* and *rhyme scheme* of a poem. Let's take a minute to go over a few more definitions:

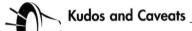

Kudos and Caveats

Aesthetic criticism that focuses on the musical qualities of a poem rather than on its meaning is a dubious undertaking. It's often helpful to see how a poem is structured in order to understand it, but don't fool yourself into thinking you can understand a poem just by appreciating how beautiful it sounds!

prosody or **versification**   The features that account for the sound and structure of verse, including meter, stanza, rhyme, assonance, and alliteration.

meter   The rhythmic structure of poetry.

stanza   A repeated pattern of lines and rhymes. Think of a verse in a song.

rhyme scheme   The pattern of rhymes in a stanza.

assonance   The repetition of vowel sounds close to each other.

alliteration   The repetition of consonant sounds close to each other.

Grains of Trivium

Between the early Middle Ages and the modern period, practically all poetry was metrical. As a result, verse was commonly referred to as "numbers," as in these lines by Alexander Pope from *An Epistle to Dr. Arbuthnot:*

As yet a Child, nor yet a Fool to Fame,
I lisp'd in Numbers, for the Numbers came.

(When I was still a child before I was made ridiculous by fame,
I talked baby talk in verse, since the verses came [when I spoke].)

Versification can require considerable skill on the poet's part. Although versification doesn't carry meaning in itself, it makes up the structure of a poem, so it helps determine how the poem's meaning is organized. Versification may reinforce the grammatical structure of a poem or work against it as a kind of counterpoint.

Rosy Rhythm

Here are the second and third of four stanzas from Edmund Waller's poem "Song" (1645), in which the prosody reinforces the sense of the lines. The speaker is about to send a shy, pretty girl a rose. He addresses the rose, telling it what to "tell" the girl to draw a comparison between the rose's beauty and the girl's:

> Tell her that's young,
> And shuns to have her graces spied,
>   That hadst thou sprung
> In deserts, where no men abide,
> Thou must have uncommended died.
>
>   Small is the worth
> Of beauty from the light retired;
>   Bid her come forth,
> Suffer herself to be desired,
> And not blush so to be admired.

(6–15)

The form of this poem is quite graceful, combining long and short lines that reinforce the rhythm and sense of the phrases in regular, repeated stanzas of five lines and two rhymes each.

Rhyme schemes are often represented with capital letters: A, B, C, etc. The rhyme scheme Waller uses in "Song" is ABABB, with the two A's representing the rhyming short lines ("young" and "sprung"; "worth" and "forth") and the B's representing the three longer lines in each stanza ("spied," "abide," and "died"; "retired," "desired," and "admired"). More rhymes per stanza are represented with more letters of the alphabet—ABACBCDD, etc.

Like most English poetry, the meter of Waller's "Song" is iambic. An *iamb* is a unit of verse (called a *foot*) made of two syllables with an accent on the second syllable: *ba-DUM*. The first and third lines of each stanza have two feet (two *ba-DUMs*, or *iambic dimeter*). The second, fourth, and fifth lines have four feet each (*iambic tetrameter*).

> **Grains of Trivium**
>
> The most common traditional metric form in English is *iambic pentameter*—five iambic feet per line: *ba-DUM ba-DUM ba-DUM ba-DUM ba-DUM.*

Of course, the actual language of the poem is not strictly metrical, but is fluid and flexible in its rhythm. For example, the line "Small is the worth," metrically speaking, isn't *ba-DUM ba-DUM*, but more like *BA-dum ba-DUM*. That's okay; the basic form of the line is still iambic dimeter.

Lines Through Time

English prosody wasn't always based on metrical syllables. In the early Middle Ages, Anglo-Saxon poetry was based on alliterative stresses in each line. Alliterative stress lines are recited with stress placed on alliterative syllables:

umbly DINK DONK mumble   BINK rumbly BONK.

Stressed Out

Here are a couple alliterative stress lines from the Old English poem *Beowulf*:

> Đa him <u>Hro</u>þgar ge<u>wat</u>   mid his <u>hæ</u>leþa ge<u>dryht</u>,
> <u>eo</u>dur <u>Scyl</u>dinga,   <u>ut</u> of <u>healle</u>;
>   (662–3)

> (Then Hrothgar left with his heroic followers,
> defender of the Scyldings, out of the hall;)

These lines are in Old English, a language that differs from modern English. Note the archaic letters. The underlined syllables are recited with a stress. Two stresses occur before and after a break in the middle of the line called a *caesura*. Often the stressed syllables are alliterative ("Hroþgar" and "hæleþa"). Unlike in syllabic meter (which was developed centuries later and has a fixed number of syllables per line), the number of unaccented syllables per line can vary.

def•i•ni•tion

A **caesura** is a pause or break in a line of verse. It usually occurs when a grammatical pause, coupled with a comma or period, falls within the line. Contrast *enjambment*, which is the continuation of the grammatical flow from one line to the next. For an example of each, here are the first two lines from "Ode to a Nightingale" (1819) by John Keats:

> My heart aches, and a drowsy numbness pains
> My sense, as though of ether I had drunk …

A caesura falls in the first line after "aches." An enjambment occurs after "pains."

Coupling

Medieval poet Geoffrey Chaucer (1343–1400) made extensive use of syllabic meter. He wrote his *Canterbury Tales* in a form that came to be known as *heroic couplets*.

These are lines of iambic pentameter (five iambic feet per line) that rhyme in pairs.

After Chaucer, eighteenth-century Augustan poets polished the heroic couplet to a glossy, crystalline finish. Here are some lines from the "Prologue Spoken by Mr. Garrick, at the Opening of the Theatre in Drury Lane" (1747) by Samuel Johnson:

def•i•ni•tion

Heroic couplets are rhymed pairs of iambic pentameter lines used in much heroic tragedy of the Renaissance and in Augustine narrative poetry.

> Ah! Let not Censure term our Fate our Choice,
> The Stage but echoes back the publick voice.
> The Drama's Laws the Drama's Patrons give,
> For we that live to please must please to live.
>
> (51–54)

These lines were written for the occasion of the opening of a new theater in London. They were intended to be spoken by an actor who asks critics not to blame the theater for putting on tasteless plays. It's not their fault, he says; they're only giving their audience what it wants! This kind of careful, elegant apportionment of sound and sense within heroic couplets was all the prosodic rage in Johnson's day.

Grains of Trivium

Heroic couplets became the form of choice for most English narrative poetry during the seventeenth and eighteenth centuries, and got their name in the late seventeenth century, when they were used extensively in heroic dramas. Since the late eighteenth century, the form's importance subsided, although it hasn't disappeared completely.

Shooting Blanks

Another important verse form is *blank verse*. Blank verse consists of unrhymed iambic pentameter lines. Like heroic couplets, blank verse is highly serviceable in poetic drama and in narrative poetry.

John Milton (1608–1674) was a poet pre-eminent in the use of blank verse. His epic poem, *Paradise Lost*, written in blank verse, has wowed readers with its grandeur for centuries. Here's a description of a battle in

def•i•ni•tion

Blank verse is unrhymed iambic pentameter poetry and is often used in poetic drama and narrative verse.

heaven that takes place before the creation of the world between rebellious angels and angels loyal to God:

> … now storming fury rose
> And clamor such as heard in Heav'n til now
> Was never, Arms on Armor clashing bray'd
> Horrible discord, and the madding Wheels
> Of brazen Chariots rag'd; dire was the noise
> Of conflict; over head the dismal hiss
> Of fiery Darts in flaming volleys flew,
> And flying vaulted either Host with fire.
> So under fiery Cope together rush'd
> Both Battles main, with ruinous assault
> And inextinguishable rage; all Heav'n
> Resounded, and had Earth been then, all Earth
> Had to her Centre shook.
>
> (VI; 207–219)

Milton depicts the warring angels as something like ancient Roman warriors with chariots. They also wear armor and fire some kind of powerful angelic artillery. Good thing Earth didn't exist yet, or the whole planet would have been shaken!

Free and Easy

Iambic pentameter, the meter of blank verse and heroic couplets, is the most widely used meter in English poetry even today, when conventional forms are routinely ignored. Actually, it's difficult to write verse without at least a loose metrical pattern of some kind and still make it sound like poetry. Such poetry is often called *free verse*—poetry with only the loosest of metrical form. It came into vogue during the Modern period, around the turn of the twentieth century.

Here are the opening lines from the poem "In a Garden" by Amy Lowell (1874–1925), which answer to the description of free verse:

def•i•ni•tion

Free verse is poetry that has no fixed meter, although it has rhythmic lines and line breaks and is, therefore, presumably composed with rhythmic qualities in mind. This style of poetry became popular in the modern period.

Gushing from the mouths of stone men
To spread at ease under the sky
In granite-lipped basins,
Where iris dabble their feet
And rustle to a passing wind,
The water fills the garden with its rushing,
In the midst of the quiet of close-clipped lawns.

Notice there's no regular meter or end-line rhyme scheme. Even so, the lines are musical and poetic, rather than simply random or chaotic.

All in all, there is no simple set of rules for interpreting poetry. Each poem must be read on its own terms—its particular structure and sense—and according to the priorities of the reader. It can often help to compare poems and poets to see how they do things similarly or differently. In any case, the more you read, the more experience you'll get in seeing what poets can do with language.

The Least You Need to Know

- Whether it's the poet or a persona, the speaker is the one doing the talking in a poem.

- Figurative language—including metaphor, symbolism, and irony—is language that means something other than what it literally says.

- Prosody, or versification, refers to the sound and structure of poetry, including meter, rhyme, assonance, and alliteration.

- Free verse is not the absence of metrical structure, but the presence of variety and irregularity.

Chapter 9

Stage Lights

In This Chapter

- ◆ Understanding drama
- ◆ Seeing drama in relation to literature in general
- ◆ Western drama's beginnings in ancient Greece
- ◆ A history of English drama

Drama has a rich and varied history and a special, privileged place among the arts. It's so important that it's a major focus of literary study, even though most of it is intended to be performed rather than read. Drama can speak directly to the human predicament like no other form, or evoke a way out through stagecraft and symbolism.

Because it's performed for an audience, drama reflects and expresses its cultural context in unique ways, depending on the religious, political, and economic forces that shape it. It costs money, takes time and energy, and risks public censure and political censorship. Yet on the whole, drama is well worth the trouble.

Serious Play

Staged drama has a more direct impact on the senses than other kinds of literature. In fact, it's closely related to *pageant*, spectacle, and musical performance, all of which may be part of a dramatic work. Because drama is not simply a literary form, but includes performative elements and an audience, it often reflects culture in unique and important ways. Historically, much drama is interesting not only because of what it presents, but because of how, by whom, on what occasion, and for what purpose it is presented.

def•i•ni•tion

The word *pageant* originally referred to a platform wagon used for transporting and staging medieval mystery plays, which would be performed in various locations successively on the same day. More recently, the term has come to refer to any public procession or a staged celebration of a historical event.

Two Major Occasions

Drama is especially well suited for the depiction of intense human situations. Traditionally, much drama focuses on situations that lead up to one of two sorts of intense human experiences: sex (usually via marriage) and death. Drama that resolves in marriage is comedy. Drama that resolves in death is tragedy.

Drama as a written literary form grew out of ritual celebrations of sex and death held in ancient Greece. These were rites performed as part of the cult of Dionysius, a god associated with wine, fertility, death, and rebirth. Some of these rites involved animal and perhaps even human sacrifice. Cult members aimed to achieve an ecstatic state by undergoing group frenzy. In other rites, participants wore large leather phalluses in celebration of fertility. Both these sorts of rites involved music and dancing.

Canon Fodder

Well-known ancient Greek tragedians include Sophocles (495–405 B.C.E.), author of *Oedipus the King* and *Antigone;* Euripides (5th century B.C.E.), author of *Alcestis* and *Medea;* and Aeschylus (525–456 B.C.E.), author of *Prometheus* and *Agamemnon.* The best-known ancient comic playwright is Aristophanes (450–380 B.C.E.), author of *The Birds* and *The Frogs.*

Introducing Drama

Gradually, role playing and the enactment of stories were added to these rituals, and drama eventually supplanted them. As dramas became more elaborate, they were written down. The oldest ancient Greek dramas that have survived in written form date from the fifth century B.C.E.

During this time, dramatic competitions were held, with prizes awarded to the writer of the best plays. Performances were staged by professional actors in open-air amphitheaters. Actors wore masks with stylized expressions the audience could easily see. So the audience could hear as well as see the action, the masks were fitted with brass resonators that amplified the actors' voices. Actors in ancient Greek drama were exclusively men.

Aristotle: A Man of Principles

In an influential work called the *Poetics*, ancient Greek philosopher Aristotle (384–322 B.C.E.) described and defined tragedy and comedy, as well as the principles of dramatic composition.

During the Middle Ages, Aristotle was widely recognized as an authority on anything and everything he wrote about, which was quite a bit. Even so, British playwrights have not widely followed his dramatic principles. (Neoclassical French playwrights followed Aristotle's rules more closely.) Nevertheless, his ideas are widely known and remain useful in critical discussions.

Tragic Turns

Tragedy was considered the highest form of drama. Aristotle said tragedy supplied a lofty imitation of human action, whereas comedy imitated action on a lower register. Aristotle's word for "imitation" is *mimesis*, a term that has come to refer to the way a work of literature represents reality.

According to Aristotle, the purpose of tragedy is to elicit sympathy so the audience can share, vicariously, the terror and remorse of the tragic hero. This experience is supposed to purge and purify the audience's emotions. Aristotle calls this emotional purging *catharsis*.

def•i•ni•tion

Mimesis is the ancient Greek word for imitation. Aristotle used it to describe the way drama imitates life. **Catharsis** is a purging of the emotions that, according to Aristotle, results from attending a tragedy. **Hamartia** is the human failing or "tragic flaw" of the protagonist in a tragedy.

The hero of a tragedy is someone of at least fairly high social stature but is not a god or demigod. He or she is not evil, corrupt, or depraved—after all, the audience must be able to sympathize with this person—but does have one or more personal failings, or tragic flaws. These include ignorance and impulsiveness (Oedipus, the title character in *Oedipus the King* by Sophocles), defiance and self-righteousness (Antigone, the title character of *Antigone*, also by Sophocles), and moral rigidity (Pentheus, the main character of *The Bacchae* by Euripides). Aristotle's word for "tragic flaw" is *hamartia*.

Tying Things Together

Aristotle claimed that the most effective dramas were unified in three dramatic unities:

- Plot or action
- Time frame
- Setting

Plot or action is unified if the drama focuses on a single event or circumstance. According to Aristotle, all the various scenes in a drama should relate closely to this single focus.

Time is unified if the action depicted in the drama takes place within a single day. If the first act of a play shows what happens on a Tuesday and the second act depicts events that occur on Friday, the drama isn't unified.

Setting is unified if the action takes place within a single area of space, such as a city or countryside.

Grains of Trivium

The ancient Greek stage was equipped with a crane operated with a pulley and weights that could be used to hoist, lower, and suspend actors in the air to represent gods ascending to or descending from heaven. The Latin phrase *deus ex machina* ("a god from a machine") originally refers to the character hoisted by this device. The phrase has since come to mean any unexpected turn of events in a drama or other work of literature, especially if it seems corny and improbable.

Drama's Second Start

Ancient drama died out with the rise of Christianity in Europe. Although classical drama eventually came to exert considerable influence on English drama, English drama originally developed independently. Like classical drama, however, English drama has its origins in religious ritual. Dramatic scenes came to be added to feast-day pageants, leading to the development of medieval drama.

Staging Morality

Unlike classical drama, with its focus on mimesis, medieval drama was often heavily symbolic—less concerned with imitating lived reality than with pointing to an idealized reality. Medieval drama includes ...

- *Miracle plays*, which dramatize saints' lives and miraculous events. Not many have survived.

- *Mystery plays* are plays performed by guilds that depict biblical events. They were staged in a big series or cycle on feast days. (Read more about mystery plays in Chapter 13.)

- *Morality plays*, or allegorical dramas.

Allegory is a kind of extended metaphor. For example, a story of a journey could be an allegory about living life. A fight between two characters named Love and Hate could be an allegory about an inner mental conflict. During the Middle Ages, texts that were not originally intended as allegories were sometimes interpreted allegorically.

def•i•ni•tion

Allegory is an extended metaphor used in (or read into) a drama or narrative. **Personification** is the device of presenting abstractions as human characters.

Allegories, including morality plays, typically depict virtues and vices as personified characters in conflict with one another. *Personification* is the literary device of presenting an abstraction such as "Vanity" or "Sloth" as a human character. In addition to plays, poems and narratives may also use allegory and personification.

The Subject of Morality Plays

Originally, morality plays dealt with explicitly religious themes, but by the end of the Middle Ages, they came to address moral issues in secular situations as well. They tend to be quite simple and didactic, delivering a message not through the representation of realistic interactions so much as through allegory.

The medieval play *Everyman* (fifteenth century, anonymous) is a prime example of a religious morality play. Everyman, the main character, represents humankind. God (a character) sends Death (another character) to Everyman to inform him that he must go on a pilgrimage to the grave, where he must make a reckoning of his actions in life. On the way, Everyman meets up with more characters, including Good Fellowship and Goods, who abandon him when they find out where he is headed.

> EVERYMAN: Gentyll Felawshipe, help me in my necessyte!
> We have loved longe, and now I nede;
> And now, gentyll Felawshype, remember me!

> FELLOWSHIP: Whether ye have loved me or no,
> By Saynte John, I wyll not with the go!

Goods likewise forsakes Everyman, as do Kindred and Cousin. Everyman is assisted, however, by Good Deeds, Knowledge, Confession, Beauty, Strength, and Discretion. But all these except for Good Deeds forsake Everyman as he enters the grave.

Grains of Trivium

Christian medieval playwrights felt no compunction about representing God onstage as a character. (God is a character in a number of mystery plays as well as morality plays.) Not simply God's character, but the whole play itself was understood (allegorically) as an imperfect, earthly representation of a perfect, heavenly truth.

Old Styles, New Forms

Clearly, *Everyman* has a didactic message ("you can't take it with you") and moral purpose ("do good deeds like Everyman") that have little to do with Aristotle's conception of drama. Similarly, the allegorical form differs markedly from classical dramatic form. As the native dramatic tradition developed and diversified, however, English playwrights rediscovered classical drama.

English playwrights not only translated ancient plays into English, but also drew on classical models and source material when writing new plays, many of which combined ancient and medieval approaches to characterization, plot, and message. Meanwhile, drama emerged in new contexts and for new reasons, including the school play and a courtly form known as the masque.

School Plays and Court Dramas

In the early days of the Renaissance, drama took a number of different forms. In addition to religious drama—morality plays and mystery plays—school drama and court drama emerged. As schools increased in number and diversity and became increasingly independent from the Church, school plays were performed both in schools for boys and in universities.

Meanwhile, a dramatic form known as the *masque* developed at the royal court. Both of these forms anticipated and contributed to the rise of Elizabethan drama in Renaissance England.

Production Numbers

Masques are closely related to pageants. They are performed by members of court dressed in lavish costumes and wearing masks, often amid elaborate scenery. In fact, only a blurry imaginary line separates the actors from the audience, who participate by dancing and whose members might be directly addressed by name during the performance. Masques include music, dancing, and poetic dialogue but do not usually involve much plot. They are geared more for spectacle and symbolism than for storytelling.

Typically, masques were staged to celebrate a special occasion or pay tribute to a member of the royal family. Despite their basic frivolity, masques could be lavish productions. Masques presented at the court of King James I featured machinery and effects specially designed by the court architect, Inigo Jones.

Canon Fodder

Scenes imitating courtly masques appear in several of Shakespeare's plays, including *The Tempest.* In courtly masques, actors often masqueraded as gods and goddesses of the classical pantheon in celebration of a special occasion such as a marriage. In *The Tempest,* when the daughter of Prospero the magician becomes engaged to be married, Prospero summons spirits in the forms of nymphs and goddesses to perform a masque in honor of the occasion.

Not Playing Around

Courtly drama—and the masque, in particular—exerted only a modest influence on Renaissance popular theater, but the broader influence of court power and court culture on Elizabethan drama was profound. The court sponsored theater companies, censored plays, and licensed performances. In addition, the symbolism and opulence of the court served as both a point of reference and a model for dramatic spectacle.

Although public, the theater was closely monitored by the state and generally promoted the state's public image. Private, independent theater companies were not permitted to operate at will. Instead, acting companies had to be sponsored by a member of the aristocracy. Technically, a sponsored company performed as servants or retainers of their sponsor, even while running the company essentially as a private business. Itinerate, unsponsored players were considered vagabonds and could be arrested and imprisoned.

In 1545, King Henry VIII appointed the office of the Master of Revels to arrange and supervise dramatic performances at court. When the public theaters opened, public performances were placed under the control of this office as well. The Master of Revels licensed companies to perform and licensed plays to be published. Plays were checked and censored if considered blasphemous or seditious (opposed to the Church or the state).

Drama Curriculum

School plays were performed in grammar schools and universities throughout most of the sixteenth century. Plays were initially in Latin, usually classical drama, but increasingly came to be original works written in English. Many were either translations or imitations of Latin sources such as the ancient comedies of Plautus or Terence.

School plays provided a means of education in language and in acting, as well as a forum for entertainment. Both grammar school and university plays were performed for Queen Elizabeth. A number of writers connected with universities went on to become important Elizabethan playwrights, including Robert Greene, Thomas Lodge, Thomas Kyd, and Christopher Marlowe.

The Influence of Senecan Tragedies

One important influence on school plays and on Marlowe (1564–1593) especially was the Roman philosopher and dramatist Seneca (4 B.C.E.–65 C.E.), famous for his "Senecan" tragedies. These were tragic plays intended to be read rather than acted. They featured a good deal of violence and bloodshed, as well as declamatory, hyper-serious speeches that, when pompous or overblown, came to be known derogatively as *bombast*.

Marlowe became famous in his day as a playwright who specialized in Senecan tragedy. His plays, including *Tamburlaine the Great*, *The Tragical History of Doctor Faustus*, and *The Jew of Malta*, are known for their lofty, serious poetry that effectively conveys the desperate characters and predicaments of their tragic heroes.

def•i•ni•tion

Bombast is dramatic dialogue that is pompous and grandiose, and is associated with Senecan tragedy. The term comes from an old French word used to refer to padding material used in clothing.

Doctor Faustus (1604) is the story of a legendary conjurer who sells his soul to the devil in exchange for magical powers, riches, and earthly pleasures. While he enjoys the fruits of his demonic bargain, arranged by the demon Mephistopheles, Faustus agonizes over his inevitable damnation and struggles in vain to repent before it's too late. Meanwhile, he contemplates suicide:

> My heart's so hardened I cannot repent.
> Scarce can I name salvation, faith, or heaven,
> But fearful echoes thunder in mine ears,
> "Faustus thou art damned!" Then swords and knives,
> Poison, guns, halters and envenomed steel
> Are laid before me to despatch myself,
> And long ere this I should have slain myself,
> Had not sweet pleasure conquered deep despair.
>
> (VI, 18–25)

The play takes spiritual angst to the extreme. Faust is unable to rise above his own sense of guilt, which merges in his mind with suicidal self-loathing on one hand and with a greater sense of guilty pleasure on the other. The worse he feels, the more he enjoys it—until at the end he is swept away screaming to hell by devils.

Canon Fodder

Marlowe is often credited with making influential use of blank verse. His unrhymed iambic pentameter lines have been admired and imitated by poetic dramatists ever since.

More Changes in Theater

The Renaissance was a time of great dramatic productivity and innovation in England. It was also the time when the public theater emerged. Elizabethan audiences of every stripe flocked to playhouses to see plays. Elizabethan plays might combine tragic and comic elements; realistic and symbolic modes of representation; prose and poetry; as well as didactic, dramatic, and political aims. The tremendous variety of the material and resourcefulness of the playwrights help make Elizabethan drama a major focus of lit study.

The Renaissance eventually waned amid economic hardship, political strife, and religious dissent. The monarchy was overthrown in the Puritan Revolution, and the public theaters closed in 1642 and remained so until 1660, when the monarchy was restored. During this time, playwrights ceased to write works for the stage, although a number of authors wrote closet dramas—plays intended to be read rather than performed onstage.

Limitations of the Restoration

The Restoration marked a rebirth of the theater and theatrical culture centered on the aristocracy. At the outset, Restoration drama tended toward decadence, especially with its comedy of manners, much of which portrayed sexual libertinism in a favorable light. Gradually, however, a more staid and puritanical attitude prevailed. In 1737, legislation was passed that imposed severe restrictions on the content of plays that could be performed.

The Theater Licensing Act denied theater companies from staging plays that addressed political or religious issues. Even plays favorable to Christian ideals were off limits because it was considered blasphemy to present them onstage. Political subjects were likewise forbidden. Government regulators didn't trust theater companies or theatergoers to keep these issues in perspective.

> **Grains of Trivium**
>
> Shakespeare's tragedy *King Lear* was banned from the stage during the years of the Licensing Act out of concern that Lear's madness might be construed as a commentary on the unstable mental condition of King George III.

During this time, only a few theaters, called "patent" theaters, were permitted to stage spoken drama, and government regulators carefully scrutinized and purged these dramas of any offending content. Other venues were permitted to stage musical entertainments. In general, the theater of this time focused on spectacle, scenery, and the stock plots of two popular forms: pantomime and melodrama.

Pantomime and Melodrama

Pantomime and melodrama were the mainstays of English theater during the years of the Licensing Act (1737–1843). Although as a general practice these forms are culturally interesting, individual works of either sort are not widely thought to be of much particular literary significance. (Shakespeare they're not.)

Pantomime draws heavily on the Italian tradition of *commedia dell'arte* in featuring the stock characters Harlequin (boy), Columbina (girl), Pantaloon (girl's stodgy father), and a *capitano* or *dottore* (father's pompous friend who is also boy's rival for girl). Frequently, these characters would enact a fairy tale rich with slapstick comedy, singing, and dancing. Traditionally, pantomime was performed as a "dumb show," without spoken lines. English pantomime of this period, however, included dialogue.

> ### Canon Fodder
>
> *Commedia dell'arte* is a popular dramatic form that stems from medieval Italy. English Renaissance playwrights, including Shakespeare, sometimes incorporated elements of *commedia dell'arte* in their work.

Melodrama of the time was similar to pantomime in its reliance on stock plots and characters, including virtuous young lovers and evil villains, as well as music and spectacle. It focused less on comedy and make-believe, and more on pathos, sentiment, and sensationalism. Melodrama drew heavily on gothic fiction, which was popular at the time. (See Chapter 17 for info on gothic fiction.)

The Return of Serious Drama

It took some time for serious literary drama to return to the stage in the wake of the Licensing Act, but return it did. Perhaps the greatest English dramatist since Shakespeare emerged during this time in the late nineteenth century: George Bernard Shaw (1856–1950), author of some 50 plays that use satire as a means to focus social criticism and reform.

Shaw's Socialist Satire

Shaw began his literary career as an unsuccessful novelist turned music critic before moving on to drama criticism. As a theater critic, he had the opportunity to steep himself in dramatic literature, including the work of the Norwegian playwright Heinrich Ibsen (1828–1906), whom Shaw admired. Eventually, while in his thirties, Shaw turned to writing plays of his own.

> ### Grains of Trivium
>
> Socialism attempts to eliminate the injustices inherent in free-market capitalism by taking wealth and power out of the hands of the disproportionately rich and putting them in control of the state.

Kudos and Caveats

Shaw's work is full of humorous, pithy, quotable statements. In his *Man and Superman: A Comedy and a Philosophy* (1905), he included *Maxims for Revolutionists*, which contains quite a few wry and intriguing sayings, including, "Revolutions have never lightened the burden of tyranny. They have only shifted it to another shoulder."

Meanwhile, Shaw grew interested in socialism, the political and economic view that the means of making and distributing necessary goods should be publicly owned.

Much of Shaw's writing draws on the awareness that conventional thinking tends to support or cover social injustice. Shaw attempts to show this injustice at work in realistic dramatic situations. His plays are largely concerned with relationships among class, money, and morality, concentrating on subjects such as religion and charity, prostitution, ethnicity and nationalism, and power and aesthetic taste.

Trade Secrets

Shaw is a gifted satirist whose work exposes the hypocrisy of conventional morality by dramatizing the ways it hides injustice and serves the interests of the powerful. Often he does so by playing with the assumptions and expectations of his audience, showing his characters in favorable and unfavorable lights until it becomes clear that what appears to be personally good or vicious about them is rooted in social and economic circumstances.

Here's some dialogue from the final scene of Shaw's *Mrs. Warren's Profession*, in which Mrs. Warren, a madam in a brothel, hashes it out with her daughter Vivie, who she has put through college and who has become a self-confident, independent woman. Mrs. Warren has just been complaining of Vivie's ingratitude in "stealing" her college education, bought with the mother's work that Vivie despises:

> VIVIE: I wish you wouldn't rant, mother. It only hardens me. Come: I suppose I am the only young woman you ever had in your power that you did good to. Don't spoil it all now.
>
> MRS. WARREN: Yes, heaven forgive me, it's true; and you are the only one that ever turned on me. Oh, the injustice of it! The injustice! The injustice! I always wanted to be a good woman. I tried honest work; and I was slave-driven until I cursed the day I ever heard of honest work. I was a good mother; and because I made my daughter a good woman she turns me out as if I was a leper. Oh, if I only had my life to live over again! I'd talk to that lying clergyman in the school. From this time forth, so help me Heaven in my last hour, I'll do wrong and nothing but wrong. And I'll prosper in it!

VIVIE: Yes: it's better to choose your line and go through with it. If I had been you, mother, I might have done as you did; but I should not have lived one life and believed in another. You are a conventional woman at heart. That is why I am bidding you goodbye now. I am right, am I not?

MRS. WARREN: Right to throw away all my money?

VIVIE: No: right to get rid of you. I should be a fool not to! Isn't that so?

MRS. WARREN: Oh well, yes, if it comes to that, I suppose you are. But Lord help the world if everybody took to doing the right thing!

In this intense, believable situation, neither character is simply either right or wrong. Their problems are rooted in social issues that pose a different dilemma for each of them. Both of them defy conventional morality and struggle to lead life on their own terms, only to find that they disagree with one another in doing so.

That's dramatic literature. You can read about selected plays and playwrights interspersed within the remaining chapters of this book.

The Least You Need to Know

◆ From its beginnings, drama has been concerned with the representation of intense human situations, especially those leading up to sex (via marriage, as comedy) and death (as tragedy).

◆ Written drama had its origins in ancient Greece during the fifth century B.C.E.

◆ Aristotle laid out principles of drama in his *Poetics*. These principles are more often talked about by critics than followed by playwrights.

◆ Medieval morality plays and mystery plays, and Renaissance school plays and masques, anticipate the rise of Elizabethan theater.

◆ During the years of the Licensing Act (1737–1843), English theaters were prohibited from staging plays with political or religious themes. At this time, melodrama and pantomime were popular.

◆ George Bernard Shaw is a prolific modern playwright who wrote satirical drama informed by socialist ideas.

Chapter 10

Taking Lit by the Tale

In This Chapter

- ◆ Getting a read on narrative
- ◆ Once upon a time: oral versus written narrative
- ◆ Plot, characterization, and perspective
- ◆ Old stories: epic and romance
- ◆ The truth be told via narrative

In the beginning, there was narrative. People used narrative to create and shape knowledge into a form they could remember and pass along. Then came written narrative. Knowledge held still, and people found that they couldn't believe all the narratives anymore, so they wrote new narratives about which narratives to believe for all time and which not to believe at all. But then people wrote narratives about how it doesn't make sense to believe any narratives for all time. And they all lived narratively ever after ….

Tell Me Another

Narrative is the telling of stories. Not only is narrative a major literary form, but it's a major form of communication as well. We share knowledge and ideas through storytelling. Narrative is at least as important in nonliterate cultures (those without writing) as it is in literate ones. Before writing came along, virtually anything worth remembering had to be told in narrative form. Otherwise, it wouldn't be remembered at all.

Writing the Unwritten

The narrative of oral cultures differs from that of literate cultures in a number of significant ways. Narratives from many nonliterate cultures have been written down, in some cases in recent times by anthropologists; in other cases, in ancient times as newly literate cultures drew on oral narrative as subject matter for literature. Structural anthropologist Claude Levi-Strauss conducted a famous study of the myths of the Bororo Indians of South America that has influenced the ways literary scholars think about oral narrative.

> **Grains of Trivium**
>
> Levi-Strauss is a pioneer of structural anthropology as well as of narratology, the theory and analysis of narrative.

In addition, ancient Greeks have preserved their myths and legends as their literature developed. These works have been well known to Western scholars all along and have been continually reexamined. Much ancient narrative shows evidence of a blending of written and oral features.

Speaking and Writing

Oral narrative is distinct from written narrative, in that it seems designed to be memorable specifically to preserve knowledge. At the same time, the "knowledge" it preserves can't be tested against history. In fact, "history" as we know it doesn't exist for nonliterate cultures. As a result, the information preserved is quite different from what we might think of as knowledge. It's more concrete, more poetic, and more mythic.

The concrete, poetic, and mythic features of oral narratives are evident in their plots, characters, and points of view, which tend to differ from those of written narrative. Of course, the terms *plot, character,* and *point of view* were developed to describe written narrative. As a result, you might not ordinarily talk about the way an oral narrative handles point of view, etc., except for purposes of comparison with written narrative.

But that's just what we're going to do—compare written and oral narrative using terms developed for analyzing written narrative—as soon as we define these terms. Take a look:

plot The pattern of events represented in a narrative. Plot may be linear—unfolding in a chronological (temporal) sequence. The time sequence may be interrupted with *flashbacks* and *foreshadowing*. The plot may also be structured internally by a building of tension or complexity. Plots can also be episodic, unfolding in segments.

characterization The representation of personality in a work of literature. Narrative characters can be described in all the ways actual people can be described—and in more ways, too, because not all characters are people. Character may be delineated through all manner of narrative techniques, including behavior, description, and imagery, and through interaction and contrast with other characters.

def•i•ni•tion

Flashbacks switch the timeline backward to a point in the past. **Foreshadowing** hints at events that have yet to unfold.

perspective The position of the narrator in relation to the story. Narratives may be told from a first-person perspective ("*I* did such and such"), a third-person perspective ("*He* and *she* did thus and so"), an omniscient point of view that appears to know everything, or a combination of any or all of them. In addition, a narrator may speak in his or her own voice or may adopt a fictive persona. In other words, the narrator may or may not be a character in the story.

Oral Fixations

Now let's take a look at plot, characterization, and point of view as they tend to get treated in oral narrative. Then we can do the same for written narrative.

Structured Stories

Oral narrative plots tend to be nonlinear, without much regard for temporal sequence. In fact, it can often be difficult to tell when one oral narrative ends and another begins, and whether two similar narratives tell different but similar stories or are different versions of the same story. Instead of a single story line, any number of episodes and alternative versions may be woven in.

In fact, oral narratives often come in groups in which many elements are repeated as variations are introduced from story to story. As a result, scholars often look at groups of oral narratives in relation to one another and try to determine what the narratives say about the culture that produced them. The real "story" isn't simply contained in a single narrative, but in the ways the group of narratives work together.

According to Levi-Strauss, oral myths tend to be versions of one another that restate common themes in different ways. He compares myths to molecules in a crystal that can be infinitely expanded in a spiral. Their structural similarities to one another hold them together in a larger structure. The purpose of the larger structure is to represent and resolve mental conflicts.

Telling Characters

Characters in oral narrative tend to be noticeably different from ordinary people. Gods, demigods, and animals with human attributes are typical characters in oral narrative. Their unusual status serves to shed light on what the world is like from the storyteller's perspective.

To a greater extent than written narrative, oral narrative tends to mingle and fuse elements from the natural, supernatural, and cultural spheres. Oral characters are special, in that they can occupy all these spheres at once or move among them—in and out of dreams, to and from the underworld, etc. The permeability of these spheres of existence enables the nonliterate storyteller to supply cosmic explanations for human experience, including birth, death, sex, and warfare.

Characterization as a personal quality of a main character can be important in driving the plot. Foolish or evil characters can set conflicts in motion and bring trouble on themselves. If the characters are important enough (gods, first human beings,

founders of a race or community), their attributes may help explain why things are the way they are. Adam and Eve were disobedient. Pandora was curious. Antigone was proud. Manabozho was a trickster. Scyf Scylding was wise and generous. What these characters do helps explain why life is as it is for the people who talk about them.

Spoken Perspective

Narrators in oral cultures tend to speak in their own voice and present themselves as conduits or transmitters of stories that actually happened or were already told by someone else. This is true even when the narrator serves a creative, poetic function in putting the words together. The story isn't just the narrator's; it belongs to everybody.

Oral narrators may refer to themselves in the first person as storytellers, but they're not usually important as characters in stories retold across generations. The action in traditional stories doesn't usually depend on what the narrator is like or how the narrator happened to find out what happened. Oral narratives are often told from an omniscient point of view that knows everything, even what the gods may be thinking.

The Write Place at the Write Time

Written narrative differs from oral narrative in part because knowledge changes in the process of getting written down. For one thing, it holds still. As a result, it can be compared more easily to the other narrations that proliferate in an increasingly complex, literate society. In time, a distinction gradually emerged between fictive and factual narratives. In literate cultures, fictional narratives lose much of their knowledge-transmitting function.

Story Lines

Written narrative tends to have a linear plot. In other words, the story begins at the beginning and progresses chronologically (in a time sequence) through the middle to the end. The time sequence may be varied with flashbacks and foreshadowing, but in general, written narratives unfold in a linear direction through time.

The plot of a written narrative typically builds to a climax that occurs somewhere in the middle and is resolved by the end. Written plots are longer and more fully developed. They may involve the weaving together of a number of subplots. They also tend to be self-contained and fully distinct from oral narratives.

Grains of Trivium

Nineteenth-century German novelist and dramatist Gustav Freytag (1816–1895) proposed a well-known schematic description for the plots of dramas and narratives known as *Freytag's pyramid*. Freytag describes the action in a plot as moving upward from the "exposition" of the conflict through the "rising action" to the "climax" at the top of the pyramid and then downward through the "falling action" to the "outcome."

Written Writers

More often than not, the main characters, or protagonists, in written narrative are human beings rather than gods or other supernatural beings. They are recognizably like ordinary people, and their characters may be quite subtle and complex. Characters are less likely to drive the plot and more likely to react to unfolding events.

Narrators are often characters in written narrative, giving rise to complex points of view. Perspective may be refracted through one or more characters whose point of view may be limited and even unreliable. Perspective may even hover ambiguously between a third-person narrator and one or more characters. This sort of ambiguous hovering is called *free indirect discourse*. It happens when a third-person narration blends into the thoughts of one of the characters. Often the narrator begins by relating what a character is thinking, and then, imperceptibly, the character's thoughts take over the narration.

def•i•ni•tion

Free indirect discourse is the narrative technique of shifting freely between a first-person and an interior third-person point of view.

English novelist Jane Austen (1775–1817) is often credited with developing free indirect discourse. Here's a brief example from near the beginning of Chapter 12 of her novel *Emma* (1816), dealing with Emma's strained relationship with Mr. Knightley:

> She hoped they might now become friends again. She thought it was time to make up …. She certainly had not been in the wrong, and he would never own that he had. Concession must be out of the question; but it was time to appear to forget that they had ever quarrelled ….

The narrative perspective shifts from a third-person account of Emma thinking ("she hoped … she thought") to a first-person account of Emma's thoughts ("Concession must be out of the question …"). The narrative seems to go right inside Emma's mind.

Epic Achievements

An important narrative form that emerges at the threshold between orality and literacy is the *epic*. The epic is clearly oral in its origins and exhibits a number of features associated with oral narrative. At the same time, the oldest epics we have are preserved in writing and reflect elements of literate thinking mixed in with oral tradition.

The ancient Greek epics *The Iliad* and *The Odyssey* are the best-known examples of epics that were written down at some point after a period of oral development. They were attributed to a legendary poet known as Homer but were probably composed of materials provided by many different poets over the course of several generations. These works exhibit features typically associated with the form, including ...

- An important subject of crucial national or cultural significance, together with a grand, lofty tone. Many epics tell the story of the founding of a nation or race by means of a battle or journey.

- One or more heroes who are larger than life. They may be semidivine or heroes of special interest to supernatural beings as well as to the world.

- A nonlinear beginning *in medias res*, or "in the middle of things."

- Conventional features such as an invocation to the muse, *epic similes*, a catalog of warriors, and a journey to the underworld.

def•i•ni•tion

An **epic simile** is an extended comparison that's developed in considerable detail over the course of several lines of verse. For example, in *Paradise Lost*, Satan's shield is "like the Moon, whose orb / Through Optic Glass the Tuscan Artist views / At evening from the top of Fesole, / Or in Valdarno, to descry new Lands, / Rivers or Mountains in her spotty Globe." In other words, Satan's shield is like the moon as seen by Galileo through a telescope.

Epic is a Greek term, identified by Aristotle as one of the major poetic forms.

Of course, not all epics contain all these elements. The Old English narrative poem *Beowulf* is generally considered an epic, as is the ancient Babylonian story of *Gilgamesh*. These works originated independently from the ancient Greek epic tradition.

In contrast, a number of literary epics have consciously extended the ancient Greek tradition into different cultural contexts. Most notable among these are the *Aeneid* by the Roman poet Virgil (70–19 B.C.E.) and *Paradise Lost* by John Milton (1608–1674). These works have helped, retroactively, to define the epic genre.

The Romance of Narrative

Whereas the epic occupies a lofty and privileged place as an early, foundational narrative form, it was soon followed by a form that developed since the advent of writing: the romance. The romance is a somewhat slippery form that's inextricably entwined with all kinds of narrative up to and including popular fiction for women.

The words *romance* and *romantic* have been used in many different senses over the years. They're often very loosely applied, sometimes to make general distinctions that aren't always airtight. Even so, romance is an important concept, or maybe a cluster of concepts.

The term has evolved in such a peculiar way, it might be useful to map out how its meanings have changed. One reason for the confusing shifts of meaning *romance* has undergone is that it has been repeatedly used in counterdistinction—defined in terms of what it *isn't* rather than in terms of what it *is*. And what it *isn't* has changed repeatedly over the years:

500 to the present   Romance languages are like, but are not, the Latin language. One meaning of *romance* has remained consistent since its earliest use: the use of the term to describe languages based on, but different from, Latin. The romance languages include French, Spanish, Italian, and Portuguese. The term *romance* (or *roman* or *romans*) was commonly used in Europe during the Middle Ages to refer to any text written in the vernacular—that is, not in Latin. In fact, the first Old French romances were translated from Latin texts.

1200 to 1700   The romance narrative form is like, but is not, epic. The term *romance* came to be used loosely in England as well as Europe to describe narratives that had certain characteristics, especially (but not exclusively) stories about knights—their battles, quests, courtships, and code of chivalry. *Romance* used in this sense is often distinguished from *epic*. Epic is a more lofty, serious narrative form stemming from ancient times. Epics tend to be more about war and less about love than romances. Late in this stage of the term's use, *romance* was often used to distinguish made-up stories from true ones.

1700 to 1800   A romance is like, but is not, a novel. A "new" narrative form—the novel—gradually

Grains of Trivium

Much romance writing up through the rise of the early novel is concerned with tensions between inherited status and personal virtue (birth and worth). To resolve this tension, romance heroes and heroines prove themselves to have virtuous, noble characters despite humble upbringings—only to discover at the end of the story that they are descended from nobility after all.

developed in England during the seventeenth and eighteenth centuries that was considered distinct from romance. In general, novels are more realistic and believable, less fanciful and idealistic, than romances. In France, however, this distinction wasn't made quite so sharply. To this day, the French word for "novel" is *roman*.

1800 to 1870   The Romantic period is like, but is not, the Enlightenment. For a good while in England, during the Enlightenment period of the eighteenth century, the fanciful nature of the romance narrative was considered a strike against it. People came to think that literature should be believable to be good. But feelings changed and literary reaction against the "Age of Reason" set in. The term *Romanticism* was used to describe a broad historical movement that valued the imagination in art and literature. Even so, people didn't go back to calling novels "romances." The novel was here to stay.

Today   Romance is like, but is not simply the same thing as, sex. Romance is what goes on between lovers, both in and out of the bedroom. Thus, a romance novel is a genre of popular fiction that focuses on love relationships. A contemporary romance novel doesn't necessarily have much to do with a medieval romance.

> **Grains of Trivium**
>
> Today we often think of prose as the most usual and appropriate form for fictional narrative. This attitude is a recent development, though. Prior to the eighteenth century, verse was the preferred narrative form.

Narrative Necessity

Since the rise of the novel, prose narrative has come into its own as the most widely read literary form, while poetry and drama have waned in comparison. The novel's emergence reflects a shift in literary sensibility amid the general acceptance of a scientific worldview and middle-class, bourgeois ideals. (For more about the rise and subsequent development of the novel, check out Chapters 16 through 20.) For all its importance, however, as the preeminent literary form, the novel is far from the last word in narrative.

Only within the past 50 years or so has "narrative" been identified as a subject of critical study, per se. Before then, people studied various forms of narrative—including myth, epic, romance, the short story, and the novel—but narrative in its own right had yet to be recognized as a distinct, abstract feature of literature. These days, not only is narrative seen as a key feature of literature, but it's also recognized as a significant element of nonliterary discourse.

Theorists identify narrative as a necessary way of relating ideas of all kinds, including those concerned with science, social science, and the professions. Anthropology and sociology increasingly and overtly rely on narrative to convey knowledge about culture and society. The notion of a scientific narrative suggests the degree to which scientific knowledge depends not on science, but on the limited and provisional nature of human understanding.

This sense of narrative ties in with poststructural notions of the constructed nature of discourse. There is no truth; instead, there are only narratives that show how things appear from various perspectives. French poststructuralist François Lyotard uses the term *grand narrative* to refer to the outdated idea that knowledge is true, unified, and consistent across cultures and disciplines. Instead of a single grand narrative, "knowledge" is produced through lots of little narratives.

The Least You Need to Know

- In nonliterate cultures, narrative is a means of preserving and disseminating knowledge.

- Nonliterate narrative tends to differ from literate narrative in the ways it handles plot, characterization, and perspective.

- Epic is a narrative form that shows both oral and literate characteristics.

- *Romance* has been defined in opposition to other narrative forms, especially the epic and the novel.

- Recent theory suggests that narrative is a necessary element of the production and communication of knowledge.

Chapter 11

Leave It to the Prose

In This Chapter

- An explication of literary prose
- Setting forth: the origins of literary prose
- Terms of persuasion: rhetoric and oratory
- Saints alive! Hagiography
- Nice tries: the essay and the Theophrastan character
- Words of the day: periodical essays and biography

Our contemporary conception of literary prose has a lot to do with our fascination with the lives, thoughts, opinions, and personal experiences of good writers. Literary prose nonfiction might seem like a fairly simple and obvious category of writing: it's nonfiction in the sense that it isn't "made up"; it's prose, not verse; and it's literary, in that it's artfully, stylishly written for readers who want to be entertained as well as instructed. But as with all literature, literary prose's forms and conventions have evolved out of dissimilar predecessors.

Our notion of prose as literature has its roots in ancient legal dispute, the cult of medieval saints, and the skeptical ruminations of Renaissance humanists reacting against outmoded medieval dogma. Not until the eighteenth century, when the publishing industry established itself as a shaping force and when the idea of "literature" became widely accepted as a special kind of writing, did prose, per se, become recognized as a literary form.

All Talk

The ancient Greeks and Romans loved making speeches and cultivated the art of oratory (speech making). Crucial to the success of an ancient orator was the ability to persuade his audience. *Rhetoric* is the name used in ancient times for the study of the persuasive features of language.

def•i•ni•tion

> **Rhetoric** is the art of persuasion, studied in ancient times as applied to oratory. Since then, rhetoric has been used as a way of analyzing other kinds of speech and writing, including both poetry and prose. Today the term is also commonly used in a negative sense to describe political discourse intended to persuade but without basis in fact.

Rhetoric has its origins in the legal system of ancient Greece. In fifth-century democratic Athens, litigants in legal cases hired pleaders known as *rhetors* to speak for them. Eventually, the art of rhetoric was applied to speech-making in general and, later still, to writing as well. Some lit scholars continue to study literature as rhetoric.

Nice Figures

Ancient rhetoricians identified hundreds of rhetorical tropes, or figures of speech, to describe the various ways of manipulating language. The idea was to use the right trope at the right time for maximum persuasive effect. Rhetoric furnished a bag of tricks speakers could dig into to win over their audiences. Here are just a few rhetorical tropes:

accismus   A pretended, ironic refusal of something you want or denial of something about you that is true. *No, I'm not going to eat that chocolate. I dislike the taste of sugar and cocoa butter.*

anacoluthon   A sentence that changes its grammatical structure in the middle, often to suggest disturbance or excitement. *We had almost reached the finish line and then, the race had to have been fixed from the beginning.*

anadiplosis   A repetition at the start of a sentence of the concluding word or phrase in the previous sentence. *There's only so much exercise you can get on an airplane. An airplane is not the greatest place to work out.*

chiasmus   A verbal pattern in two parts, in which the second part is a mirror image of the first. *Some people eat to live, others live to eat.*

hyperbole   An exaggeration, overstatement. *A flood of tears.*

polyptoton   A construction that brings together different grammatical forms of words that have a common root. *'Tis not through envy of thy happy lot / But being too happy in thine happiness ….* (Keats)

syllepsis   The use of a single word in two different senses at once. *I just quit smoking and my job.*

> **Grains of Trivium**
>
> Medieval scholars divided scholarship into seven liberal arts, including the quadrivium (arithmetic, geometry, astronomy, and music) and the trivium (grammar, logic, and rhetoric). Our word *trivia* is derived from the medieval *trivium*.

Eloquent Examples

The best-known and most influential of the ancient orators was Roman statesman and philosopher Cicero (106–43 B.C.E.). Renowned for his eloquence, Cicero left a prolific body of writings, including speeches, letters, and philosophy, as well as treatises on rhetoric. Cicero was admired and imitated during the Renaissance, not only in Italy, but by writers of Latin prose in England as well. Eventually, Cicero's influence extended to English prose.

Ciceronian style is known for its dignity, balance, and clarity, despite the fact that it's elaborate and full of rhetorical tropes. It includes long sentences (known as *periods*) filled with elegantly balanced and coordinated clauses. Ciceronian style is often contrasted with Senecan style, modeled after the writing of Seneca (4 B.C.E.–65 C.E.), the Roman dramatist (discussed briefly in Chapter 9). Senecan style is characterized by short, uneven sentences and abrupt transitions. It was imitated in seventeenth-century England, partly in reaction against the influence of Cicero.

Shining Lives

Writers during the Middle Ages were not as interested in—or as aware of—classical style and rhetoric as writers during the Renaissance would become. They were, however, obsessed with religion. Perhaps the most popular of all prose forms of the time emerged out of the study and worship of Christian saints. This field is known as *hagiography* (sacred writing).

def•i•ni•tion

Hagiography is the study of saints. More specifically, it is a saint's biography.

Hagiography includes all manner of lore about Christian saints. It developed as an expression of veneration to particular saints and was used as a means of teaching history and theology both in sermons and out of the Church. The term *hagiography* is used to refer not only to the study of saints, but to a particular literary form, the life of a saint.

Saints' lives include what we would call biographical information but generally focus on the holiness, miracles, and martyrdoms that show worthiness of sainthood. Saints include people from all walks of life: kings, clerks, merchants, maids, hermits, and others who lived from the days of the early Christian Church. A related form to emerge out of the saint's life has come to be known as spiritual biography, the life of someone, not necessarily sainted, who is notable for spiritual experiences.

Prose Reformers

By and large, medieval writers devoted themselves to the task of transmitting and expounding on received authority. They tended to be dogmatic in their acceptance of the writings of ancient authors. A reaction against dogmatism set in during the Renaissance as humanists began to question medieval scholarship and pay increased attention to secular life. Renaissance humanist Michel de Montaigne (1533–1595) pioneered a new prose literary form that was well suited to dealing with secular concerns in a nondogmatic way. This was the essay.

Try, Try Again

Essay comes from the French word for "attempt." Montaigne was a skeptic who questioned whether human beings were capable of knowing the truth. His essays attempted to describe personal experiences, ideas, and observations about almost anything concerned with worldly existence. Among Montaigne's numerous essays are "Of Sadness," "Of Fear," "That to Philosophize Is to Learn to Die," "Of Cannibals," "A Consideration of Cicero," and "Of the Uncertainty of Our Judgement."

Montaigne's essays became immediately popular upon their publication in French beginning in 1582. An English translation was published in 1603 that influenced English writers. In fact, Sir Francis Bacon (1561–1626) wrote a series of essays of his own. Like Montaigne's, Bacon's essays were extremely popular. And like Montaigne, Bacon was skeptical. He opposed dogma and complained about all the falsehood that results from the uncritical acceptance of ancient authorities.

Canon Fodder

Bacon outlined an ambitious program for rebuilding the store of human knowledge from the ground up in his works *The Advancement of Learning* (1605) and *Novum Organum* (*The New Instrument of Learning;* 1620). His thinking influenced the later British empiricists and marks an important early stage in the rise of science.

The essay, together with the skeptical point of view and thoughtful, personal tone that goes along with it, has exerted an important influence on literary prose ever since. Throughout the seventeenth century, much thoughtful, personal, quirky prose was written on a variety of subjects. An essaylike form popular at the time was the Theophrastan character.

Literary Characters

Theophrastus (390–287 B.C.E.) was a follower of Aristotle and was known for his writings on botany. In addition, he wrote a collection of short descriptions of character types gently ridiculing those who exhibit common human failings and foibles. His characters include the Boorish, the Pretentious, the Tactless, the Arrogant, and the Stupid.

The Theophrastan character was revived in England early in the seventeenth century and remained popular until late in the century, when it largely died out. It described all sorts of people familiar to readers of the time, supplying amusing and moralizing observations on how these types behaved and thought. They treated personality traits, but also professions, religious callings, and even peculiar circumstances.

Samuel Butler's (1612–1680) *Characters* (published 1759), for example, include a Politician, Huffing Courtier, Henpect Man, Corrupt Judge, Hunter, Cuckold, Tennis-Player, and Vapourer. Many characters focus on hypocrisy and excess, looking ahead to the outpouring of satirical writing that would come in the eighteenth century. Some, however, are laudatory.

As in the essay, however, Theophrastan characters are generally skeptical and tend to fault

---

Canon Fodder

Samuel Butler (1612–1680)—not to be confused with Samuel Butler (1835–1902), the author of the novel *The Way of All Flesh* (1903)—is best known as the author of *Hudibras* (1663), a mock-epic poem satirizing puritanical arrogance and hypocrisy.

---

people for their vain beliefs and fatuous behavior. Here's a portion of the character of Butler's "News-Monger" (a seller of printed news items):

> A News-Monger is a Retailer of Rumour, that takes up upon Trust, and sells as cheap as he buys. He deals in a perishable Commodity, that will not keep: for if it be not fresh it lies upon his Hands, and will yield nothing. True or false is all one to him; for Novelty being the grace of both, a Truth goes stale as soon as a Lye; and as a slight suit serves as well as better while the fashion holds, a Lye serves as well as Truth till new ones come up.

Butler describes the news-monger as a dealer in a cheap and "perishable Commodity" that spoils quickly and quickly goes out of fashion. Because it becomes obsolete so quickly, it makes no difference whether it's true or not!

Essay Issues

Prose as an art form came into its own in the eighteenth century, when writers cultivated elegance and taste and could hope to be paid for their efforts. The periodical essay—an ongoing series of printed works published at regular intervals—was a mainstay of popular reading for a new society. The periodical essay offered these readers advice on how to fit in with a growing middle class.

Good Morals and Good Taste

Social tensions between serious, austere, working-class English Puritans and carefree, extravagant, aristocratic libertines had been simmering since the buildup to the Puritan Revolution of the 1640s. The emerging middle class was looking for a resolution to this long-standing conflict and was ready to compromise. The periodical essay helped teach them how.

In 1709, Sir Richard Steele (1672–1729), a former soldier turned editor, started a publishing venture under the pseudonym Isaac Bickerstaff. His paper was called *The Tatler*, and it appeared three times a week and contained essays by Steele and, later, by a corroborator named Joseph Addison (1672–1719). The essays were full of witty observations about people and events, as well as moral advice and criticism.

Written in a smooth, elegant, yet casual and personable style, *The Tatler* recommended moderation and self-restraint on the one hand and an appreciation for the finer things in life on the other. *Tatler* installments were read and discussed in clubs and coffeehouses all over London, and were aimed at women as well as men, at literate merchants and clerks as well as aristocrats—anyone who might want some entertaining guidance on how to think and act in a society with a newly emerging middle class. The newly rich had to learn to think and act more like the established aristocracy, who, in turn, had to learn to accept the new social and economic realities.

The Tatler ran until 1711 and was followed closely by *The Spectator*—same writers, similar concept, different title. These publications were followed by numerous imitators, of which the most important were *The Idler*, and *The Rambler* by the poet and lexicographer Dr. Samuel Johnson.

> **Kudos and Caveats**
>
> In issue 10 of *The Spectator*, Steele set forth what he hoped to accomplish in writing his essays, saying, "I shall endeavor to enliven morality with wit, and to temper wit with morality." Did you spot the chiasmus?

Common Bonds

Johnson is known today as a consummate prose stylist as a poet, a critic, and the author of a famous dictionary. His *Idler* essays tended to be a bit more serious and formal than the offerings in *The Tatler* and *The Spectator*—more Ciceronian, in fact. Here's a sample from *Idler* number 60, in which Johnson entertains the idea of a life story for everyone who has ever lived:

> I have often thought that there has rarely passed a Life of which a judicious and faithful Narrative would not be useful. For, not only every man has in the mighty Mass of the World great Numbers in the same condition as himself, to whom his Mistakes and Miscarriages, Escapes and Expedients would be of immediate and apparent Use; but there is such an Uniformity in the state of Man, considered apart from adventitious and separable Decorations and Disguises, that there is scarce any Possibility of Good or Ill, but is common to Humankind. … We are all prompted by the same Motives, all deceived by the same Fallacies, all animated by Hope, obstructed by Danger, entangled by Desire, and seduced by Pleasure.

Johnson suggests we all have so much in common that we could all learn from pretty much anyone's life story. This attitude—that we can learn about ourselves from other people's experiences—may help explain the emergence and popularity of the novel during Johnson's time. In fact, the early novelists suggested that their readers could learn from the lives of fictional characters in much the same way Johnson imagines people learning from anyone's biography.

Canon Fodder

Johnson is the subject of perhaps the most highly celebrated literary biography ever written, *The Life of Samuel Johnson* (1791) by James Boswell (1740–1795). Boswell admired Johnson and his writing tremendously and became intimately acquainted with him in the course of gathering material for the book.

The essay has continued to be a mainstay of literary prose up to present day. The same is true of biographical writing and writings that hold biographical interest, including memoirs, letters, and diaries. These things, together with the essay, depend on the uniquely modern ability to take an interest in the worldly experiences and personal thoughts of other people—even (and especially) ordinary people.

The Least You Need to Know

- Literary prose evolved out of classical oratory, medieval hagiography, and skeptical Renaissance humanism.

- Rhetoric is the art of persuasion and the study of the persuasive elements of discourse.

- Hagiography is the study of saints and writing about their lives.

- The essay is a prose form originated by French Renaissance humanist Michel de Montaigne.

- The Theophrastan character was extremely popular during the seventeenth century but has since died out.

- Prose became widely accepted as an art form in the eighteenth century, thanks in large part to the periodical essay.

Part 3

Way Back When

The chapters in Part 3 sketch the development of English literature from its ancient antecedents through the Augustan period. They touch on a few of the most memorable writers and works, broaching a few of the many issues they raise and suggesting a small part of what their significance is and why. Many of the issues that come into play have long since disappeared; many others are still with us in altered form.

The chapters in this part trace the emergence both of individual authors and of a sense of individual authority as writers wrestled imaginatively with social ideals in an effort to continually renew or transform them into something they could believe in and live by. The result is something that approaches modern Anglo culture.

"We don't want the bloody grail! We want chivalric romance!"

Chapter **12**

Old School

In This Chapter

- The foundations of English lit: the Bible and the classics
- Religious slants: neo-Platonism, allegory, and typology
- The importance of classical models and influences on English literature
- Shaking the faith: secularization

Throughout the many centuries of the Middle Ages and into the Renaissance, literate people understood themselves and their world very differently from the ways we do. Their way of thinking was strongly influenced by a hybrid of Christian theology and ancient Greek philosophy known as neo-Platonism. Neo-Platonism offered a way to understand reality as the expression of Christian divinity shining through the veil of a sinful, fallen world.

Neo-Platonism provided a peculiar, powerful set of guidelines for interpreting written works, especially the Bible and classical literature. It also enabled medieval and Renaissance writers to present their writings as part of an overarching symbolic universe that united fallen humanity with divine creation. Writers found symbols of divinity everywhere and put them together into stories that evoked the religious destiny of humankind.

Of course, this way of thinking didn't last beyond the Renaissance. It gradually subsided over a long period of time—as part of a historical process known as secularization. Secularization took place amid religious reform, political upheaval, and scientific discovery, as well as amid the proliferation of printed books and new points of view. In fact, the Bible and the classics continued to exert a powerful influence on the history of English lit well after the last gasp of neo-Platonism in the seventeenth century.

In the Beginning ...

Around 300 B.C.E., the ancient Greeks lived not terribly far from the ancient Hebrews. (Considering how close they were, it's kind of surprising how different their cultures were.) Eventually, both came under the yoke of the Roman Empire. Greek and Hebrew cultures began to merge, but by then each had already produced its distinctive foundational literature. The languages those works were written in are dead now, but the lore they contain remains.

The Christian Empire Emerges

Already, the Romans had absorbed Greek lit, together with everything else about the Greeks. Then, at the dawn of the Common Era, a small enclave of radical, rebellious Jews sparked a movement that would absorb the Western world. The Romans sacked Jerusalem. The Goths and Vandals sacked Rome. Then a newly emerged cult—which began with the promise that God would quickly bring an end to the world but grew into a belief in the mystic power of the bodily remains of its martyrs—swept across Europe. This "cult" is known today as Christianity. Many Christians were persecuted and put to death under ancient Roman law.

When the persecutions against Christians dwindled and the martyrdoms abated, the early Christians looked around for guidance and found their Bible and their Church. Christianity gradually spread throughout Europe, and a Christian empire was established. The ruling hub of that empire was right on top of the old Roman capital, which meant the Christians had custody of Greco-Roman literature. And in place of the decayed relics of martyrs, they had the wisdom literature of Christ and of the Hebrew law and prophets.

A Mixed Bag

Since the beginning of the Middle Ages, writers combined elements of biblical (Judeo-Christian) and classical (Greco-Roman) thinking into a way of understanding both the world and literature. Christian thought exerted an inescapable hold on the medieval mind. In general, classical ideas that supported the Christian worldview were embraced, while those that didn't fell by the wayside.

> **Grains of Trivium**
>
> Aristotle was a leading classical influence on medieval thought. Several of his works were kept alive not by European Christians, but by Muslim Arabs.

This fully Christian, partially classical worldview made sense of the natural world and the social order, as well as handed-down written traditions. It was so rich, comprehensive, and harmonious that it required centuries of faith-shaking discovery, disillusionment, and adjustment to leave it behind. Classical literature exerts an ambiguous influence throughout this process of secularization.

On one hand, medieval writers skillfully incorporated a great deal of classical lore into their Christian tradition. On the other hand, much classical thought and lit provided models for non-Christian outlooks on reality. Eventually, these models led readers to question previously accepted aspects of the Christian faith and the Christian worldview.

Mental Mergers

Both the Judeo-Christian and Greco-Roman traditions are large and complex in their own right. They are also more or less distinct from one another, even as they become merged in European thought and literature. And they do, in fact, get merged at a very early stage in European history. Latin became the common language of medieval Europe as Christianity gained acceptance.

> **Canon Fodder**
>
> Much surviving ancient Roman literature was copied and preserved during the reign of Charlemagne (742–814), the Christian emperor who conquered and converted much of Europe. In the process of rooting out paganism and spreading Christianity, Charlemagne promoted scholarship among the clergy. The cultural activity of this period is known as the Carolingian Renaissance.

In addition, in the philosophy of ancient Greece, medieval Christians found ideas that appeared consistent with and complementary to Christian theology. Pagan philosophy and Christian theology were seen to go hand in hand as "faith" and "reason."

Plato and Aristotle, in particular, were revered as authorities throughout the Middle Ages. Platonic thought was wedded to Christianity as neo-Platonism. Meanwhile, Aristotle's thought and writings served as a model for medieval scholarship.

All Signs Point Up

Neo-Platonist thinking had an enormous impact on medieval and Renaissance literature. It formed the basis of strategies for reading the Bible that were widely applied to literature in general by readers and writers alike. In addition, thanks to neo-Platonist thought, reality itself could be "read" in much the same way as the Bible to yield an overarching Christian message.

Grains of Trivium

Medieval Christians were extraordinarily comfortable with the idea that a piece of writing could "mean" something very different from what it "says." This idea is expressed in the legal distinction between the "letter" (what is written) and the "spirit" (what is intended) of the law.

What's the Big *Ideal?*

Plato regarded ideals as real things. Platonic ideals include not only abstract virtues such as courage and justice, but ideal forms as well. Physical things, both living beings and inanimate objects, are imperfect expressions of their ideal forms. Plato believed that ideal forms existed on a higher plane of reality than material, physical things. Human beings—especially philosophers—can learn to see past the imperfect material world and appreciate ideal reality.

To the early neo-Platonist Christians, Plato's ideal reality resonated with notions of holiness, heaven, and God. They believed that physical reality had existed in a fallen state ever since Adam and Eve, the first human couple, disobeyed God in the Garden of Eden. The fallen, physical world, if interpreted correctly, could point the way to the divine truth of Christian salvation.

The "fallen world" included not only the physical objects that make up the material world, but also subjects of written texts, especially including topics covered in the

Hebrew Bible. To the neo-Platonists, the Old Testament (Hebrew Bible) pointed the way to divine truth, but it required skillful interpretation to get there—to see how the characters and events it describes symbolize and foreshadow Christian ideals.

Typecasting

The medieval study of biblical symbolism is known as *typology*. From a typological standpoint, biblical events and characters were seen as symbols that could be understood as types of an ideal, divine truth. And what, do you suppose, that divine truth was?

def•i•ni•tion

Typology is the study of biblical symbolism. Biblical "types" could be found not only in the Old and New Testaments, but in nature and society as well.

To medieval Christians, the essence of divine truth was to be found in the life, teachings, death, and resurrection of Christ—all of which are recounted in the New Testament. They saw the Old Testament as a symbolic prefiguring of the New. The Old Testament not only has its literal meaning as a history of the Jews before the coming of Christ, but it also has a higher typological significance as a prefiguring of Christianity.

Thus, many Old Testament characters were seen as "types" of Christ. For example, Jonah, who was swallowed by a whale and remained inside it for three days and nights, prefigured Christ, who spent three days and nights in the tomb before his resurrection. Isaac, who was bound and about to be slaughtered by Abraham as a sacrifice to God, is a type of Christ, who was crucified as a sacrifice to atone for the sins of humanity.

Déjà Vu

Typological readings of the Old Testament uncovered all kinds of parallels to the New:

♦ The Tree of Knowledge in the Garden of Eden prefigures the cross on which Christ was crucified.

♦ Moses bringing the Ten Commandments down from Mt. Sinai prefigures Christ expounding the ten beatitudes in the Sermon on the Mount.

Grains of Trivium

Medieval Christians believed that the cross on which Christ was crucified was made of wood taken from the actual Tree of Knowledge.

- ◆ The flood that destroyed all creatures except those on Noah's Ark prefigures the Apocalypse—the end of the world. The ark itself prefigures the Church. Surviving the flood represents baptism.

- ◆ The 40-year journey the Israelites made through the wilderness prefigures the 40 days and nights Jesus spent fasting in the wilderness.

Medieval Christians saw not only the Bible, but the world itself, as a symbolic embodiment of divine truth. Yearly feasts were held on days that symbolized Christian events. More broadly, the spring season symbolized the Resurrection, when Christ emerged from the tomb.

Biblical symbolism could be found in secular and pagan writings as well:

- ◆ The legendary King Arthur was a type of Christ because both Arthur and Christ were expected to make a second coming.

- ◆ The legendary phoenix typified the resurrection of Christ through its rebirth out of its own ashes.

- ◆ The panther symbolized Christ because it was supposed to sleep for three days after feeding.

Neo-Platonism gave Christians a way to interpret reality in general as an interconnected system of signs pointing to Christian truths. Whatever didn't fit the paradigm could easily be ignored.

A Tale of Types

"The Merchant's Tale" from Geoffrey Chaucer's (1343–1400) *Canterbury Tales* provides an indication of typological thinking at work in medieval English lit. The story sets up a whole series of correspondences between a number of married couples, all of whom can be interpreted as types of Mary and Joseph, the earthly parents of Christ. The story draws from biblical lore, classical mythology, and contemporary stereotypes about married men and women. Thus, it brings ancient symbolism to bear on an up-to-date domestic scenario.

Each of the *Canterbury Tales* is told by one of a group of pilgrims bound for Canterbury, and each is framed by dialogues and prologues introducing the story as well as the teller. The merchant is an unhappily married man, so it's fitting that the tale he tells concerns a troubled marriage. The merchant complains that his wife is a shrew—a typical complaint lodged against married women of the day. His story tells of another, closely related typical complaint: infidelity.

Kudos and Caveats

Arguably, Chaucer is *not* typical in the way he uses types; he pushes the typological envelope to exploit gaps between symbols and what they symbolize to a shockingly amusing degree. Then again, shockingly amusing types *are* typical of medieval carnivalesque literature that stems from such rituals as the Feast of Fools.

A January–May Romance

"The Merchant's Tale" concerns a 60-year-old knight named January who falls in love with a teenage girl named May. He decides to marry her after long debate with himself and his friends. She agrees, as the marriage stands to improve her social station. She's not attracted to him, however, and isn't satisfied by him after they're married.

January is a suspicious, jealous husband who fears that some younger man may lead his young wife astray, so he builds a walled garden to keep her in. As it turns out, his fears are justified because his young squire, Damyan, falls passionately in love with May and writes her love letters that she reads in secret.

Meanwhile, as fate would have it, January goes blind. He laments the loss of his sight but congratulates himself all the more on having built his walled garden, where he thinks he can keep his wife safe from interlopers as well as enjoy her in private. One day he calls her to join him there. May signals to Damyan to slip in ahead of them, and he does so, hiding in a pear tree.

Sitting in the garden with January, May implies that she's pregnant and has a sudden, powerful craving for green fruit. She asks January to get her a pear from the tree. He says he is unable to on account of his blindness but agrees to help her climb up into the tree on his back. There she meets the waiting Damyan and the two have sex.

Grains of Trivium
In addition to being a "type" of Adam, the biblical first man, January also resembles a type character from Roman comedy—the *senex iratus*, or jealous husband.

Mythic Figures

While this is going on, it just so happens that Pluto and his wife, Proserpina, arrive on the scene. Chaucer describes them as the king and queen of Fairyland, although they are better known as figures from Greek mythology. (Pluto, the god of the underworld, abducted Proserpina and took her back underground with him as his bride. She refused to stay with him, but because she swallowed seven pomegranate seeds while in the underworld, she was obliged to spend half of every year with him—the winter months.)

Pluto, seeing that May was cheating on January, became indignant at how untrustworthy women invariably are. He decided to expose May's infidelity by restoring January's sight. But Proserpina sympathized with May and vowed to grant to her, and to all women caught cheating, the ability to bold-facedly answer their husbands with arguments and excuses.

> **Grains of Trivium**
>
> Damyan is apparently named for St. Damian, known for the miraculous healing of many illnesses, including blindness.

January regains his sight and sees May and Damyan having sex in the pear tree. He complains to May that she's cheated on him. She says he is mistaken and that the reason she's struggling with Damyan in a tree is to restore January's sight. Although he was doubtful at first, May eventually persuades January that whatever she was doing with Damyan was for his benefit!

True and False

There's a practical moral here, somewhere—probably something to do with what happens to lustful old geezers who marry young girls and then become "blind" jealous husbands. There's also a "higher," Christian moral to be pieced together out of the story's symbolism. Oddly enough, May's tryst with Damyan in the pear tree appears to symbolize Christ on the cross, especially because, according to May, it heals January of his blindness:

> Up peril of my soule, I shal nat lyen,
> As me was taught, to heele with youre eyen,
> Was no thyng bet, to make yow to see,
> Than strugle with a man upon a tree.
>
> (2371–2374)

Like Christ's struggle on the cross, May's "struggle" with Damyan helps January (who, named for the first month, represents the first man) "see" that human beings are all guilty of original sin, and this is why men and women are so often unhappy together. The tale brings together symbolic and literal evidence of original sin found in Hebrew scripture, gospel legend, Greek myth, and a salesman's dirty joke. In fact, it refers to, alludes to, or recounts no fewer than four different stories about a man, a woman, and a fruit:

- January discovering May's infidelity in the pear tree.

- Adam and Eve in the Garden of Eden, where first Eve and then Adam taste the fruit of the Tree of Knowledge.

- Pluto and Proserpina in the underworld, where Proserpina eats the seeds of a pomegranate.

- An old Christian legend that tells of Joseph and a pregnant-with-Jesus Mary. The couple stops in a cherry orchard on their way to Galilee, and Mary asks Joseph to get her some cherries, telling him she is pregnant (much as May asks January to get her a pear). Joseph is angry to learn that Mary is pregnant because he knows he's not the father, so he says, "Let the father get cherries for you." At that moment, the cherry branches bend down to Mary of their own accord.

> **Canon Fodder**
>
> "The Merchant's Tale" is highly allusive and refers as well to the Greek mythic couple, Pyramis and Thisbe, and to Priapus, an ancient Greek fertility god.

Born-Again Classicism

Although traces of neo-Platonism persisted well into the Renaissance, it gradually began to fade. Various factors led to this fading, including economic instability and increased social mobility; scientific and geographic discoveries that contradicted biblical accounts of the world; and growing experience with texts of all kinds, thanks largely to the invention of the printing press. Even so, neo-Platonism persisted as a rationale for Renaissance humanism, which fueled a growing and renewed interest in the arts of letters of ancient Greece and Rome.

Virgil's Vocation

Humanists regarded human creativity in a positive light as a reflection of God's creativity in making the world. This notion supplied a rationale for reading and imitating the ancient Greek and Roman poets. Classical literature came to be widely read and admired all over Europe and served as a stylistic model and source of subject matter for poets as well as critics. Aristotle's *Poetics* received newfound respect among Elizabethan dramatists, and lyric and narrative poets consciously adopted classical poetic genres, including the ode, the elegy, the satire, and the epic.

The literature of Greece came to be recognized for its ecstatic and inspired qualities, and the literature of Rome known for its urbanity. Throughout medieval Europe, the Roman poet Virgil (70–19 B.C.E.) was widely regarded as the world's greatest poet. By the Renaissance, his epic poem *The Aeneid* was considered an exemplary poetic achievement. Virgil established his poetic vocation by writing *eclogues*, *georgics*, and *epics* (poems about shepherds, farmers, and heroes, respectively). This program was imitated, more or less closely, by English Renaissance poets Edmund Spenser (1552–1599) and John Milton (1608–1674).

def•i•ni•tion

Eclogues are pastoral lyrics—poems that idealize the life of shepherds. **Georgics** are poems about farming. **Epics** are heroic poems.

Much as Virgil's *Aeneid* tells of the founding of Rome, Spenser's *The Faerie Queene* (1596) attempts to codify the ideals of Protestant England under Queen Elizabeth, drawing on chivalric romance as well as conventions of classical epic. Milton's *Paradise Lost* (1667) even more ambitiously tries to "justify" a Protestant worldview in treating major biblical themes in classical epic form.

Echoes of Virgil

Here's the first stanza of Spenser's *The Faerie Queene*, loaded with Virgilian echoes:

> Lo I the man, whose Muse whilome did maske,
> As time her taught, in lowly Shepheards weeds,
> Am now enforst a far unfitter taske,
> For trumpets sterne to chaunge mine Oaten reeds,
> And sing of Knights and Ladies gentle deeds;
> Whose prayses having slept in silence long,
> Me, all too meane, the sacred muse areeds
> To blazon broad emongst her learned throng:
> Fierce warres and faithfull loves shall moralize my song.

The speaker says that he (like Virgil) once wrote pastoral poetry and is now turning to epic romance. Spenser had, in fact, written pastoral poems after classical models.

So did John Milton, Andrew Marvell, Alexander Pope, Percy Bysshe Shelley, and Matthew Arnold, to name a few writers of the seventeenth, eighteenth, and nineteenth centuries. Pastoral themes figure into quite a lot of English literature.

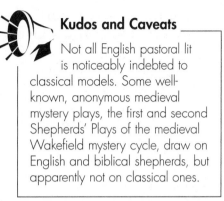

Kudos and Caveats

Not all English pastoral lit is noticeably indebted to classical models. Some well-known, anonymous medieval mystery plays, the first and second Shepherds' Plays of the medieval Wakefield mystery cycle, draw on English and biblical shepherds, but apparently not on classical ones.

English pastoral literature draws not only on classical shepherds, but on Christian symbolism as well (Christ is a lamb of God and a shepherd to his Christian flock). In addition, English pastoral poetry sometimes refers to real English shepherds. The wool trade was a mainstay of the English economy for many years. As a result of the resonance of pastoral images, the mode became steeped in conventions that successive generations of poets could work with and against.

Polished Models and Deism

Up into the twentieth century, most English schoolboys studied Latin. Ancient Roman lit was especially admired—and its urbane, polished style was imitated—by the English "Augustan" poets of the "neoclassic" eighteenth century. These writers self-consciously identified themselves with the Roman poets who wrote during the reign of Emperor Augustus, especially Virgil, Horace, and Cicero. They aimed at producing literature that displayed reason, taste, moral judgment, and elegance.

Broadly speaking, this eighteenth-century focus on classical style signaled a declining interest in Christian faith and doctrine. Neoclassicism was partly a reaction against the Puritanical zeal that plunged England into violent revolution in the seventeenth century. As a corrective against excessive religious "enthusiasm" (with which the Puritans helped justify their protests against royal power), many English gentlemen cultivated interest in scientific experiments and rationalist philosophy.

A religious outlook known as *deism*—the belief that God exists but does not intervene in the natural course of things—emerged as a compelling, rational alternative to Puritan enthusiasm, Catholic "superstition," and Epicurean atheism. It was a theological and philosophical view that saw God as a

def•i•ni•tion

Deism is the view that God, the creator of the universe, exists but does not continue to influence the natural order.

real but remote creator of humankind, best appreciated through reason rather than through revelation. (God's word is said to be "revealed" in the Bible.) A common image of the deist God is as a watchmaker. He made the universe and wound it up, but then he just lets it run.

Alexander Pope's "The Universal Prayer" (1738) indicates something of this view:

> What Conscience dictates to be done,
>   Or warns me not to doe,
> This, teach me more than Hell to shun,
>   That, more than Heav'n pursue.
>
> (13–16)

Grains of Trivium

Deistic thinking is behind the call for separation of church and state in the Constitution of the United States.

Pope somewhat paradoxically asks God to teach him to be guided by his own conscience rather than by the theological stick and carrot of Heaven and Hell. The prayer is "universal" because it does not look to God from the perspective of any particular religious creed, but with the idea that all human beings are endowed with sufficient reason to believe in God.

Rite and Wrong

Renaissance humanism and eighteenth-century deism can be seen as stages in a long, gradual, and untidy historical process called *secularization*—the decline of religion as a controlling force within society. It can be traced in a broad, general way in the history of English lit as well as in the history of philosophy and the history of laws pertaining to religious practice.

def•i•ni•tion

Secularization is the gradual, historical decline of religion as a controlling social force.

Secularization advanced further during the nineteenth century. If eighteenth-century deism regarded the world as a self-regulating piece of clockwork, nineteenth-century evolutionary thought saw the world as a constantly changing, organic sort of growth. The creator's (God's) hand was no longer evident in the design of "creation."

Christian doctrines of all sorts—redemption from original sin, divine judgment and eternal damnation or salvation, and election through baptism—became increasingly subject to doubt and criticism. This was especially the case within well-educated liberal society. Of course, religion didn't simply disappear, but it had a decreased influence on people's lives and thinking.

Christ Victorian

Even so, religious feeling and poetic feeling continued to reinforce one another into the Victorian period. Catholic poet Gerard Manley Hopkins (1844–1889) wrote religious verse. In addition, the famous elegy by Alfred Lord Tennyson, *In Memoriam A. H. H.*—widely considered his greatest work—chews over deep religious issues.

The poem laments the untimely death of Tennyson's best friend, Arthur Hallam, and searches for consolation. In the process, it ruminates on religious doubt on many fronts, including questions raised by scientific evidence that species become extinct. In fact, the poem raises many questions that it doesn't answer directly, while clinging to faith in God—his feelings prompt him to believe even though his reason cannot support his faith.

> Our little systems have their day;
> They have their day and cease to be;
> They are but broken lights of thee,
> And thou, O Lord, art more than they.
> We have but faith: we cannot know,
> For knowledge is of things we see;
> And yet we trust it comes from thee,
> A beam in darkness: let it grow.
> Let knowledge grow from more to more,
> But more of reverence in us dwell;
> That mind and soul, according well,
> May make one music as before,
> But vaster. We are fools and slight;
> We mock thee when we do not fear:
> But help thy foolish ones to bear;
> Help thy vain worlds to bear thy light.

(17–32)

> ### Grains of Trivium
>
> Queen Victoria greatly admired Tennyson's work. She found *In Memoriam* a source of comfort following the death of Prince Albert in 1861 and arranged for a personal meeting with Tennyson.

The speaker addresses God and asks God to help humanity remain reverent even as human knowledge about the universe increases. As he does so, he hearkens nostalgically to a time when "mind and soul, according well" (reason and faith, working together) made "one music." The speaker hopes that the lost harmony between faith and reason might be restored "as before" and grow "vaster."

From Nostalgia to Irony

Tennyson's poem is an elegy, a work written to mourn the death and memorialize the life of someone who died. It imparts the sense of grief, not only for the loss of Arthur Hallam, but for the historical loss of unity between a rational and a faith-based worldview. The poem attempts to accommodate reason to faith in the face of increasing knowledge conflicts with traditional beliefs ("little systems"). Finally, however, the speaker's faith feels more like nostalgia than conviction.

In the following century, this sort of nostalgia would harden to irony, as in these lines from T. S. Eliot's "Preludes":

> Wipe your hand across your mouth, and laugh;
> The worlds revolve like ancient women
> Gathering fuel in vacant lots.

This dramatically self-conscious attempt to conceive of an impersonal universe in human terms succeeds only by representing human activity as a pathetic search for the means of light and warmth. Although "ancient" and purposeful, there's no assurance of continued success or that success even matters.

Of course, the large and gradual shift in belief from a religious to a secular worldview is not simply complete, even today. Nor is it a straightforward, linear process. But a broad overview of the changing interrelationship between literature and religious belief from the Renaissance down to our times shows a clear, slow trend toward secular thinking.

The Least You Need to Know

- English lit has roots in the Judeo-Christian and Greco-Roman traditions.
- Neo-Platonism combined ancient Greek philosophy with Christian theology.
- Renaissance humanists wrote works modeled consciously on classical literature.
- Secularization is the long, slow historical process through which religion loses its influence on society.

Chapter  13

Monks and Warriors

In This Chapter

- ◆ An overview of the literature of the Middle Ages
- ◆ Dusting off Old English literature
- ◆ Keeping the faith with early Anglo-Latin literature
- ◆ Anglo-Saxon charms and riddles
- ◆ *Beowulf* basics

One of the many fascinating things about Old English literature is its mystery. Because it was composed so long ago and because it survives in forms that imperfectly, incompletely reflect its oral roots, it can be a real challenge to interpret. And that makes it all the more intriguing.

Old English lit comes to us in old manuscripts that contain traces of even older traditions. These traditions reflect three broadly distinct cultures whose influences get blended in the literature: Anglo Saxons, Celts, and Romanized Christians.

Although these cultures made war on one another at various times in history, the battle lines become blurred in the surviving manuscripts. As a result, it's often hard to tell just what these people were thinking. Even so, the works of the period richly reward study, even in modern translations.

"Dark" Is Beautiful

Medievalists tend to get annoyed when you refer to their period as the "Dark Ages" or suggest that nothing of any great interest or importance got written down until the Renaissance, when classical learning and letters were "reborn." In fact, even a brief overview of medieval lit shows an impressive and intriguing variety of work. Spanning 1,000 years, from about 500 to 1500, and amid circuitous change in languages, culture, and politics, the literature of the Middle Ages has a lot to say for itself.

Hard to Fathom

The literature of the "Dark Ages" really is "dark" in the sense of being more difficult to understand than literature of more recent periods. Here's why:

♦ The languages medieval lit was written in were different from ours, were less standardized, and were more grammatically complex.

Kudos and Caveats

Medieval culture often gets a negative reputation from diverse and sometimes conflicting sources. According to the Renaissance humanists, the Middle Ages neglected the Greek and Roman classics. According to English Protestants, the Middle Ages nurtured Catholic superstition.

♦ Dating individual works and tracing their history through available manuscripts is often a challenge. Many works were passed along orally and written down only centuries later, sometimes more than once and sometimes in incomplete form. Some texts were damaged, and much, undoubtedly, has been lost.

♦ The cultural contexts of medieval texts can be fluid and are not always well understood.

♦ People thought, acted, and interpreted texts and reality differently from the ways we do today— very differently.

Of course, medievalists are drawn to these challenges. They like puzzling over textual mysteries, piecing together shreds of evidence, and fleshing out vague and sketchy understandings of peculiar patterns of thought and culture. It doesn't bother them that the literature they study doesn't really fit the mold of "English lit" that would later come to be taken for granted as a thriving, largely self-sufficient, and eminently legible tradition.

Will the Real "English Lit" Please Stand Up?

Literary output in the various dialects of Old and Middle English was often less vibrant and prolific than writing in other languages such as Irish and Welsh early on, French later, and Latin throughout most of the period. As a result, medievalists who study "English" lit often study literature written in these other languages, too. After all, in addition to English dialects, people who lived in the British Isles spoke Irish, Welsh, French, or Latin. So you might say "English lit" was still in its early stages of development and had to prop itself up with other languages and traditions.

This isn't to say that there weren't quite a few important works written in English during the Middle Ages. There were. But these works aren't the whole story of what was going on in England at the time.

> **Canon Fodder**
>
> Old English lit was rivaled by Old Irish lit and Old Welsh lit. The Old Irish Ulster cycle includes the *Cattle Raid of Cooley*, an important epic telling of the deeds of the hero Cuchulain. The Old Welsh *Mabinogion* includes tales of the legendary King Arthur.

The Whole Story

Once upon a time, there was the *Old English period* (500–1100). The dates of this period correspond with the time the Old English language was in use, although not all writing (and not even all the best writing) of this period was in Old English. This period is known for "heroic" narrative poetry, especially *Beowulf,* and for the gradual reacceptance of Christianity in England.

Then came the *Anglo-Norman period* (1066–1350). As a result of the Norman conquest of England, French became the language of the English royal court, paving the way for a profound French influence on English literature.

> **Canon Fodder**
>
> Most Old English lit is of unknown authorship. Some has been dubiously attributed to two shadowy—perhaps legendary (made-up)—figures named Caedmon and Cynewulf.

Meanwhile, the *Middle English period* (1200–1500) came along as the Old English language mingled with French and Latin, and evolved into the language called Middle English. English lit took many forms, including popular ballads, religious allegories and dream visions, bawdy stories, "mystery" plays, romances, and more. Eventually, English came to be spoken at court, and England got its first great poet, Geoffrey Chaucer. English lit was written mostly in English ever after.

From Tribal to Scribal

From the first to the fifth centuries, the country now known as England was an outpost of the Roman Empire called Britannia, after the conquered Britons who lived there. The Britons spoke Celtic, submitted to Roman rule, and embraced Christianity after the conversion of Charlemagne. Their poetic traditions were oral; Celtic lit was not written down until many centuries later.

> ### Grains of Trivium
>
> The noted scholar and theologian Alcuin (753–804) was educated in England at a school in York, where he eventually became headmaster. He later met Charlemagne and became head of the famous Palace School and a leading figure in the Carolingian Renaissance.

Fighting and Writing

When the Roman Empire collapsed and the Romans went back home to pick up the pieces, Britannia was invaded by Germanic tribes, predominantly Angles and Saxons. The Anglo-Saxons pushed the Celts to the outskirts of Britannia, into present-day Scotland, Wales, and Ireland. They also brought paganism, a love of heroism in battle, and a tradition of narrative poetry that was sung or spoken to the accompaniment of the harp.

Examples of this poetry were preserved in writing centuries later by Christian monks, but not before the great Irish sagas were written down. Ireland remained a stronghold of Christianity as much of Europe was beset by pagan tribes. Responding in large part to the influence of missionaries from Rome and Ireland, the Anglo-Saxons adopted Christianity starting in the late sixth century. From this period, they began to produce writing, mostly in Latin, that still survives.

Caedmon: In Your Dreams

Surviving writing from this time includes the works of a learned monk known as the Venerable Bede (673–735). Bede was a scholar best known for his *Ecclesiastical History of the English People*. Here he tells the story of Caedmon, the first English poet to be known by name, although we're not sure if he really existed.

Caedmon was an illiterate laborer who was ashamed of his lack of prowess as a singer. At feasts, when people took turns singing, passing the harp around to share songs and stories, Caedmon would run off. Although he felt ashamed, he was actually disgusted by the foolish and useless subject matter of the secular (nonreligious) songs that were sung. As a result, he never bothered to learn to sing them.

One day, after escaping another song session, he went off to sleep in a cattle shed. In a dream, a figure appeared to Caedmon and bid him to sing religious verse. Caedmon found that he could do so easily, and when

> **Kudos and Caveats**
>
> Old English writing combines the Roman alphabet with Anglo-Saxon runes. Unlike some dialects of Middle English, it's virtually incomprehensible to modern English speakers without training. Much Old English lit, however, has been translated into modern English.

he woke, he retained the ability. According to Bede, Caedmon went on to compose beautiful verses on God, the creation, and biblical history. It was clear to all that Caedmon's newfound ability was a gift from God. A cycle of narrative poems based on biblical stories appears in a manuscript that dates from the tenth century. It's traditionally attributed to Caedmon.

Strong Survivors

Much of the most important Old English poetry is contained in four manuscript collections dating from the tenth century. These are known as the *Exeter Book*, the *Vercelli Book*, the *Junius* manuscript (containing the works attributed to Caedmon), and the *Beowulf* manuscript. Not much that existed before these books were compiled has survived, but a number of minor poems, charms, and riddles written in Anglo-Saxon English remain.

> **Grains of Trivium**
>
> The *Beowulf* manuscript was partially destroyed by fire in 1731 before it was ever copied. As a result, some of the lines of the poem have been lost forever.

It's possible that many Old English texts were destroyed in Viking raids on England during the eighth and ninth centuries. It's also possible that only a small portion of the songs and stories from the Anglo-Saxon oral tradition were ever written down. Bede's story of Caedmon suggests that many of the monks able to write may have felt an aversion to secular literature. In any case, it's certain that more poetry was composed than got written, and more was written than has survived.

The Anglo-Saxon poetry that's been preserved incorporates a puzzling blend of pagan and Christian ideas. It's difficult to tell whether this blend reflects a partially

Christianized culture that existed at the time it was written, or the adding of Christian elements to pre-Christian oral poetry at the time it was written down.

Charmed, I'm Sure

A particularly intriguing Old English literary form is the charm, a combination of a song, prayer, magic spell, and folk remedy. Several surviving charms are intended to help recover lost cattle. One supplies a cure for a stitch; another shares a procedure to get bees to swarm.

> **Grains of Trivium**
>
> The "land remedy" charm makes the only known mention of Erce. It's hard to say whether she was a pagan goddess or a metaphoric personification of Earth.

The best-known charm is the "land remedy" for infertile land, which includes directions on how to prepare a magical remedy made from milk, honey, yeast, oil, and trees. It also includes instructions on how to prepare and place a crucifix on the land, and how to perform incantations that include prayers to God. In addition, it includes appeals to a mysterious figure called "Erce, the earth mother":

> Erce, Erce, Erce, eorþan modor.

After chanting to Erce, the user of the remedy is instructed to plough the first furrow through the soil with a plough that has a seed placed on it. The charm then exhorts the earth mother to "be fruitful in God's embrace":

> Hal wes þu, folde, fira modor!
> Beo þu growende on godes fæþme,
> fodre gefylled firum to nytte.

Next, the user is instructed to bake a loaf of bread made with holy water and place it in the furrow, followed by more chanting.

The charm suggests that Earth's fertility results from a kind of sexual union between God and the earth. This union is both symbolized and enacted by the plough and the bread, which represent the penetration and fertilization of the earth. And no doubt the chanting to God and to Erce helps put both of them in the mood!

Riddle Me This

Another Anglo-Saxon literary form is the riddle, a poem that supplies clues to its subject matter and then asks the listener to guess what it is. Many of these riddles are difficult to solve, even if you know how to read Old English. The texts of these riddles don't include the answers, so scholars have to puzzle them out. Many solutions remain conjectural or unknown.

Probable solutions to Old English riddles include animals, plants, weapons, farm implements, and natural phenomena (storms, fire, an iceberg). The riddles invite the listener to look at these things in special ways, often by merging the spheres of nature and culture into one. In many riddles, the thing to be guessed at speaks, describing itself and asking the listener to identify it: "Say what I am called."

One riddle describes a creature that devours knowledge, but is no wiser for having words in its mouth. (A moth or bookworm?)

Another describes a miracle on the waves: water turned to bone. (An iceberg?)

Another claims not to bite anyone "unless he bites me." (An onion?)

In general, riddles create playful, metaphoric descriptions of the solutions they represent. Often they treat inanimate things as living creatures, and vice versa. Sometimes they evoke feelings through pathos or irony. The bookworm riddle may be construed as an ironic depiction of human knowledge. Another riddle represents a war-weary shield, bemoaning the many battles and blows it's forced to undergo.

You Know It

In representing concepts and things through metaphoric images, riddles resemble a poetic devise commonly used in Anglo-Saxon and Old Norse narrative poetry known as the *kenning*. Kennings are stock phrases that provide figurative descriptions of people, things, and concepts. The term comes from the Old Norse word *kenna*, which means "to know." A closely related device is the *kend heiti*, or a "characterized thing." This stock phrase provides a literal description of a thing. Both terms come from a medieval treatise on poetry by Snorri

def•i•ni•tion

A **kenning** is a figurative stock phrase used to describe something in Old English and Old Norse narrative poetry. A **kend heiti** closely resembles a kenning, except it's literal instead of figurative.

Sturluson (1178–1241) of Iceland, famed author of the *Heimskringla,* a poetic chronicle of Norse mythology.

Here are some kennings:

◆ Bone house—human body

◆ Bone locks—joints or ligaments

◆ Battle light—sword

◆ Sword storm—battle

◆ Swan's road, whale road—the sea

◆ World candle—the sun

◆ Word hoard—speech

Kennings are figurative. A body isn't literally a house made of bone; it merely resembles a house in certain ways. A kend heiti, in contrast, is literal. Here are a few:

◆ Helmet-wearer—warrior

◆ Heath stepper—stag

◆ Ring giver—king

> **Canon Fodder**
>
> Old English kennings are comparatively simple compared to many Old Norse kennings. An Old Norse kenning for gold is *Frodi's meal.* This refers to a legend about a Danish king named Frodi who had a meal that could magically grind out gold.

Kennings and kend heiti were originally used in narrative poems that were recited by memory. They would probably have helped the poet remember the poem in addition to making the poem more vivid for the listeners. All the kennings and kend heiti listed here are from the Old English epic poem *Beowulf.*

Beowulf: Old Hero

Although recorded in a tenth-century manuscript, *Beowulf* was originally performed orally at a much earlier time. While it tells us much of what we know about pre-Christian Anglo-Saxon culture, it has Christian notions woven into it. It may well have been sung and modified repeatedly before it was written down, with Christian ideas added to the older story somewhere along the way.

Praise and Blame

Beowulf contains what appears from a modern perspective to be an uneasy mix of tribal values and Christian ideals. The heroic poem extols the virtues of warriors: bravery, prowess in battle, and loyalty to king and clan. These values reflect the way of thinking of people whose livelihood depended on the spoils of war and whose survival depended on resisting attack.

In keeping with these tribal values, those who succeed in battle can expect to be rewarded by the king, who distributes war loot to his warriors. They can also hope to be glorified by *bards* who might recount their deeds and sing their praises at feasts. Bards can also sing verses that hold up cowards and weaklings in battle to public ridicule.

def•i•ni•tion

A **bard** is an Old English minstrel—musician, poet, and storyteller. Years after the Old English period, "the Bard" was used as a popular honorary epithet for William Shakespeare.

Old English heroic poetry is intended to encourage warriors to fight well and speaks from a culture in which fighting was considered important. Gradually, however, people may have come to see that fighting, in the long run, was a no-win situation. In any case, despite marriages between tribes intended to foster peace, intertribal violence continued.

Men and Monsters

Beowulf makes clear references to bards and their singing, to kings and their generosity, and to warriors and their courage as it glorifies the exploits of the hero, Beowulf. It's interesting, however, that although Beowulf is a warrior, he doesn't fight against other warriors, but against a man-killing monster named Grendel. According to the story, Grendel is descended from Cain, the biblical character who murdered his brother Abel. Cain and Abel were sons of the first human couple, Adam and Eve.

In recounting the hero Beowulf's fight with a monster descended from the world's first murderer, is the story trying to say that killing people as a way of life is wrong? Maybe. But if so, killing the monster doesn't solve the problem. Beowulf kills Grendel and goes on to kill Grendel's mother as well, but he dies in the process. Beowulf's death is much lamented by his kin, the Geats, a tribe from southern Scandinavia. In addition to grief, his death elicits dire predictions of tribal warfare between the Geats and the Swedes, Franks, and Frisians. On the whole, *Beowulf* is a dark and violent work. It appears that life among the Geats will remain dark and violent even though Beowulf has killed Grendel and his mother.

Beowulf is the first of many important master works of English literature. Stay tuned for more to come.

The Least You Need to Know

◆ During the Old English period, "English" lit was written in several different languages, including Old English, Latin, Old Welsh, and Old Irish.

◆ Most of the surviving literature was apparently composed orally and revised repeatedly before finally getting written down.

◆ Anglo-Saxon poetry, including charms, riddles, and the epic *Beowulf*, exhibits a blending of Christian and pagan influence.

◆ *Beowulf* comes from a poetic tradition that glorifies warriors who are courageous in battle.

Chapter 14

Quests and Visions

In This Chapter

- An overview of Middle English lit
- The French connection: Anglo-Norman lit
- Arthurian romance and *Sir Gawain and the Green Knight*
- Chaucer and *The Canterbury Tales*
- Worker's rites: Medieval mystery plays

The Middle English period was the age of chivalry, when French romance exerted its influence in England through the Anglo-Norman connection. Tales about knights in shining armor helped spread the ideals of a powerful nobility. At this time, the legend of King Arthur returned to England as an inspiration to English poetry.

Late in the period, England's first major poet emerged. Geoffrey Chaucer's unprecedented achievements set a high standard for subsequent poets to aim for, and his *Canterbury Tales* continues to intrigue and entertain. His innovations paved the way for the Renaissance.

Middle English drama included the mystery cycles, a form that brought Christian theology to bear on contemporary working life. This writing reflects and promotes the cohesion of clerical and secular activity at the time and provides a fascinating view of medieval society.

Stormin' Normans

In the eleventh century, England was conquered by a force led by the Duke of Normandy, subsequently known as William the Conqueror. The success of the Norman invasion was decided at the Battle of Hastings in 1066. The new King William helped bring French language and culture to England. Before long, English writers began tapping into French literary traditions, the romance chief among these.

A Day of Knights

If you haven't checked it out already, you might want to flip back to the "The Romance of Narrative" section in Chapter 10, which explains the various ways the term gets used at various moments in history, including in the Middle Ages. At this time, romances were generally stories about knights. Battles often figured into romances, but more often, romance plots centered on quests and courtships. Such stories, read predominantly by the upper classes, expressed and celebrated an idealized code of honor and behavior known as *chivalry*.

def•i•ni•tion

Chivalry is the idealized code of the medieval nobility. It stressed honesty and integrity in living up to one's social obligations, courtesy to others, and deference to ladies.

Chivalry derives from *cheval*, the French word for "horse." But chivalry is much more than just good horsemanship. It's largely concerned with morality and etiquette—so much so, you might almost think of it as a sort of supplemental religion for the medieval nobility. Heroes of chivalric romance typically face tough moral choices. They are sometimes guided by Christian precepts, but more often the important factors are chivalric values—keeping one's word, upholding personal commitments to one's lord, and respecting the chastity of ladies.

Hello, Ladies

Why the concern for the ladies? To violate a lady's chastity was, in effect, to despoil the property—and the future lineage—of another nobleman, either her father or her husband. The fact was, nobly born women of the Middle Ages had very little control over their relationships with men. Marriages were arranged, usually in the interest of forging alliances between clans.

The codes of chivalry call for deference to women not because women had personal power over men, but because their chastity preserved the purity of aristocratic, patrilineal bloodlines. In theory, these bloodlines set the nobility apart from the commoners. (And if you're wondering, yes, some—but not all—noblemen made their daughters wear chastity belts.)

> **Kudos and Caveats** _____
>
> Historically, many "virtues" have served sociological functions. The virtue of womanly chastity helped preserve the purity of patrilineal bloodlines. Celibacy among the clergy helped keep Church men devoted wholly to the Church and to Church business, without families to claim their time and resources.

Conquered and Conquering Kings

Within and beyond knightly, chivalric doings, medieval romance generally focused on one of three large, legendary, and historical subjects: the matter of France, the matter of Greece and Rome, and the matter of Britain. The matter of France concerned Charlemagne. The matter of Greece and Rome concerned the Trojan Wars and Alexander the Great. The matter of Britain concerned King Arthur and his knights.

Stories from the Round Table

King Arthur was a legendary king who may well have had a historical antecedent— a Celtic Briton who defended Britannia unsuccessfully against the Anglo-Saxons. Lore and legend about Arthur developed in Wales and traveled to France, where it became subject matter for romance. From there, Arthurian romances in French returned to England with the Normans before eventually being penned in Middle English.

The most complete treatment of Arthurian legend in Middle English is Sir Thomas Malory's *Le Morte d'Arthur* (c. 1470). Perhaps the best Arthurian romance in Middle English, however, is *Sir Gawain and the Green Knight* (c. 1400), a tale in which the chivalry of one of Arthur's knights is put to several tests. Passing all of them at once proves difficult.

Off with His Head!

On Christmas day, when Arthur and his knights are feasting together, a supernatural figure rides into the hall. He is a huge knight, larger than anyone else present, and except for his red eyes, he is completely green—hair, skin, clothing, even his horse.

Canon Fodder

The only medieval source for *Sir Gawain and the Green Knight* is an anonymous manuscript dating from about 1400 that also contains three other poems—*Patience, Purity,* and *The Pearl.* It may be that all four poems were written by the same poet.

He wears no armor and is unarmed, save an enormous green ax. He demands to speak with Arthur in order to propose a Christmas "game." The game he proposes is that one of Arthur's famous knights should strike at his neck with the ax. In return, after the passing of a year and a day, the Green Knight gets to take a whack at the knight. Sounds fair!

The Green Knight is a multivalent symbol that unites the ideal of chivalry with the mystery of nature while suggesting conflict between the two.

His game is both playful and serious. On one hand, it links chivalry to the courteous enjoyment of the pleasures of court life. On the other hand, it links chivalry to the ideal of keeping one's word, even to the death.

The Green Knight challenges King Arthur and his court to live up to their chivalric reputation. Goaded by the knight's taunting challenge, Sir Gawain agrees to the proposal. As Arthur's most highly respected knight, Sir Gawain is obligated by his own ideals to be courteous to the knight and to stand up for himself, his king, and his comrades. Taking up the ax, Gawain swings it and chops the Green Knight's head clean off!

Perhaps this beheading suggests the attempt, on the part of the chivalrous individual, to subdue his own nature. Chivalry demands a sacrifice. But although his head rolls across the floor, the Green Knight appears completely unharmed. His body retrieves his head and mounts his horse. The severed head then tells Gawain to come and find him at the Green Chapel in a year's time to receive a blow with the ax in return. With that, the Green Knight rides out of the hall.

Nobody's Perfect

As the following Christmas approaches, Sir Gawain sets off to find the Green Chapel. Along the way, he stops to rest at a castle. The lord of the castle tells Gawain that the Green Chapel is close by and invites Gawain to stay with him three nights until it's time for his appointment with the Green Knight. Like the Green Knight, Gawain's host proposes a courteous game: he will go out hunting and give Gawain anything he shoots in exchange for whatever Gawain may happen to get over the course of three days in the castle. Gawain agrees.

The young wife of the lord of the castle puts Gawain's chivalry to the test in a new way: she tries to seduce him. Gawain resists her but accepts a love token from her—a green girdle (that is, a belt) that has the power to protect anyone who wears it from harm. Although it's a breach of courtesy to accept the girdle without giving it to his host, Gawain does so, hoping its power will protect him from the Green Knight.

At last, it's time for Gawain's appointed meeting with the Green Knight. Gawain bares his neck, the Green Knight swings his ax … and he barely nicks Gawain. As it turns out, the host of the castle and the Green Knight are one and the same. The Green Knight knows Gawain accepted the girdle from his wife and kept it secret. The nick with the ax was punishment for Gawain's falsehood.

Gawain confesses his fault and is pardoned by the Green Knight, who, to the last, retains his courtesy and sense of humor. He also praises Gawain for resisting the advances of his wife. Gawain played the Green Knight's game well, although not flawlessly. After Gawain returns to Arthur's court and tells of his adventures, King Arthur commands all his knights to wear green girdles in honor of Gawain and as a token of humility.

Tales for the Road

Since the Renaissance, Geoffrey Chaucer (1343–1400) has been called the "father of English poetry." Although, obviously, he wasn't the first English poet, his writing brought new qualities to poetry. For one, he brought a new awareness of syllabic meter (see Chapter 7). He is especially known for his ability to write about his own society—fourteenth-century England—in all its diversity. And he brought a broad knowledge of literature and literary conventions to bear in his works.

As briefly mentioned in Chapter 11, Chaucer's greatest work, *The Canterbury Tales*, is a collection of stories united by a narrative frame in which a diverse group assembled from all over England gathers in London in preparation for a pilgrimage to Canterbury. There they intend to pay homage to the Christian martyr St. Thomas Becket, the twelfth-century archbishop who was murdered in Canterbury Cathedral. To pass the time along the journey, the pilgrims agree to trade stories.

Narrative Frame

The pilgrims include 30 men and women from all walks of medieval English life. Chaucer's plan was for each to tell four tales—two on the way to Canterbury and two on the way back. Chaucer never completed the cycle, however, and only 24 tales make up the collection. Even so, they offer considerable variety in subject matter as well as form, including such medieval genres as romance, fabliau (a humorous tale), beast fable, and saint's life.

The tales reflect the interests and backgrounds of the various pilgrims who tell them. The knight, for example, tells a courtly romance, while the miller tells a scandalous fabliau. What's more, the tales subtly respond to and comment on tales told previously. Some are linked with intervening dialogues and prefaced with prologues that help relate the tales to their tellers.

Kudos and Caveats

Although medieval readers clearly appreciated poetry, authors had to be careful not to seem to intrude on the prerogative of the Church. Chaucer's poetry is remarkable for the freedom and tact with which it plays with religious teachings and explores social attitudes toward the Church. While he is unprecedented as an English author, Chaucer often qualifies his own authority by claiming his work is intended merely to amplify Christian doctrine. In fact, *The Canterbury Tales* concludes with a famous "retraction" in which Chaucer asks God to forgive him for writing and translating "worldly vanitees."

Lightening Up

"The Nun's Priest's Tale" provides a good illustration of how *The Canterbury Tales* respond to one another and reflect the backgrounds of the pilgrims who tell them. It follows "The Monk's Tale," a series of tragedies, which the other pilgrims found tedious and depressing. In contrast, "The Nun's Priest's Tale" is humorous and pointedly mock-tragic. It thus supplies a kind of answer to the preceding tale.

The nun's priest is employed at a convent and is subordinate to the head nun, or prioress. His job is to perform priestly functions for the nuns that women were not allowed to fill, even for themselves, including saying Mass and hearing confession. He thus has spiritual authority over the nuns, even though he's not in charge of the convent.

By implication, the nun's priest appreciates the instructive moral purpose behind the monk's tragic stories. At the same time, he's not inclined to provide heavy-handed moral guidance for his nuns, but is capable of taking a warmer, lighter view of things. He can adapt the bleak outlook of medieval Christianity to the presumably simple spiritual requirements of the convent.

Birds of a Feather ...

The tale the nun's priest tells is deftly analogous to his own situation: it concerns a rooster in a hen-house belonging to a temperate old widow. The tale is a beast fable, endowing animals with human personalities in order to draw moral conclusions from their behavior and poke fun at human foibles.

As the tale unfolds, it's easy to identify the nun's priest with the rooster (even though the nun's priest and the nuns are apparently celibate, while the rooster and the hens are not!). The rooster's crowing is "merier than the merye orgon / On massedays that in the chirche goon" (merrier than the church organ / that is played on Mass days). The hens are described as "his sustres and his paramours" (his sisters and his lovers).

The rooster's name is Chaunticleer, and, like the nun's priest, he loves spouting moral wisdom he has gleaned from the Bible and theological writings. In fact, although he's a bit pretentious (after all, he is a rooster), he's rather clever and engaging in discussion with his favorite hen, Pertelote.

Chaunticleer tells Pertelote about a dream that frightened him and asks her to help him interpret it. He dreamt that "a beest ... lik an hound" (i.e., a fox) threatened to kill him. Pertelote tells him not to be such a coward as to fear his dream. A discussion ensues in which Chaunticleer offers scholarly support for his view of the providential nature of dreams. Pertelote, however, attributes the dream to "fume," or gas caused by overeating, and recommends he take an herbal "laxitif"!

After some debate, the tale smoothly defuses the disagreement without resolving it. Chaunticleer declines the laxative and gallantly declares that Pertelote's beauty has quelled his dread. He defies his dream and goes off into the chicken yard to peck for corn.

But the dream comes true and the fox appears. The nun's priest, narrating the tale, weighs in and ruminates on fate, divine foreknowledge,

> **Canon Fodder**
>
> A common literary device during the Middle Ages is the dream vision. The poet falls asleep and envisions an allegorical scenario that may be supposed to represent a higher, idealized truth. Dante's *Divine Comedy* is a major dream vision. Chaucer wrote several shorter dream visions, including "The Legend of Good Women" and "The Parliament of Fowls."

and free will, citing his authorities, the Bible, and the Church fathers at every step of the way. He goes on to blame "Wommennes conseils" (women's advice) for all human woe by leading to the fall of Adam in paradise.

He deflates this tragic tone (as if it needed further deflation) by reversing himself. He apologizes, lest he has offended any women who are listening, and attributes the condemnation of women to Chaunticleer. Thus, both narrator and rooster appear at least somewhat critical of women, yet ingratiating.

In any case, Chaunticleer sees the fox and is about to fly away. But the fox speaks, telling Chaunticleer how much he admires good singing and how he used to enjoy listening to Chaunticleer's father, who, according to the fox, sounded especially fine when he closed his eyes and stretched out his neck.

> **Grains of Trivium**
>
> The rooster is a Christian symbol of watchful readiness. Its crowing at dawn anticipates the trumpet call that will announce the final judgment and the apocalypse.

Chaunticleer falls for the fox's flattery and begins to sing in the posture suggested by the fox: eyes shut and neck outstretched. The fox immediately clamps his teeth around Chaunticleer's neck, swings him up on his back, and carries him out of the chicken yard. The hens let out a mock-tragic cackling, rousing the entire household, which sets off in pursuit.

Striking a note of pathos, and playing on the fox's pride, Chaunticleer tells the fox that if he were the fox, he would defy the pursuers and eat the rooster then and there. The proud fox answers, "In faith, it shal be doon." As the fox speaks, Chaunticleer frees himself and flies into a tree.

In conclusion, both fox and rooster curse themselves for their mistakes—the rooster, for keeping his eyes shut; the fox for keeping his mouth open. The narrator identifies both these failings with flattery and advises his hearers to accept the morality of his tale and reject its folly.

Chaucer's Trade Secrets

The Canterbury Tales occasionally suggests that people of different stations in society take differing but equally valid perspectives on shared beliefs. An important form of medieval drama suggests this even more strongly (although with less elegance and sophistication than Chaucer): the mystery play. Mystery plays are staged by members of different professions called guilds and portray different episodes taken from biblical history.

Works and Plays

Mystery plays show the profound significance of Christian belief at work within the fabric of medieval society. These beliefs were not merely taught, but performed. They were performed not merely by actors, but by craftsmen who felt a sense of continuity between their work and the dramas they performed. Although these plays are intended strictly to represent biblical events, they put biblical lore to cultural uses the earliest Christians never could have imagined.

Canon Fodder

Other forms of medieval drama include morality plays and miracle plays. Morality plays are allegorical dramas that typically depict virtues and vices as personified characters in conflict with one another; the medieval play *Everyman* is a prime example. Miracle plays dramatize saints' lives and miraculous events. Few English miracle plays have survived. (See Chapter 9 for more on both types of plays.)

In a number of European towns and cities, including several English towns and cities, mystery plays were performed on ritual occasions such as the festivals of Whitsuntide or Corpus Christi. These simple enactments of biblical stories intended to educate illiterate churchgoers on the Christian themes of the creation, fall, and redemption of humanity. At first they were performed in church by the clergy. Gradually, the laity got involved, and eventually, performances moved outside the churches and were taken over by the guilds.

Each guild was responsible for one play, supplying a text (revised as needed from previous performances), a wagon that worked as a stage, actors, and costumes. All the plays together made up a *cycle*, which told more or less the whole story of Christianity. The plays were performed on carts that were moved to successive performance locales around town. After staging a performance in one location, a guild moved its cart to a new place and performed the play again. Over the course of a day or so, audiences in several locations could see the whole cycle.

def•i•ni•tion

Cycle is a term used for collections of works on a common theme such as Charlemagne or the Trojan War. They typically represent the work of several different authors brought together into a group. Cycles are often groups of romance narrative, although mystery plays are dramatic cycles.

In time, the texts of the plays evolved to reflect aspects of each guild's trade and relation to society. In York, shipbuilders performed a play about Noah's Ark. In Chester, a play on the same subject was performed by men who drew and delivered water. Many plays exhort people to do good work, pointing to the holy "works" of God and the saints as a model and suggesting that work and worship of God are closely equated. Thus, the plays represent as well as embody the idea that the work of the guilds carries out a moral, religious function.

Here are some of the plays that make up the 47-play York cycle, together with the guilds that put them on (some make more sense than others):

- The Creation—plasterers

- The Expulsion (of Adam and Eve from the Garden of Eden)—armorers

- The Flood—fishermen and seamen

- Moses and Pharaoh—hosiers (stocking-makers)

- The Baptism—barbers

- The Last Supper—bakers

- The Road to Cavalry (on the way to the Crucifixion)—sheepshearers

- The Crucifixion—pin makers

- The Death of Christ—butchers

- The Resurrection—carpenters

- The Last Judgment—mercers (textile dealers)

> **Grains of Trivium**
>
> Much of what we know about mystery plays comes from town records. Apparently, town officials oversaw the guilds, okayed play manuscripts, and made sure performances squared with the plays as written. They could also impose fines for bad acting!

Family Feud

The plays are not dry, austere, solemn shows. Instead, they often represent biblical characters as contemporary people with dialogue that links the action to contemporary events. Many are enlivened with farce—physical, slapstick comedy that resorts to buffoonery, exaggeration, and improbable events for the sake of laughs.

The Wakefield *Killing of Abel* presents Abel's murderer, Cain, as comically foulmouthed, selfish, dissatisfied, and childishly uncooperative. When Abel suggests they go to offer sacrifice to God, Cain responds:

Shuld I leife my plogh and all thyng,
And go with the to make offeryng?
Nay, thou fyndys me not so mad!
Go to the dwill and say I bad!
What gifys God the to rose hym so?
Me gifys he noght but soro and wo.

ABELL: Cayn, leife this vayn carpyng,
For God giffys the all thy lifyng.

CAYN: Yit boroed I never a farthing
Of hym—here my hand.

Grains of Trivium

Mystery play texts were continuously revised. Some manuscripts have references to the pope and Catholic sacraments crossed out, evidently in an effort to keep the tradition alive into the Protestant Reformation.

CAIN: Should I leave my plough and everything
and go with you to make an offering?
No, you don't find me as crazy as that!
Go to the devil and say I sent you!
What does God give you to get you to speak so highly of him?
He gives me nothing but sorrow and woe.

ABEL: Cain, stop this vain carping,
because God gives you all your livelihood.

CAIN: But I never borrowed a farthing [coin worth ¼ of a penny]
from him. Believe me.

Cain is obsessed with having and keeping worldly wealth. Although he believes in God, he has no respect for him. Later, when he hears God speak to him from heaven (God is a character in the play), Cain says, "Who is that hob over the wall?" A "hob" is a hobgoblin, a mischievous elf. The wall may be literally a wall or railing at the edge of the stage. Thus, Cain is amusingly out of step with the cosmos, yet reminiscent of a common, carping malcontent. It's easy to imagine the play's audience hissing and booing Cain, just for fun.

Culturally speaking, the Middle Ages grew increasingly vital and eventually overflowed into the Renaissance. Religious thinking continued to dominate in life and in literature, but space gradually made way for secular attitudes as well. Often these new secular attitudes developed amid religious and political conflict. To learn more, keep reading!

The Least You Need to Know

- The Norman invasion brought the influence of French literature, including the romance tradition.

- Chivalry is an idealized moral code for the nobility that is often reflected in medieval romance.

- Medieval romance tends to concern itself with the quests and courtships of knights.

- Geoffrey Chaucer is the first major English poet we know by name. His *Canterbury Tales* are framed with a narrative about a band of pilgrims.

- Mystery plays were presented by guilds on feast days. They depict important events in Christian history.

Chapter  15

Courtiers and Cavaliers

In This Chapter

- ◆ The flourishing of Renaissance literature
- ◆ Petrarchan lyric and Elizabethan court poetry
- ◆ Spenser's *Fairye Queene*
- ◆ Metaphysical versus Cavalier poetry
- ◆ Milton's epic, *Paradise Lost*

The Renaissance was a vital and innovative epoch when culture mushroomed. It marked the discovery of new continents and new scientific truths, and the rise of a more economically and politically powerful English nation. It also marked the rediscovery and revival of the literature of ancient Greece and Rome, as well as the borrowing of new literary fashions from Italy.

Literature flourished at court and in public theaters. Poetry came to be regarded as an important and serious undertaking that could win lasting fame for the poet and for the subject of his poetry. The lyric emerged as a poignant and subtle means of expressing and testing the ideals of the age as the epic powerfully enshrined them.

But idealism waned as political, economic, and religious rifts divided society. The Puritan Revolution pulled down the monarchy and chastened an increasingly libertine aristocracy. After that, the pervasive mutual reinforcement of state power and poetic symbolism that characterized the English Renaissance was never again possible.

Brave New World

The European Renaissance was ushered in by a flourishing of material and literary culture in fifteenth-century Italy, where trade and banking enabled powerful families to become fabulously wealthy and sponsor artistic, technical, and intellectual accomplishments of all kinds. Italian poets looked to ancient examples set by the Greeks and Romans, and drew on them as models and inspiration. Appreciation of classical thought and culture also provided a rationale for celebrating worldly achievement and for sidestepping austere Christian morals that frowned on human ambition.

Renaissance humanism quickly spread north out of Italy, fueled by the invention of the printing press in the 1470s. Bold new thinking took on revolutionary proportions in 1511, when German cleric Martin Luther spoke out against corruption in the Church and sparked the Protestant Reformation in Northern Europe.

Meanwhile, thanks to the discovery of the New World, gold and silver plundered from the Americas poured into European coffers.

Fame and Finesse

The great Italian poet Dante (1265–1321) constructed a magisterial, monumental dream vision, *The Divine Comedy* (1320), in which his beloved Beatrice symbolizes divine revelation as Christian destiny plays itself out against the backdrop of the Christian cosmos.

> ### Canon Fodder
>
> In *The Divine Comedy,* Dante's guide through hell and purgatory is none other than the ancient Roman poet Virgil (70–19 B.C.E.), who stands for "Reason." Contrast Beatrice, who guides him into heaven as "Revelation."

But even with Dante's unquestioned importance, he exerted far less influence on English poets than his younger fellow Florentine Petrarch (1304–1374), who praised his beloved Laura in a sequence of short lyrics called the *Canzoniere*. In this sequence, Petrarch rediscovered a classical poetic idiom that was widely imitated all over Europe, including England.

The Petrarchan lyric, especially the sonnet, provided a model that enabled courtiers and civil servants to veil their professional aspirations and political criticisms in artful, decorous love "plaints."

The Petrarchan sonnet also provided a quasireligious rationale for itself by uniting the poetry, the poet, and the poet's beloved in an equation intended to produce undying fame for all three. For Petrarch and his imitators, this fame was powerfully symbolized by the laurel, a plant Petrarch identifies with his beloved Laura.

Boy Meets Girl, Boy Gets Tree

Petrarch and his contemporaries knew the Greek myth telling the story of Daphne, or Laurel, thanks to the Roman poet Ovid's (43 B.C.E.—17 C.E.) *Metamorphoses*. Daphne, a mountain nymph, attracted the attention of the god Apollo, who was smitten with love for her—or lust, at any rate. Apollo chases after Daphne, who runs away and prays to her mother, Earth, to protect her. Her prayer is granted—in a way—as she is transformed into a laurel tree. Disappointed but not defeated, Apollo breaks a branch from the tree and makes himself a laurel crown.

In honor of Apollo, the Greeks awarded laurel crowns to victors in games and contests. Thanks to Petrarch, the laurel crown came to be associated with poetic achievement.

In Petrarchan poetry, the laurel crown elegantly symbolizes many things at once. For one, it represents the beloved's sexual purity. Because she's a tree, she's unobtainable. Perhaps ironically, the poet admires his beloved all the more because of her refusal to yield to him. Therefore, the laurel also symbolizes the poet's sincerity. His love remains steadfast even though there's apparently no hope of requital.

> **Grains of Trivium**
>
> "Poet Laureate" became an unofficial title in England during the Renaissance and became an officially recognized honor bestowed for the first time on John Dryden in 1668.

On top of these, the laurel is an evergreen. Because its leaves don't wither and die with the changing seasons, they symbolize the undying fame the beloved deserves to have because of her beauty and purity—and which the poet deserves also because of the power of his love and the genius of his verse. Kind of nifty, isn't it?—once you get past Apollo's attempted rape!

Order in the Court

English courtiers had started translating and imitating Petrarch's poetry by the mid-sixteenth century. From the beginning, they exploited its potential as a subtle, decorous way to air hopes and frustrations attendant upon their courtly profession. If they succeeded in pleasing or impressing their sovereign, they could be preferred to lucrative posts. If they did or said the wrong thing, however, they could be turned out into the cold—or worse. Attending at court was tricky business.

Queen and Country

Whereas the Petrarchan vein was a clever, amusing, and suggestive novelty at the court of King Henry VIII, it became the common language under Queen Elizabeth (reigned 1558–1603). Directly and indirectly, "The Virgin Queen" inspired an outpouring of verse in which devoted love and political loyalty could be understood as pretty much the same thing.

> **Canon Fodder**
>
> Three great English sonnet sequences were written during the Renaissance: Sidney's *Astrophil and Stella,* Edmund Spenser's *Amoretti,* and William Shakespeare's sonnets (published 1609). Shakespeare wrote his sonnets after the initial vogue, for the form had already subsided.

The most accomplished Elizabethan court poet was Sir Philip Sidney (1554–1586), who led a brilliant political career while distinguishing himself with his sonnet sequence, *Astrophil and Stella* (published 1591). Sidney also penned an essay, "The Defense of Poesy," in which he argued for the cultural and spiritual benefits of poetry against those inclined to see it as immoral (e.g., Puritans).

But Sidney's work was outshone by that of a provincial, courtly wannabe named Edmund Spenser (1552–1599). Spenser longed for preferment at court under Elizabeth but instead found himself entrenched as aid and secretary to the Lord Deputy of Ireland. Hoping to get noticed in London, he not only wrote the sonnet sequence *Amoretti* (published 1595), but he also completed just over half of a phenomenally ambitious cycle of verse narratives intended to glorify Elizabeth and her court: *The Faerie Queene* (published 1590, 1596).

The Faerie Queene draws heavily on romance, epic, and Petrarchan conventions in attempting to idealize courtliness as the legacy of a time-honored chivalric code that reaches its apex under Queen Elizabeth. Elizabeth is represented allegorically as the Faerie Queen, Gloriana, whose knights represent the virtues of courtliness, including holiness, temperance, chastity, friendship, justice, and courtesy, as they go off in pursuit of wrongs to redress.

Old-Fangled Language

In keeping with the markedly traditional nature of the poem, Spenser wrote elaborate, lush, and deliberately archaic-sounding verse fraught with outdated words and spellings. Many poets during and since Spenser's day have regarded his verse as quintessentially poetic. Many others have seen it as lamentably affected. Ben Jonson's opinion that Spenser "writ no language" may stem partly from jealousy, but also from his sense of poetry as a way for living people to communicate.

Here's a stanza from *The Faerie Queene* that introduces Canto V of Book III, "Of Chastity":

> Wonder it is to see, in diverse minds,
> How diversely love doth his pageants play,
> And shews his powre in variable kinds:
> The baser wit, whose idle thoughts always
> Are wont to cleave unto the lowly clay,
> It stirreth up to sensual desire,
> And in lewd slouth to wast his carelesse
>   day:
> But in brave sprite it kindles goodly fire,
> That to all high desert and honour doth
>   aspire.

> **Canon Fodder**
>
> The verse form Spenser used in *The Faerie Queene*, known today as the Spenserian stanza, has been widely admired for its elegant rhyme scheme and its potential to combine narrative utility and lyrical effects. This form was revived during the Romantic period by a number of poets, including Shelly, Keats, and Byron.

These lines draw on a Petrarchan distinction between carnal desire and idealized love. Love "plays" its "pageants" or shows itself differently in different people. Love makes "The baser wit" (the low-born mind) lustful. "In brave sprite" (in a noble spirit), love incites noble ambition. Note the use of only three rhymes within nine lines of verse. Also note that the last line is one iamb longer than the others. This form has become known as the Spenserian stanza.

> **Grains of Trivium**
>
> *The Faerie Queene* seems practically to deify Queen Elizabeth by praising her as a sovereign, invoking her as a muse, and holding her up as an example and source of her nation's virtue. In fact, Queen Elizabeth enjoyed something like cult status among many of her subjects. It's possible that some of the ardent devotion commonly expressed for St. Mary by English Catholics before the Protestant Reformation was transferred to the Virgin Queen as England shifted from a Catholic to a Protestant nation.

The Queen Is Dead! (and Other Changes)

The death of Queen Elizabeth in 1603 marked the end of an era that, although fraught with its share of social and economic upheaval, remained idealistic. The idealism of the period is evident in the way much of its literature testifies to a belief in a divinely ordered universe. The natural world, human society, and God and angels were widely regarded as layers in a continuous, harmonious cosmos united in a great chain of being.

Many people still regarded the world as the center of the universe, with humanity occupying a key, central place in divine creation. Despite an upswing in social mobility, conventional thought regarded the social order as ideally fixed in a way that resonated with the order of nature and God's intentions. The monarch ruled by divine right, and the privileges of gentility were accorded to them by virtue of their noble blood. By the end of Elizabeth's reign, these ideals were starting to lose their luster.

def•i•ni•tion

Metaphysical poetry is characterized by elaborate, sometimes bizarre use of metaphor, rough and rugged versification, dramatic speakers, and paradoxical reasoning. Cavalier verse is characterized by smooth elegance, a focus on beautiful things (including women), and an interest in life's pleasures as opposed to moral virtue.

English poetry of the early seventeenth century reflects the waning of these ideals in different ways—especially through two different styles or schools of poetry: *metaphysical* and *cavalier*. The metaphysical poets remained intensely interested in the old ideals, even while recognizing that they were severely challenged by new ideas. In contrast, the cavalier poets were more interested in manners than beliefs.

The metaphysical poets tested the limits of the belief in a divinely ordered cosmos while portraying it as less harmonious and more fraught with tension and paradox than previously thought. Their poetry often seems strained, both formally and intellectually, as if written amid a struggle to keep the disintegrating cosmos in one piece. Use of bizarre imagery and rough-sounding meter are hallmarks of the metaphysical school.

Getting It Donne

The preeminent metaphysical poet is John Donne (1572–1631). Much of Donne's work seems intentionally outrageous as he challenges, refutes, and parodies conventional wisdom about love and morality, often by drawing on esoteric theological or philosophical notions. (The use of esoteric philosophical allusions gives metaphysical poetry its name.)

In the lyric "Loves Alchymie," for example, Donne compares an idealized, Petrarchan attitude toward love to the pseudoscience of alchemy. Alchemists hoped, and sometimes pretended, to find a way to transmute base metal into gold or to find a formula for eternal youth. Alchemy was widely regarded as a hoax by the time Donne wrote his poem, which suggests that idealized love is, like alchemy, a sham. Meanwhile, Donne's alchemical terminology is humorously erotic:

> Oh, 'tis imposture all:
> And as no chymique yet th'Elixer got,
>   But glorifies his pregnant pot,
>   If by the way to him befall
> Some odoriferous thing, or medicinall;
>   So, lovers dreame a rich and long delight,
>   But get a winter-seeming summers night.

These lines say that love and alchemy are both "impostures," or pretenses. Just as "chymiques," or alchemists, delude themselves and others with false claims about their discoveries, lovers "dreame" of lasting happiness when all they get is an experience that is paradoxically cold like winter and short like a summer night.

Grains of Trivium

Donne's life was fraught with wrenching experiences. Born a Catholic, he faced a tortuous moral decision in converting to Anglicanism and eventually becoming a Protestant minister in a society where Catholicism was a crime punishable by death and where Catholics were viciously persecuted. Donne also married young without the blessing of his father-in-law and struggled to support his wife and live down what many of his contemporaries regarded as a foolish decision. In any case, much of Donne's poetry expresses moral and spiritual angst consistent with an embattled conscience.

Now or Never

While metaphysical poetry is largely concerned with the testing of ideals, thoughts, and beliefs, cavalier poetry is concerned with style and manners. It tends to be smooth and elegant, and often draws on poetic ideals as mere conventions, without either challenging or defending them. It can be somewhat personal, often addressed specifically to an individual or a group of the poet's friends.

When it deals, as it often does, with love and other worldly pleasures, cavalier verse commonly exhibits a relaxed moral attitude, focusing on the joys of earthly existence rather than on the means to salvation in the afterlife. A common cavalier motif is known as *carpe diem*, or "seize the day." This is typically an exhortation addressed to a young, attractive female to take advantage of her youth and beauty while she still has them. More broadly, it's any reminder that life is fleeting. A prime example can be found in the poem "To the Virgins, to Make Much of Time" by Robert Herrick. It begins:

def•i•ni•tion

The **carpe diem** motif originates with a phrase used in an ode by the ancient Roman poet Horace (first century B.C.E.) meaning "seize the day." It was widely used by the English cavalier poets.

> Gather ye Rosebuds while ye may,
>   Old time is still a-flying;
> And this same flower that smiles today
>   Tomorrow will be dying.

Severed Head of State

The term cavalier was used to refer not only to a school of poetry, but also to a socio-political class of English gentlemen who found themselves in heated conflict with the Puritans. English Puritans became increasingly militant and antiroyalist as the first half of the seventeenth century progressed. They opposed the moral laxness of the cavaliers and of the king of England, Charles I.

The Puritans blamed the king for misrule amid mounting economic difficulties. They opposed him all the more vehemently on account of his ties and sympathies with the Catholic Church. The Puritans gained control of Parliament as civil war broke out. At the height of the revolution in 1649, the king was tried and executed for treason.

Justifying the Ways of God to Men

In the waning days of the Renaissance and, as it were, amid the ashes of the Puritan Revolution, Puritan poet John Milton composed *Paradise Lost* (1667), what many believe is the greatest epic poem—if not the greatest poem—ever written. This grand work tells the biblical story of the temptation and fall from grace of the first human couple, Adam and Eve, interweaving it with an account of Satan and the fallen angels' revolt in heaven against God.

Readers on both sides of the Puritan conflict have tried to draw parallels between Milton's great poem and political events of the time, but *Paradise Lost* is much more than a comment on current events. It attempts, in the poet's words, "to justify the ways of God to men" by presenting a coherent and compelling account of humanity's place in God's creation as Milton understood it. In Milton's telling, mankind's original sin has less to do with sex than with disobedience of God's commands.

> **Grains of Trivium**
>
> *Paradise Lost* was not the first classically styled seventeenth-century epic to treat biblical subject matter. That distinction goes to Abraham Cowley's *Davideis* (1656). Cowley's four-book epic recounts the life of King David in heroic couplets.

Devilish Doings

In the poem, Adam and Eve are banished from paradise not because they had sex (in *Paradise Lost*, they do so before the fall with no adverse consequences), but for disobeying God by eating the fruit of the Tree of Knowledge. The silver lining is that now humanity can participate in its own salvation; each person is free to choose between good and evil. This freedom of choice contrasts with the condition of the fallen angel, Satan, whose fall is irredeemable.

Although most of the action in the poem is based on stories from the Bible, the poem itself is modeled on the classical Virgilian epic, complete with invocations to the muse, journey to the underworld, catalog of heroes, and other elements of the genre. One of the great achievements of the poem is the way it synthesizes a vast, diverse quantity of classical, biblical, and historical lore into a compelling, unified vision of human destiny.

Although steeped in the copious literary knowledge Milton acquired through decades of reading, *Paradise Lost* is surprisingly clear and easy to read, even to today's readers. Milton's blank verse has a grand, lofty weightiness that Augustan poets of the following century widely admired and imitated. His characterization of Satan is especially intriguing, and it inspired the famous comment that Milton "gives the devil his due."

> **Canon Fodder**
>
> Milton's biblical source for the fall of Satan was the last book in the Bible, *Revelation*. His biblical source for the fall of Adam and Eve was *Genesis*, the first book in the Bible.

See what you think of these lines describing Satan:

> Th' infernal Serpent; hee it was, whose guile
> Stirr'd up with Envy and Revenge, deceiv'd
> The Mother of Mankind; what time his Pride
> Had cast him out from Heav'n, with all his Host
> Of Rebel Angels, by whose aid aspiring
> To set himself in Glory above his Peers,
> He trusted to have equall'd the most High,
> If he oppos'd; and with ambitious aim
> Against the Throne and Monarchy of God
> Rais'd impious War in Heav'n and Battle proud
> With vain attempt. Him the Almighty Power
> Hurl'd headlong flaming from th' Ethereal Sky
> With hideous ruin and combustion down
> To bottomless perdition, there to dwell
> In Adamantine Chains and penal Fire,
> Who durst defy th' Omnipotent to Arms.
>
> (I; 34–49)

Renaissance poetry exhibits an urgency and idealism that faded by the end of the seventeenth century as writers lost the sense that God, nature, and humanity were united in a common purpose. In contrast, the next literary period, the Augustan age, tended to turn away from divine themes to focus squarely and specifically on human society. What the writers of this period saw in their fellow human beings was not always pretty! Read on to learn more.

The Least You Need to Know

- Renaissance poets idealized literary ambition as fame, understood as the fruit of the poet's selfless love.

- Conventions of Petrarchan lyric enabled poets to write about courtly ambitions and disappointments in a politically acceptable fashion.

- Metaphysical poetry wrestles with moral and religious issues and exhibits the strain of emotional and intellectual struggle.

- Cavalier verse tends to be smooth and elegant, and concerned with life's pleasures rather than moral concerns.

- *Paradise Lost* presents the biblical theme of the fall as an epic modeled on the classical style.

Chapter 16

The Bard

In This Chapter

- Shakespeare, his achievement, and his reputation
- Drama on the Elizabethan stage
- The Tudor Myth and the history plays
- *As You Like It:* nature mirroring culture
- Hamlet: a little too late and way too early

William Shakespeare (1564–1616) is, by many accounts, the greatest poet who ever lived. He was tremendously resourceful with words, and as a Renaissance playwright, he was well situated to use those words to great poetic and dramatic effect. He produced a large and rich body of work that has elicited about as much criticism as that of all other English writers combined, if you count the many critical studies written in India, Japan, and elsewhere.

Shakespeare's reputation rests on his literary, cultural, and national importance. Studying Shakespeare means studying great writing, as well as studying the remarkable cultural context in which he wrote. It also involves coming to terms with a national icon of enormous stature. After all, great writing is an important facet of English culture and a great source of national pride. All these things come together in Shakespeare more strongly than in any other figure.

Yet despite his importance and—to many scholars—his familiarity, assessing Shakespeare's work is an ongoing critical challenge. His work is of such scope, depth, subtlety, and complexity that it's continued to reward study for hundreds of years.

William Who?

We know fairly little about Shakespeare's life. He was the son of a textile dealer, was married, and had children. Otherwise, it seems that he was almost wholly taken up with the theater.

Strokes of Genius

Shakespeare belonged to several theater companies during the course of his career—not only writing plays, but acting as well—and eventually obtained part ownership of at least one of the companies he worked with. Shakespeare worked closely and at length with some of the best actors of his time. He also had a chance to see, immediately and firsthand, what sort of things pleased his socioeconomically diverse audience.

Kudos and Caveats

Most Shakespeare scholars see no reason to doubt that Shakespeare actually wrote the plays attributed to him. Claims that someone else wrote them—Francis Bacon or Edward de Vere, Earl of Oxford—are not well substantiated and smack of sensationalism. Then again, perhaps the Loch Ness monster wrote them!

Like other poets and dramatists of his day, Shakespeare drew heavily from source material when constructing his works. He borrowed ideas and subject matter from everywhere—ancient and recent history; biography; romance; poetry and drama; travel accounts; essays; treatises on such things as witchcraft, rhetoric, and the military; and the Bible and other religious writings.

He also drew on a wide variety of literary conventions in his plays—romance, epic, classical tragedy, Roman comedy, Italian *commedia dell'arte*, masque, mystery and miracle plays, picaresque narrative, pastoral, and Petrarchan poetry. Yet Shakespeare was apparently less formally educated than some of his playwright contemporaries, such as Christopher Marlowe and Ben Johnson, and his work often appears less concerned with formal considerations. Thus, he has traditionally been seen as a more "wild," "free," and "natural" poet than any of his contemporaries.

Although his work reflects the ideals and prejudices of his day, Shakespeare appears concerned with entertainment value primarily and moral value secondarily. Moral issues pervade his writings, and on the whole, his work upholds the moral perspective of the ruling classes of his time. But many of his readers have found Shakespeare unusually disinterested and able to sympathize universally with the human condition in all of its variety.

Shakespeare wrote at a special time, when ideas, language, and society were changing, subject to a rich diversity of influences, and holding promise of important discoveries. Shakespeare clearly sensed this and was interested in bringing ideas, images, and issues together in new ways. Like other writers of his time, he was a humanist, someone who believed that human creation resonated with divine creation.

His was also a time many writers and readers of literature have looked back to with nostalgic admiration. A country as rich and powerful as England has been since the Renaissance likes to have cultural icons that demonstrate how great it is. Shakespeare works very well in that regard.

> **Grains of Trivium**
>
> Writing in 1818, literary critic William Hazlitt said of Shakespeare that his mind "had no one peculiar bias, or exclusive excellence more than another. He was just like any other man, but that he was like all other men. He was the least of an egoist that it was possible to be. He was nothing in himself; but he was all that others were, or that they could become."

> **Kudos and Caveats**
>
> Annoyed with what he considered his contemporaries' excessive admiration for Shakespeare, British playwright George Bernard Shaw (1856–1950) coined the term *bardolotry* to make fun of Shakespeare worship.

That's Show Biz

The English Renaissance theater provided a dynamic venue for the multifaceted dramatic literature of the period. Despite city officials' puritanical restrictions that limited where and by whom plays could be performed, and despite periodic outbreaks of the plague, which forced theaters to close for a time, Renaissance Londoners had a voracious appetite for plays. It's possible that thousands of plays were performed in public during Shakespeare's 25-year career (1589–1613), although many plays presented during this time were never printed and did not survive. Shakespeare wrote 38 plays that have survived in print.

Before the rise of Elizabethan theater, drama in England was closely tied to religious ritual. Much of it was performed in various towns by the various guilds during feast days. (See Chapter 9 for more on the history of English drama.) In time, as the

Protestant Reformation took hold in England, religious drama died out. Plays might be performed by traveling troupes mixed in with juggling, tumbling, and other forms of popular entertainment. These traveling performers often gravitated to London, which was fast becoming one of the largest cities in the world.

Unless they were sponsored by a member of the nobility, traveling performers were considered vagabonds in the eyes of the law and were subject to arrest, fines, and imprisonment. In order to perform legally, a dramatic company needed a noble patron. As supposed members of the household of their sponsors, theater companies were able to present plays in public and charge admission. They also gave performances at court and occasionally at private houses.

> **Grains of Trivium**
>
> It's possible that the Elizabethan stage helped take up political slack and fill a religious void left in the wake of Catholicism, which was brutally purged and proscribed by the Protestant King Henry VIII and his Protestant daughter, Elizabeth I. In any case, this was a time of less religious ritual and more theatricality than previously.

Shakespeare's Playbook

The body of Shakespeare's work is known affectionately as "the *corpus*" (*corpus* means "body"). His plays were company property, and it was generally not the policy for theater companies to publish plays they might still perform. According to the thinking at the time, people were less likely to pay to see them performed if they could read them.

Paper Trail

Some of Shakespeare's plays were published in pirated editions during his lifetime. Pirated editions were apparently reconstructed from memory by actors who had been involved with a performance. These works tended to be faulty, full of omissions, substitutions, and mistakes. Such an edition, published singly in its own volume, is known as a *bad quarto*.

It wasn't until 1623, seven years after Shakespeare's death, that members of his theater company collected *fair copies* of his plays and published them in a single volume, known to scholars as the *First Folio*. This volume remains the best original source of most of Shakespeare's work, although some additional poems and plays have since come to light that were not included in it.

def•i•ni•tion

A **bad quarto** is a published, pirated play reconstructed from memory by someone who acted in it. *Quarto* refers to how a big sheet of paper was folded to yield four pages per sheet in a book (*quarto* = "four"). **Fair copies** were manuscripts of plays professionally prepared by a scribe for a theater company or a publisher. Contrast *foul papers*, the messy manuscripts drafted by a playwright. The **First Folio** is the 1623 collection of Shakespeare's plays published after his death by members of Shakespeare's acting company. *Folio* means "fold." Just as a quarto is made of big sheets folded into four, a folio is made of big sheets folded in two.

The First Folio divides Shakespeare's plays into four genres:

- Comedies
- Histories
- Tragedies
- Romances

A number of plays, however, could fit equally well in more than one category. (Shakespeare was not a stickler for formal rules of drama.)

Playing with the Past

The so-called history plays include 10 plays concerned with English history focusing on the lives of kings. Shakespeare wrote plays dealing with Roman history as well, but these are traditionally grouped with the tragedies. Two of the history plays are called tragedies—*The Tragedy of Richard II* and *The Tragedy of Richard III*—but they are grouped with the history plays.

Shakespeare's histories are among the first plays we know of written in English to deal with recent historical events. Although such plays may have been written by other playwrights and subsequently lost, Shakespeare is often credited with inventing this sort of play. In fact, the first four plays we know Shakespeare wrote were history plays. They form a group, sometimes called the *minor tetralogy* (in contrast to the *major tetralogy*, written later), that treats English history at an earlier stage. Both of Shakespeare's tetralogies deal with what has come to be called the "Tudor Myth."

def•i•ni•tion

A **tetralogy** is a group of four works.

The Tudor Myth

The Tudors were the ruling dynasty in England from 1485 to 1503, starting with the reign of Henry VII and ending with the death of Elizabeth I. Henry Tudor became King Henry VII after defeating Richard III in the Battle of Bosworth Field. Henry VII, related by marriage to the House of Lancaster, married a daughter of the Yorkist King Edward IV and so united the two houses. Got that?

According to the Tudor Myth, the Tudor dynasty brought an end to the Wars of the Roses between the House of York and the House of Lancaster over succession to the throne. Furthermore, says the myth, the Wars of the Roses were divine retribution for Henry IV's having murdered and succeeded Richard II in 1398. In usurping the throne of a lawful king, Henry IV doomed England to a long series of civil wars. Finally, Henry VII came along as a divinely sanctioned king and inaugurated the "Tudor peace."

Grains of Trivium

A special performance of the history play *Richard II*, depicting the deposition of an incompetent king, was commissioned at the Globe Theater on February 7, 1601, by associates of Robert Devereaux, the Earl of Essex. The day after the performance, the earl led a failed rebellion against Queen Elizabeth. Elizabeth suspected that the staging of *Richard II* might have been intended to muster popular support for her overthrow. She ordered an investigation, but no charges were brought against Shakespeare or the acting company. Instead, the company was invited to court to perform before the queen—on the day before Essex was executed for treason!

The Tudor Myth was widely accepted in Shakespeare's day, thanks to a general willingness to agree with the ruling dynasty's point of view and, more specifically, thanks to a number of historical accounts commissioned by Henry VII to serve as propaganda that would legitimize his claim to divine right kingship. Shakespeare drew on these accounts as source material for his two tetralogies and may well have believed them. In any case, Shakespeare's history plays enjoyed great success in his time, and many of them are highly regarded to this day.

Shakespeare began writing his history plays in the wake of patriotic fervor in England following the defeat of the Spanish Armada in 1588. This surprising naval victory shifted the balance of power at sea decisively in England's favor. It may well have encouraged belief in the Tudor Myth as well.

Bad Rap

Chronologically, the final episode of the Tudor Myth is presented in *Richard III*. This play tells of the defeat of the evil King Richard III by the noble Henry Tudor. According to the Tudor Myth—and Shakespeare—Richard III is a selfish, ugly, wily, scheming, duplicitous, demented, murderous tyrant. He is disfigured from birth with a hump back and crooked legs, and, partly on account of his ugliness, he is spiteful and envious of everyone. As a result, he takes twisted pleasure in making people suffer, especially when he does so through schemes that benefit him politically.

The body of King Henry VI, whom Richard murdered, appears on the stage in scene two of the first act. There Henry's daughter-in-law, Lady Anne, bemoans his death and curses his murderer. In the process, she curses the murderer's future wife and child, little suspecting that she herself will end up marrying the murderer, Richard.

She addresses the corpse ("thee"), but the speech is, in effect, a *soliloquy*—a speech directed toward the audience rather than toward another character in the play that reveals the thoughts of the person making the speech. She refers to "my young lord," her husband, whom Richard has also murdered:

Kudos and Caveats

Richard III is the best play of the minor tetralogy. (The others, Shakespeare's earliest plays, are not considered brilliant.) On the whole, the second tetralogy is much better: *Richard II*, *Henry IV* parts 1 and 2, and *Henry V*.

def•i•ni•tion

A **soliloquy** is a speech that conveys the private thoughts of the character who delivers it.

> More direful hap betide that hated wretch
> That makes us wretched by the death of thee
> Than I can wish to wolves—to spiders, toads,
> Or any creeping venom'd thing that lives!
> If ever he have child, abortive be it,
> Prodigious, and untimely brought to light,
> Whose ugly and unnatural aspect
> May fright the hopeful mother at the view,
> And that be heir to his unhappiness!
> If ever he have wife, let her be made
> More miserable by the life of him
> Than I am made by my young lord and thee.

(1,2; 17–28)

Anne wishes more bad luck on Richard than she could wish on spiders and toads—creatures considered venomous and symbolic of Richard's envious nature. She goes on to wish that Richard's child might be stillborn or so unnaturally deformed so as to frighten its mother. Then she hopes Richard might make his future wife more miserable than she has been made by the deaths of her husband and father-in-law.

It's a doleful speech that becomes all the more horrible when you realize she's unwittingly cursing herself. As the play unfolds, Richard takes impish satisfaction in manipulating her into marrying him. I suppose next to Richard III, Henry VIII doesn't seem quite so bad!

Signs of the Times

Shakespeare wrote at a time when English society tended to see itself in idealistic terms well suited to poetic representation. The hierarchical social order was understood as a natural and harmonious system of relationships based on bloodlines and cemented with wholesome and natural feelings of love and duty. Low-born servants had a duty to obey their nobly born masters and were expected to do so out of love and respect rather than for financial gain or personal advantage. Similarly, wives and children were expected to show love and duty to their husbands and fathers, just as subjects owed love and duty to the king or, as it happened, to Queen Elizabeth.

Status Symbolism

Social mobility—the potential for the low-born to rise above their inherited station and for the high-born to fall in status—was seen as a threat to the "natural" social order involving a failure or corruption of the "natural" feelings of love and duty that held the social order in place. Aspects of both the ideal order and threats to it could be represented through an abundance of poetic images uniting natural and cultural spheres.

For example, horticultural imagery was often used to describe social relations. In these lines from Shakespeare's comedy *As You Like It*, the hero, Orlando, sympathizes with Adam, the old servant of Orlando's evil brother Oliver. Adam has been cast off after years of faithful service:

> **Grains of Trivium**
>
> In a book titled *Patriarcha, or the Natural Power of Kings* (1680), Sir Robert Filmer claims that kings are (or should be) direct descendents of eldest sons stretching all the way back to Adam, the first man, on whom God conferred the right to rule. Thus, kings rule by divine right.

O good old man, how well in thee appears
The constant service of the antique world,
When service sweat for duty, not for meed!
Thou art not for the fashion of these times,
Where none will sweat but for promotion,
And having that do choke their service up
Even with the having. It is not so with thee.
But, poor old man, thou prun'st a rotten tree,
That cannot so much as a blossom yield
In lieu of all thy pains and husbandry.

(2,3; 56–65)

Orlando praises Adam for serving his brother not for gain ("meed") or for social advancement ("promotion"), but out of duty. His master Oliver, in contrast, is a rotten tree, because he does not respond to Adam's dutiful service with noble beneficence, represented as a "blossom" on a fruit tree.

Back to Nature

As You Like It focuses on breakdowns in the social order caused by the "unnatural" feelings of two contrasting but similarly vicious characters, Oliver and Duke Frederick. Oliver doesn't show appropriate care for his younger brother, Orlando, or for his servant, Adam. Duke Frederick has usurped the dukedom from his older brother, the rightful Duke Senior, who must live in exile in the Forest of Arden.

Both these characters are spurred on to evil treatment of others by "envy." They are surrounded by worthy, noble, virtuous, and dutiful characters at whom they lash out because they feel themselves inferior to and in competition with them. The virtuous characters—including Duke Senior and his followers, Orlando, Adam, and Duke Senior's daughter Rosalind (disguised as a man)—all end up retreating into the forest.

Grains of Trivium

A number of Shakespeare's comedies, including *A Midsummer Night's Dream* and *A Winter's Tale*, show characters retreating into woods and fields from troubled social situations. In a natural, bucolic setting, the plays' problems work themselves out before the characters return to their civilized lives. Literature critic Northrop Frye has identified the settings of these plays as Shakespeare's "green world," a marvelous place where rejuvenation and metamorphoses take place.

Doings in the forest provide Shakespeare with the opportunity to demonstrate his poetic talents in many ways. He plays with conventions of pastoral poetry in contrasting the innocence of an idealized bucolic existence with the guile and duplicity often associated with life at court. He plays with conventions of the love lyric in having Orlando write love poems to Rosalind and hang them on trees in the forest. And he draws parallels between the hardships of nature and human unkindness.

Here's a speech Duke Senior makes on life in the forest:

> Now, my co-mates and brothers in exile,
> Hath not old custom made this life more sweet
> Than that of painted pomp? Are not these woods
> More free from peril than the envious courts?
> Here feel we not the penalty of Adam,
> The season's difference, as the icy fang
> And churlish chiding of the winter's wind,
> Which when it bites and blows upon my body
> Even till I shrink with cold, I smile and say,
> "This is no flattery: these are counselors
> That feelingly persuade me what I am."
> Sweet are the uses of adversity
> Which like the toad, ugly and venomous,
> Wears yet a precious jewel on his head;
> And this our life, exempt from public haunt,
> Finds tongues in trees, books in the running brooks,
> Sermons in stones, and good in everything.
>
> (2,1; 1–17)

The duke compares and contrasts bad weather and human unkindness. The cold blast of the winter wind, although unpleasant, compares favorably to the flattery of "envious" courtiers because, unlike the courtiers, the wind doesn't lie, but lets him know what he is—a mortal human being. The "venomous toad," a conventional symbol of envy, is presented as an image of "adversity"—the hardship of life in the forest. The jewel on the toad's head apparently stands for the philosophical benefit to be derived from adversity. Thus, the duke derives wisdom from things in nature, including "trees," "brooks," and "stones."

While the good characters are experiencing the natural world as an altered version of society, the envious Duke Frederick and Oliver make plans to kill the gentlemanly Orlando. Oliver sets out into the forest to look for his brother but is attacked by a lion. Orlando arrives just in time to rescue Oliver, who changes his attitude and resolves his differences with Orlando.

Soon afterward, Rosalind's true identity is revealed. She and Orlando get married in the forest together with two other couples. At that moment, word arrives that Duke Frederick has repented his sins and plans to go off to live in a monastery, leaving the dukedom to his older brother, the rightful duke.

Depth of Character

As a playwright, Shakespeare has been especially acclaimed for his copious and expressive use of language and for his ability to portray a great variety of characters with convincing depth and complexity. Although his characters generally speak more like inspired poets than ordinary people, they seem to have personalities and lives of their own. Sometimes referred to as "inwardness" or "interiority," this subtle quality of many Shakespearean characters is virtually absent from literature written before Shakespeare's time.

Blue-Blooded and Blue

Among the most subtle, deep, and complex of Shakespeare's characters is Prince Hamlet, the "melancholy Dane." Hamlet is intriguingly dissatisfied with life. A sensitive, intelligent, and accomplished young nobleman, he pretends to be mentally deranged to disguise his animosity toward his uncle, King Claudius, whom he plans to kill to avenge his murdered father.

But Hamlet is not simply pretending to be crazy. He's a little unbalanced at the outset! The inner mental workings of this slightly disturbed prince, who pretends to be even more disturbed than he really is, has fascinated not only audiences and critics ever since, but philosophers as well. Anyone who has ever felt vaguely dissatisfied and falls to brooding has something in common with Shakespeare's prince.

While Hamlet's character is easy to relate to, even centuries after Shakespeare created him, Hamlet's problems can be difficult to understand. They cause him to drag his feet and fail

> **Canon Fodder**
>
> Sensitive, intelligent, and somewhat disaffected people—guys who think too much—find it easy to identify with Hamlet. The poet Samuel Taylor Coleridge (1772–1834) confessed, "I have a smack of Hamlet myself."

to act when he has the opportunity to take his revenge. Hamlet's delay proves fatal, and he is killed in the end (along with most of the characters in the play) after King Claudius senses that Hamlet poses a threat and lays a plot to kill him.

A Chip Off the Old Chopping Block?

For centuries, critics have labored to come to terms with Hamlet's inner problem, and theories and speculations abound to explain his hesitation to avenge his father. Apparently, Hamlet is a character profoundly ahead of his time, exhibiting existential angst like a nineteenth- or twentieth-century philosopher. He's slow to take revenge because he's so early to take to existentialism.

Does Hamlet think like a nineteenth-century philosopher? Yes, but not before the nineteenth century. During Shakespeare's day, Hamlet's problem reflected an issue of Shakespeare's time: a vicious cycle of succession to the throne by regicide (murder of a king). Perhaps Hamlet was reluctant to kill King Claudius (who became king by killing another king, Hamlet's father, who, in turn, won half his kingdom by killing another king, Old Fortinbras) because he (Hamlet) dimly realized that doing so would make him a king fated to be killed by the subsequent king.

> ### Grains of Trivium
>
> Shakespeare wrote *Hamlet* near the end of Queen Elizabeth's reign. Eleven years before Shakespeare penned the play, Elizabeth consolidated her power by having her sister, Mary Queen of Scots, put to death. Sounds like a harsh way to treat family, but Elizabeth had a good role model: their father, Henry VIII, had several of his wives executed. So two sixteenth-century Tudor monarchs resorted to trimming the family tree to keep their own branches in the sun. It's not exactly the same as succession by regicide, but it's pretty close.

Hamlet suggests that if Hamlet *had* killed Claudius sooner, he would have taken the throne, married Ophelia, and been murdered by Ophelia's brother Laertes, who then would have become king. Hamlet wasn't pleased with the prospect, so he procrastinated. And yes, in addition, he thinks too much.

The Least You Need to Know

◆ Shakespeare was an actor and shareholder in the theater, as well as a playwright.

◆ Shakespeare's history plays uphold the "Tudor Myth": that Henry Tudor (Henry VII) restored divine-right kingship (and recovered divine approval for the English monarchy) by defeating the supposedly evil Richard III and uniting the houses of Lancaster and York.

◆ Much of Shakespeare's imagery blends natural and cultural spheres and suggests that the social order has a "natural" basis.

◆ Hamlet pretends to be crazy, but he is actually a little unbalanced to begin with.

Chapter 17

August Personages

In This Chapter

- ◆ An overview of the Restoration and the eighteenth century
- ◆ Drama makes a comeback
- ◆ No one is safe from Augustan satire
- ◆ The beginnings of the British novel

Eighteenth-century English literature tended toward refinement and elegance on one hand and, paradoxically, toward carping and ridicule on the other. The refined elegance is evident in the learned and stately neoclassical verse of the "Augustan" poets. The carping and ridicule was evident everywhere—in verse, prose, and drama.

This was the golden age of English satire, when everyone was a critic and critics were impossible to please. Everywhere they looked, writers saw signs of pride, selfishness, lust, guile, hypocrisy, idiocy, and insanity. They considered it their duty to alert, instruct, and reform society, whether they themselves were middle-class Puritan moralists or aristocratic libertines (libertines believed in the pursuit of personal pleasure).

Amid the critical fray, a new literary form emerged that would help make all the squabbling moot by presenting social issues within a whole new fictional framework. It's called the novel, and it changed the way people thought and felt about literature.

King and Stage Restored

In 1660, after a bloody civil war and a period during which England was ruled by a "lord protector" rather than a king, the British monarchy was restored to the throne. And almost immediately, the British theater, which had been banned since 1642, was restored as well. In general, Restoration theatergoers were aristocratic, anti-Puritanical, and cynical.

Good Manners

London playhouses of the day staged revivals of Elizabethan plays as well as newly written heroic plays, tragedies, and comedies. Comedies were by far the most popular. The Restoration *comedy of manners* emerged as a distinctive and successful mode of drama.

def•i•ni•tion

The **comedy of manners** is a dramatic form concerned with the social conventions of polite society. It may make fun simultaneously of those who abide by these conventions and those who don't.

Restoration comedy was staged with music and lavish costumes in indoor theaters equipped with sliding panels of painted scenery. Witty and elegant, it focused predominantly on the social preoccupations of its aristocratic audience: moral hypocrisy on one hand and sexual freedom on the other.

Good Boys Behaving Badly

In the wake of the Puritan Revolution, English nobility were not inclined to be especially respectful of religious dogma or puritanical morality. Instead, they exhibited a growing sense that moral claims were generally self-serving and hypocritical. Restoration comedy helped expose and ridicule moral hypocrisy.

Grains of Trivium

Women were barred from acting on the Renaissance stage, and female roles were commonly played by boys. In contrast, female actresses served a vital function in contributing to the sexual energy and dynamics of Restoration theater. It was not uncommon for actresses to become mistresses of wealthy theatergoers.

In the comedy of manners, an excess of moral scruples showed an inability to think and act for oneself. Similarly, excessive sexual prudishness on the part of women suggested they were either unattractive and sought to make a "virtue of necessity," or else were angling for other, richer lovers. Much Restoration comedy explores, and even celebrates, sexual libertinism—the pursuit of sexual pleasure for its own sake.

One clear expression of libertine values is the figure of the Restoration rake-hero. A "rake," or "rakehell," is an unprincipled, pleasure-seeking man who typically spends his time and money chasing women, gambling, and drinking. In the moralistic thinking of Puritanical sorts, rakishness leads to all sorts of social and spiritual ills. In Restoration comedy, however, the rake is elevated and idealized. He understands human nature and is witty and energetic enough to expose hypocrisy and succeed in his sexual exploits.

Potent Pretence

One particularly outstanding rake-hero is Horner, a leading character in William Wycherley's *The Country Wife.* Horner spreads false rumors about himself that he is impotent in order to fool jealous husbands into letting him become intimate with their wives. The trick also lets him ferret out married women interested in extramarital sex—namely, those who are disgusted and disappointed by impotency!

Grains of Trivium

Characters in Restoration comedy tend to be types rather than individuals. Often their names indicate what sort of type they represent. Horner is someone who gives "horns" to other men, i.e., cuckolds them. Other types in Wycherly's play are the jealous husband Pinchwife, the would-be wit Sparkish, and the hypocritical self-styled "virtuous gang" of ladies, including Lady Fidget and Mrs. Squeamish.

Horner's ruse works perfectly. He succeeds in duping jealous husbands and in seducing and exposing (at least, to themselves) the hypocrisy of their wives. Horner's escapades serve as a foil for a more idealized, restrained, and far less interesting romance between Horner's friend, Harcourt, and the virtuous beauty Alithia.

Satire: The Best Medicine

Restoration drama faded after a few sparkling decades, as theatergoers grew increasingly middle class. A central element of the comedy of manners persisted, however, in the prose and poetry of the eighteenth century, which came to be a hallmark of the age. This was satire.

High Standards, Low Expectations

Satire is a literary mode that stems from ancient Greece and Rome and crops up sporadically throughout much of the history of English lit. It came into its own during the eighteenth century, however, when all the age's best writers wrote extended satirical works. Satire exposes and denounces vice and folly, holding them up to derision.

Satire became an appealing literary attitude during the time because traditional religious and social ideals were proving difficult to live up to, especially insofar as they called for selflessness and equated desires and passions with folly and derangement. After all, it's hard to be selfless if you have a self, and it's hard not to desire anything—no matter how much you may want to!

> **Canon Fodder**
>
> In an allegorical, poetic satire called *The Fable of the Bees: or, Private Vices, Publick Benefits* (1714), Gerard Mandeville argued that personal vices had a positive impact on society by encouraging trade and industry. This work was officially declared a public nuisance by a civil jury.

The rationalist philosophers—Descartes and his followers—made a clear, theoretical separation between reason and desire. Reason was pure, objective, and independent of motive or point of view. Desire was subjective and rooted in physical processes, and took multifarious, unreliable forms. In theory, this distinction made perfect sense and convincingly explained a great deal about human behavior. In practice, however, it proved impossible to act rationally in ways that satisfied everyone's judgment.

Reason in action was elusive, especially amid widespread doubts about religious and aristocratic values. In contrast, self-serving, ambitious, egotistical, and other desirous behavior was evident practically everywhere. Satire of the time exposed and ridiculed this behavior, often without suggesting clear alternatives.

Swift Kicks

Among the most accomplished of eighteenth-century satirists was Jonathan Swift (1667–1745). He was skilled at ridiculing vice and folly from all sides at once while sitting squarely in the middle of it. Arguably somewhat misanthropic, Swift's works tend to take a dim view of humanity and human pretensions.

In his ingenious, freewheeling fable *Tale of the Tub*, Swift sets out to satirize "the numerous and gross corruptions in Religion and Learning." He makes fun of doctrinal divisions between Catholicism, Lutheranism, and Calvinism by representing the three branches of Christianity as brothers—Peter (St. Peter was considered the first pope), Martin (Martin Luther), and Jack (John Calvin and, more generally, Puritan separatists). Each brother inherits a coat (representing religious doctrine) from their father (God).

In his will, their father tells the brothers not to make alterations in their coats, but, wanting to keep abreast of changing fashions, the brothers have their coats embellished with all manner of new "points," "fringes," and "embroideries." In this way, Swift ridicules doctrinal innovations introduced by the Church since the beginnings of Christianity.

Peter gradually becomes rich and powerful—so much so that he eventually goes crazy as a result: "what with pride, projects, and knavery, poor Peter was grown distracted." His brothers become exasperated with him and strike out on their own. Wishing to distinguish themselves from Peter as much as possible, they begin to remove the added embellishments from their coats. Jack, in his zeal, goes too far and tears his coat to shreds in the process. With this, Swift suggests that, in trying to undo the abuses of Catholicism, the Puritan separatists have lost sight of the basic unifying significance of the Church.

> ### Canon Fodder
>
> In addition to *Tale of the Tub,* Swift's satires include "A Discourse Concerning the Mechanical Operation of the Spirit" (a satire on empirical philosophy and religious enthusiasm) and "A Modest Proposal" (facetiously proposing to end hunger and poverty by means of cannibalism). His best-known work, *Gulliver's Travels,* is highly satirical as well.

Here's more about Jack:

> He would stand in the turning of a street, and, calling to those who passed by, would cry to one, "Worthy sir, do me the honour of a good slap in the chaps";* (*The fanatics have always had a way of affecting to run into persecution, and count vast merit upon every little hardship they suffer.) to another, "Honest friend, pray favour me with a handsome kick on the arse"; "Madam, shall I entreat a small box on the ear from your ladyship's fair hands?" "Noble captain, lend a reasonably thwack, for the love of God, with that cane of yours over these poor shoulders." And when he had by such earnest solicitations made a shift to procure a basting to swell up his fancy and his sides, he would return home extremely comforted, and full of terrible accounts of what he had undergone for the public good.

In this passage, Swift makes the Puritans' willingness to suffer persecution as testimony to their godliness seem like hilarious lunacy. Not surprisingly, Martin ends up looking the least ridiculous of the three brothers. (Swift strongly supported the Anglican Church.) Even so,

> ### Canon Fodder
>
> Since the Middle Ages, the Church has been represented allegorically as the bride of Christ. Obviously, Swift's allegorical image of three coats is deflating.

the satire strikes at Christianity in general. *Tale of the Tub* makes the history of the Church look like an ongoing series of absurd and petty family squabbles.

Wry Lines

While Swift wrote his most important satirical works in prose, much eighteenth-century satire is in verse. The leading poets of the early eighteenth century were consummate stylists. They were urbane, lucid, and driven to interpret and evaluate social types and social behaviors. In doing so, they turned to classical models for urbanity and polish, especially the Roman writers who lived during the reign of Emperor Augustus (27 B.C.E.–14 C.E.): Horace, Virgil, and Ovid. Roman satirist Juvenal (c. 100 C.E.) was also widely admired. As a result of its debt to these writers, eighteenth-century neoclassical verse is often called "Augustan" poetry.

The English Augustans made unstinting use of heroic couplets, which they considered flexible, dignified, and well suited for serving up poetic and critical insights in a controlled yet musical manner. As you might remember from Chapter 7, heroic couplets are rhymed pairs of iambic pentameter verse. They are called "heroic" because they were commonly used since the Renaissance in heroic tragedy. (If you'd like to read about rhyme and iambic pentameter, turn back to Chapter 8.)

Following are some choice heroic couplets from the poem "The New Dunciad" (1742) by Alexander Pope. The poem ridicules all those who pretend to possess knowledge, wit, or virtue but succeed only in being dull. Pope represents dull people mockingly as devotees of the goddess Dullness. These lines refer to the practice of sending young English gentlemen, accompanied by a tutor, on tours to Europe to gain experience and sophistication. Here the goddess leads a young man on such a tour:

> Led by my hand, he saunter'd Europe round,
> And gather'd ev'ry vice on Christian ground;
> Saw ev'ry court, heard ev'ry king declare
> His royal sense of Op'ra's or the fair;
> The Stews and Palace equally explor'd,
> Intrigu'd with glory, and with spirit whor'd ...
>
> (311–316)

Instead of acquiring knowledge and culture, the young man learns vices. He hears a lot of small talk, goes to brothels ("Stews"), and distinguishes himself by getting involved in underhanded schemes ("intrigues") and by his drunken, enthusiastic ("with spirit") patronizing of prostitutes. A few lines later, he fails to learn any foreign languages while forgetting how to speak English properly!

The poem concludes with cynical, histrionic lines that lament the utter failure of thought and culture to live up to their aims as chaos takes over:

> Thus at her [Dullness's] felt approach, and secret might,
> Art after Art goes out, and all is Night.
> See skulking Truth to her old Cavern fled,
> Mountains of Casuistry heap'd o'er her head!
> Philosophy, that lean'd on Heav'n before,
> Shrinks to her second cause, and is no more.
> Physic of Metaphysic begs defense,
> And Metaphysic calls for aid on Sense!
> See Mystery to Mathematics fly!
> In vain! they gaze, turn giddy, rave, and die.
> Religion blushing veils her sacred fires,
> And unawares Morality expires.
> Nor public Flame, nor Private, dares to shine;
> Nor human Spark is left, nor Glimpse divine!
> Lo! thy dread Empire, CHAOS! is restor'd;
> Light dies before thy uncreating word:
> Thy hand, great Anarch! lets the curtain fall;
> And Universal Darkness buries All.

Novel Ideas

As poets of the period hearkened to classical antecedents, prose fiction became increasingly popular among a growing middle class. Meanwhile, it underwent many gradual but profound changes. In general, narratives became more concerned with incidents drawn from daily life and ordinary experience, and less concerned with the acts of idealized people of long ago and far away. They focused less on marvels and supernatural doings, and more on events that might actually happen. Fictional narratives with these characteristics came to be recognized as novels.

True to Life—Sometimes

Unlike satire, the novel was generally a serious form. Early novels often had prefaces claiming they were morally instructive. They might have happy or unhappy endings, depending on whether the main character made appropriate or inappropriate moral choices along the way. Often they were larded with *sentiment*, expressions of emotion that aim to suggest the inherent goodness of individual characters or humanity in general.

Compared to earlier works of fiction, the early novel's generally serious tone was less a result of the particular views of morality it reflected than it was of its realistic subject matter—its *verisimilitude*. In fact, standards of virtue had become confused and conflicted. It had become increasingly difficult to portray virtue in ways that everyone could approve of and appreciate.

def•i•ni•tion

Sentiment is the expression of any emotion that means to imply the goodness of a character or of humankind. **Verisimilitude** is the semblance of truth, a quality that helps distinguish the early novel from fable and romance.

Meanwhile, standards of truth were becoming increasingly aligned with scientific—as opposed to moralistic—thinking. With its verisimilitude, the novel reflected emerging standards of empirical possibility. You might say readers of the early novel came in looking for direction on how they should behave but came away with perspective on what they could believe.

While drawing on a long, rich tradition of narrative fiction that included romance and epic, the eighteenth-century novel incorporated more recent elements borrowed from nonfictional texts, including biography, travel accounts, history, news, personal correspondence, and diaries. Borrowing ideas from these kinds of texts, novelists constructed fictions that tended to seem as though they might be true even though they were made up.

Just Desserts

Of the many groundbreaking early novels of the late seventeenth and early eighteenth centuries, Samuel Richardson's (1689–1761) *Pamela; or Virtue Rewarded* (1740) is perhaps most often pointed to as the first fully realized modern English novel. Richardson was a printer, so he had a privileged view of the reading public of his day. Early in his writing career, he wrote "familiar letters" intended to be used as models for middle-class people wanting to write social correspondence of various kinds.

def•i•ni•tion

Epistles are letters, usually formal. An **epistolary novel** is a novel made up of correspondence between characters.

From his experience as a letter-writer, Richardson developed the idea for a work of fiction constructed out of letters, with correspondence, or *epistles*, between characters put together into a story. This form of narrative is known as the *epistolary novel*.

Pamela consists mostly of the letters written by a humble but virtuous servant girl to her parents, together with entries from her journal. She is pursued (today we might say *harassed*) by her employer (her "master"), known as Mr. B., whose intentions are not honorable—that is to say, he wants to have sex with her but has no intention of marrying her (at least, not at first). After all, Pamela is only a servant.

But the virtuous Pamela stoutly refuses to be seduced, despite the threats and lies of Mr. B. Eventually, however, Mr. B. comes to admire and respect Pamela's virtue and asks her to marry him. She accepts (after all, he's rich) and is thereby "rewarded" for her virtue.

Pamela; or Virtue Rewarded was a big hit. Eighteenth-century readers appreciated the work's detail, intimacy, and sentiment. In contrast, today's readers might be inclined to wonder why anyone would want to work for, much less marry, a creep like Mr. B. Virtue *rewarded?*

Actually, *Pamela* was harshly criticized soon after it was published. Richardson's contemporary, fellow novelist, and sometime playwright Henry Fielding (1701–1754) regarded Pamela not as virtuous, but as calculating and hypocritical in parlaying her chastity into a rich marriage above her station. He wrote a satirical send-up called *Shamela* (1741) that makes fun of the moral pretensions of Richardson's novel. *Virtue* rewarded?

The Least You Need to Know

- Restoration drama's comedy of manners expressed the libertine attitude of its aristocratic audience.

- Augustan lit hearkens back to the Augustan period of the Roman Empire in cultivating a polished, urbane style.

- The eighteenth century was a golden age of English satire.

- Poets refined the art of heroic couplets—rhymed pairs of iambic pentameter verse, used copiously in eighteenth-century verse.

- In the eighteenth century, the novel emerged as a narrative form concerned with events taken from ordinary life that might actually happen.

Part 4

These Days

Part 4 discusses representative works and features of English literature from the Romantic period to the present and relates them to such social developments as the industrial revolution and the rise of the middle class. During this long sweep of history, literature emerges as a largely independent sphere of activity, increasingly set apart from religion and politics as such, although scarcely empty of political and spiritual concerns.

In general, however, the concern with ideals exhibited in the literature of previous periods gives way to an interest in experience. As social life becomes increasingly complex, English lit responds through a series of formal innovations and experiments. Writers seek new ways to come to terms with changing reality and with the gap between reality and writing.

"I'd give anything for something postmodern."

Romantic Moods

In This Chapter

"The Romantic period" is a phrase used to refer to a time of profound changes in thought and society that took place throughout Europe. Applied to English literature, it dates from the late eighteenth to the mid-nineteenth century. The Romantic period marks a time when art and literature received impetus from a newfound appreciation of the imagination.

In widespread reaction against the constraints on creativity imposed by an excessive concern with "reason," Romantic writers saw value in the creative process for its own sake. They found much to admire in the strange and curious literature of the Middle Ages that had gone unappreciated in the Augustan age. And they looked with fresh curiosity into the workings of their own minds, generating ideas that laid a foundation for modern psychology.

It was a fruitful time for literature in general and for lyric poetry in particular, as poetic insight and Romantic feeling were well suited to one another. Meanwhile, the novel reached early maturity. In general, people had a sense that their world was changing fast. They were right.

Rising Tides

At the start of the Romantic period in Europe, the most drastic and dramatic change was the French Revolution, in which an effete and disengaged French aristocracy was violently overthrown by peasants and replaced by a regime led by Napoleon Bonaparte. Following in the wake of the American Revolution, the French Revolution helped incite democratic and egalitarian fervor among many British and awakened antagonism toward social change among many others.

Growing Pains

In England, the Industrial Revolution brought rapid and often painful economic changes, as wealth shifted from aristocratic landowners to urban merchants and industrialists. Many agrarian laborers lost their livelihoods and became impoverished. Populations grew rapidly in manufacturing centers, where unskilled laborers with few legal rights and protections lived in slums and worked in sweatshops.

> **Grains of Trivium**
>
> Economist Thomas Malthus (1766–1834) put forward the theory (the "Malthusian doctrine") that population increases at an exponential rate, whereas the means of feeding the population increases much more slowly. He concluded that unless the growth of population can be checked, humanity will be faced with famine.

Poets and novelists of the time responded to these changes in various ways, but the trait most often associated with Romanticism is imagination. Many sensed that the changing times brought a need for heightened individuality and creativity, both to take advantage of new opportunities within an increasingly democratic society and to rise above the dehumanizing effects of mechanization and social displacement. Thus, faith in the imagination became a creed of most (but not all) writers of the period, whether they were radical or conservative in their political views.

All, All Alone

Although Romanticism in England emerged gradually out of the prior Augustan age, its defining characteristics contrast markedly with those of eighteenth-century neoclassicism, especially where the imagination and individuality are concerned. Augustan writers placed great value in reason and objectivity. They generally regarded imagination as a symptom of social isolation and a door to madness rather than a means to creative insight.

In contrast, Romantic writers regarded the imagination as a wholesome, healthy human capacity. It could yield the personal benefits of insight and creativity, as well as the social benefits of shared feelings and intuitive sympathy. At the time and since, this Romantic attitude has been seen as liberating. Some would argue, however, that Romantic ideals are merely a positive spin on the increased alienation of the modern individual. As people become less closely and fully connected to others in society, they seek consolation in a romanticized individuality.

Wordsworthy Sentiments

Of course, there was continuity as well as contrast between the English Romantic and Augustan periods. Augustans and Romantics both appreciated the *sublime*—a combined sense of grandeur and mystery—in art as well as in nature. *Sensibility*—a susceptibility to powerful feelings—was also a strain of Augustan literature that contributed to Romantic ideals, especially when it appeared in nature poetry. In fact, both of these qualities were important in the criticism and poetry of one of the key innovators of the Romantic movement, William Wordsworth (1770–1850).

def•i•ni•tion

The **sublime** is a characteristic of art or of nature that inspires a feeling of grandeur and mystery— ancient ruins, a storm-swept landscape, or the fall of Satan in Milton's *Paradise Lost* (see Chapter 15). **Sensibility** is susceptibility to powerful feelings, a literary quality that emerged during the late eighteenth century.

Theory and Practice

Wordsworth helped put English Romanticism on a secure footing with *Lyrical Ballads* (1798), a work he published jointly with fellow poet Samuel Taylor Coleridge (1772–1834). This collection of poems helped solidify a change in attitudes toward literature in departing, both in style and subject matter, from poetry written previously.

Wordsworth described his view of the changes and his sense of what poetry ought to be in the preface to *Lyrical Ballads* (second edition, 1802). He took issue with many poetic conventions that had come to be taken for granted and that, according to Wordsworth, stood in the way of creative spontaneity. Instead of hearkening to outmoded conventions, poets should work with "language really used" by people of the day and should treat themes taken from "common life." By writing poems about "humble and rustic life," Wordsworth hoped to convey the "essential passions of the heart."

Canon Fodder

Not only were Romantics disposed to appreciate poems about "humble and rustic life," but they were also receptive to humble and rustic poets. Scotsman Robert Burns (1759–1796) was greatly admired as a rustic, peasant poet, despite his education. Somewhat less successful (and less educated) was John Clare (1793–1864), who enjoyed brief notoriety for his unpolished, untaught verse.

Wordsworth wanted to link poetry with the natural tendency of human beings to think, feel, and imagine. In fact, he believed that nature exerted a pervasive and healthy influence on forming his own poetic abilities. Many of his poems deal with his experiences in nature, especially as a boy, and suggest that his special appreciation of nature helps make him a special poet.

Formative Years

In the poem "Lines Composed a Few Miles above Tinturn Abbey," Wordsworth describes the experience of returning to a natural setting familiar to him from child-hood. In these lines, he contrasts his appreciation for nature as an adult with his less-reflective sense of nature as a boy:

> ... I have learned
> To look on nature, not as in the hour
> of thoughtless youth; but hearing oftentimes
> The still, sad music of humanity,
> Not harsh or grating, though of ample power
> To chasten and subdue. And I have felt
> A presence that disturbs me with the joy
> of elevated thoughts; a sense sublime
> Of something far more deeply interfused,
> Whose dwelling is the light of setting suns,
> And the round ocean and the living air,
> And the blue sky, and in the mind of man:

A motion and a spirit, that impels
All thinking things, all objects of all thought,
And rolls through all things.

(88–102)

Wordsworth writes of nature here with something like religious reverence. It is a higher power or "spirit" that suffuses existence and both "chastens" and "elevates" the poet's thoughts. It links his thoughtless boyhood experience with his mature sense of his common bond with "humanity."

All for One

Wordsworth's attitude toward nature and his sense of poetry as a natural activity was tremendously influential. Many writers embraced Wordsworth's reverence for nature, and most came to rely on the notion that poetry is, at least to some extent, a natural, organic activity that reflects the individual character of the poet as well as the age in which the poetry is written.

This poetic turn toward nature enabled writers to express opposition to social and artistic conventions without necessarily being thought insane or seditious. Nature, in this view, is not simply opposed to society—although social conventions, including poetic conventions, can stand in the way of a profound appreciation of nature and its influence. Thus, personal experience and individuality are important correctives to social norms.

> **Grains of Trivium**
>
> In addition to poetry and criticism, Wordsworth wrote *A Guide through the District of the Lakes for the Use of Tourists and Residents* (1810), a travel guide to his native Lake District (Cumberland and Westmoreland in Northern England).

In some ways, this view reflects an emerging democratic attitude toward poetry. All poets may have equal potential to tap into their natural creative abilities. At the same time, however, it marks a growing separation of poetry from social and political concerns. Just as the poet is no longer bound by conventions, the reader is no longer expected to be guided by the poet in any specific way. The decadent idea of "art for art's sake" that emerged late in the century had its roots in this attitude.

Byron: Alone with Others

Ironically, while Wordsworth helped redefine the purpose of poets and poetry, the writer of the day who most strongly typified the Romantic poet in the minds of his contemporaries was not a Wordsworthian nature poet, but a satirist whose work, like that of the eighteenth-century satirists, is primarily concerned with social attitudes. This was George Gordon, Lord Byron (1788–1824).

Fitting the Profile

Byron the poet is commonly identified with the heroes of his poems. He was a rakish aristocrat who courted scandal, sought pleasures compulsively, and despised conventional morality. The same can be said of his best-known characters, Childe Harold (from *Childe Harold*, 1808–1817) and Don Juan (from *Don Juan*, 1819–1824). They are restless, proud, dashing, and dissatisfied, despite being overindulged with sex, wine, and worldly travels. They are passionate and volatile but jaded. Brooding yet witty, they seem to celebrate life by mocking it.

> **Canon Fodder**
>
> Of all the major Romantic poets, including Byron, Wordsworth, Coleridge, William Blake, Percy Shelley, and John Keats, Byron's work was the least concerned with the imagination and the most concerned with the social consequences of one's actions.

This type of character is known as the Byronic hero and has been linked with numerous fictional characters since Byron's time, including Heathcliff from Emily Brontë's *Wuthering Heights* (1847) and Jay Gatsby from F. Scott Fitzgerald's *The Great Gatsby* (1925, American). Dark, turbulent, and willful, Byronic heroes avoid seeming petty and selfish on account of their self-destructiveness and their dislike of the world's complacence.

A Hopeless Romantic

While Byron's satires mock the hypocrisy of his time, his heroes also mock themselves for pursuing pleasures that offer them no satisfaction. Their hopelessness shows a sensitivity and humanity that rakes of the eighteenth century generally didn't exhibit. Thus, they are true romantics, despite their familiarity as rake-heroes. (See Chapter 17 on Restoration rake-heroes.)

> **Grains of Trivium**
>
> Byron's wife left him after less than a year of marriage, claiming (with apparent reason) he was having an incestuous affair with his half-sister. He left England for good amid the ensuing scandal.

Here are some lines from *Childe Harold's Pilgrimage* (1812), a poem that recounts the adventures of an aristocratic wastrel traveling restlessly through Europe:

For he through Sin's long labyrinth had run,
Nor made atonement where he did amiss;
Had sighed to many though he loved but one,
And that loved one, alas! could ne'er be his.
Ah! happy she! to 'scape from him whose kiss
Had been pollution unto aught so chaste;
Who soon had left her charms for vulgar bliss,
And spoiled her goodly lands to gild his waste,
Nor calm domestic peace had ever deigned to taste.

(1; 5)

Childe Harold is hopelessly in love with a woman he knows he would only ruin—economically and morally—if he could have her. So it's good for her that he can't. But why can't he? He's too proud!

Plain Jane

Not all great writers of the Romantic age are philosophically, or even temperamentally, romantic. Perhaps the greatest novelist of the period successfully resisted the vogue of impassioned individualism in creating heroines known for their good sense and self-restraint. Meet Jane Austen (1775–1817).

Even Keel

Austen wrote novels about the gentry living in the English countryside. At a time when land enclosures were changing the face of rural England and undermining the livelihoods of the laborers who worked there, Austen's novels reassuringly suggested that social ills are the fleeting results of minor human foibles and misunderstandings, and can be corrected with a little patience and good judgment.

Focusing largely on insular, isolated, village life, Austen depicts the lives of a small group of characters with perceptive detail within a carefully constructed plot focused mainly on courtship and marriage. A good marriage is crucial to the happiness and well-being of Austen's

> **Grains of Trivium**
>
> Jane Austen never married. She had an "understanding" with a man whose parents disapproved of her on financial grounds. She later accepted the proposal of an old friend, only to withdraw her acceptance the next day.

main characters. Whether they marry well or badly depends on their ability to control their own impulses and to understand those of others.

Off Again, on Again

Austen's *Sense and Sensibility* (1811) contrasts the lives and characters of two sisters, Elinore Dashwood (known for her sense) and Marianne (known for her sensibility), whose family is left penniless upon the death of their father. They move to a relative's cottage in the country as their mother nurtures hopes that they will find suitable husbands.

Faced with false hopes, faithless suitors, jealous rivals, shifting fortunes, and major misunderstandings, the sisters must continually weigh their feelings about men, money, and honor. Both end up happily married, although Marianne must adjust her sights and rethink her romantic attitude toward love. Elinore, in contrast, turns out to have had the right approach all along.

Gothic Novels: Scary Stories

Gothic novels—novels about gruesome doings and supernatural horrors, usually set far away and long ago—became increasingly popular during the Romantic period. The form emerged during the eighteenth century but gained popularity and respectability in the nineteenth, as the imagination came to be more highly regarded.

Grave Ideals

Gothic novels are typically set in such places as medieval castles and monasteries. In addition to ghosts; inanimate objects that move; prophecies, omens, and curses that come true; and other supernatural elements, Gothic novels typically focus on the corrupt, demented behavior of aristocrats and Catholic priests—often in fiendish pursuit of one or more helpless young females. Thus, the form serves to denounce the outmoded and decayed ideals of chivalry and Catholicism for middle-class, Protestant readers.

These outmoded ideals, of course, don't simply disappear from society as economic and religious views change, but they come back to "haunt" people in the form of supernatural fears. Gothic novels express these fears. Some Gothic novels provide rational explanations for the apparently supernatural occurrences they portray. Others do not.

Seeing Things

Ann Radcliffe's (1764–1823) *The Mysteries of Udolpho* (1794) is set in a mouldering sixteenth-century Italian castle, home to a sinister chief of a band of freebooters named Montoni. He is visited by Emily St. Aubert, the niece of the woman he married in hopes of inheriting her property. Attempting to get Emily to relinquish her inheritance to him, he imprisons her in his castle.

> **Canon Fodder**
>
> Jane Austen's novel *Northanger Abbey* (1818) concerns the adventures of a young lady whose imagination has been excited by reading Ann Radcliffe's Gothic novel *The Mysteries of Udolpho* and who consequently jumps to frightened (but false) conclusions about the cause of death of her host's wife.

Although she is threatened by Montoni and his bandits, her worst fears are imaginary, as her excited emotional state prompts her to suppose that eerie and supernatural things keep happening. It turns out, however, that the apparitions are merely the result of her anxious mind working on ordinary reality. At last, she is rescued from the castle by her lover.

The Romantic period remains a special and important time in literary history, a time when many new literary attitudes emerged that are still cherished today. In particular, the concept of the literary imagination has continued to strike a note with readers and writers ever since.

The Least You Need to Know

- The Romantic period marked a newfound appreciation for the imagination.

- Wordsworth's preface to *Lyrical Ballads* calls for poetry to adhere more closely to ordinary speech, humble and rustic life, and spontaneous feeling.

- Byron is easily identified with the "Byronic hero" of his poems—jaded, dissolute, willful, and restlessly dissatisfied.

- Jane Austen wrote well-crafted novels featuring level-headed heroines who keep romance, fashion, and money worries in perspective.

- The Gothic novel, featuring macabre doings in a medieval setting, rose in popularity during the Romantic period.

Works for Victoria

In This Chapter

- ◆ A look at the Victorian period
- ◆ Rifling through some Victorian novels
- ◆ Picking up cues from the dramatic monologue
- ◆ *The Importance of Being Earnest*

Victorian England has a somewhat unsavory reputation for prudery, priggishness, stodginess, and hypocrisy. Although not entirely deserved, this bad rep stems in part from the phenomenal economic success of the English middle class and the equally phenomenal political power of England as a nation. If Brits in general seemed to be walking around with their noses in the air, they had their reasons.

Rather than simply flaunt their good fortune, Victorians tried to appear worthy of it by cultivating attitudes of dignity, control, and competence. As they did so, they looked around at their world and noticed many problems. And they read about these many problems in Victorian novels.

During the Victorian age, the novel ripened to maturity and became, overwhelmingly, the form of choice for most readers. Early in the period, the novel exhibited a hopeful, confident attitude toward social challenges. But as the twentieth century approached, the novel and other literary forms became increasingly fraught with uncertainty.

Pride and Power

During the reign of Queen Victoria (1837–1901), England became a major world power with one of the largest mercantile and industrial economies on the planet, plus an expansive empire that included many colonies abroad. England's thriving middle class relied increasingly on emerging technologies, including the telegraph, steam engine, and camera. Their faith in progress, science, and themselves fostered liberal and *laissez-faire* attitudes toward a rapidly changing society.

Fueled by this growing and largely literate middle class, the novel emerged as the dominant literary form of the period. Types and subgenres of the novel proliferated. For the most part, however, the Victorian novel dealt with contemporary society in all of its aspects.

From *Bildungsroman* to Sci Fi

Here's a list of some of the different kinds of novels popular during the Victorian period:

bildungsroman   A novel that traces the development of a young person from childhood or adolescence to maturity, often written in the form of an autobiography. Charles Dickens wrote several, including *David Copperfield* (1850) and *Great Expectations* (1860).

condition of England novel   A novel concerned with the negative social impacts of industrialism. Two by Elizabeth Gaskell are *Mary Barton* (1848) and *North and South* (1855).

> **Grains of Trivium**
>
> In addition to a number of new sorts of novels, how-to books came on the scene, including Samuel Smiles's *Self-Help* (1859), which provided advice on how to be a stodgy, self-reliant Victorian.

fashionable novel   Sometimes called the "silver fork" novel, it focused on the lives of the rich and elegant. Theodore Hook's *Gilbert Gurney* (1836) is one of many examples.

detective novel   Urban crime proliferated in England as cities grew. Detective fiction emerged to portray efforts to bring criminals to justice. Wilkie Collins's *The Moonstone* (1868) paved the way for Arthur Conan Doyle's (1859–1930) Sherlock Holmes novels.

sensation novel   A melodramatic novel devoted to scandalous doings, guilty secrets, and lurid intrigues. Prominent examples are Wilkie Collins's *The Woman in White* (1860) and Mary Braddon's *Lady Audley's Secret* (1862).

science fiction   Probably you've heard of it. Best known among Victorians in sci fi is H. G. Wells, who wrote *The Time Machine* (1895), *The War of the Worlds* (1898), and others.

Keeping It Real

Victorian novelists and novel readers were fascinated by their society and by the moral, economic, and romantic positions of men and women within it. Novels portrayed people dealing with one another and with society as a whole as they confronted the various challenges Victorian life might present.

Published novels were widely available in bookstores and lending libraries. Many were also published in serial form in periodicals. Quite a few were published in three volumes, known as "triple-deckers." Writing early in the twentieth century, novelist Henry James complained that many Victorian novels were "large, loose, baggy monsters."

Novelists of every sort made a self-conscious attempt to write true-to-life, believable fiction—work that could be appreciated for its *realism*. As the period progressed, novelists tried to refine and improve on prevailing notions of realism in fiction. As a result, the form of the novel evolves somewhat in response to new attempts to write in a realistic manner.

def•i•ni•tion

Broadly, **realism** in fiction is the concern with representing life as it might actually be lived. The term is problematic, however, as modes of verbal representation keep changing over time together with cultural conceptions of reality.

Shifting Standards

Early in the period, novels tend to suggest that human beings and their lives are reasonably easy to understand and that narrators can be trusted to convey this understanding. Many such novels are written from an omniscient point of view. Everything that matters is made plain. Events unfold in an easy-to-follow chronological sequence. Idealized characters and sentimental scenes are common.

Later in the period, novels increasingly suggest that the world is too complex to be easily understood. Narrative perspective may shift from one subjective point of view to another. Time frames may shift as well, with flashbacks and gaps in the unfolding of events. Moral ambiguity becomes common.

Going to the Dickens

One of the most popular and prolific novelists of the early Victorian period was Charles Dickens (1812–1870). Dickens is best known for *bildungsromans* set in London that explore urban social problems, including poverty, crime, and corruption. Dickens often linked these themes to specific events and institutions of his day: work houses and the passage of the poor law, the legal system, English schools, and others.

These important social concerns indicate Dickens's interest in realism. Even so, Dickens's work is infused with idealism as well—even to the point of sentimentality. His main characters are often improbably virtuous—wholesome, innocent youngsters who seem incapable of doing wrong, but whose struggles and hardships highlight the evils of a corrupt society. An example is the title character from the novel *Oliver Twist* (1838).

It's a Twisted World

Oliver Twist is a foundling who is sent to a workhouse as a small boy. There, Oliver and his companions are overworked and underfed while the trustees and administrators pad their salaries by skimming goods and money intended to support the boys. Oliver's labor is eventually purchased by an undertaker whom he serves as an apprentice. After he is treated cruelly by a fellow apprentice, Oliver runs away to London, where he falls in with Jack "the Artful Dodger" Dawkins and a group of boy pickpockets led by Fagin, a receiver and seller of stolen goods.

> **Grains of Trivium**
>
> The Poor Law, passed in 1834, required impoverished orphans to be institutionalized in workhouses where they were to be clothed and fed and put to work for the public good. Oliver Twist dramatizes the abuses to which the workhouse system was susceptible.

The novel paints a vivid and compelling picture of the London underworld and its petty criminals. Oliver, however, remains implausibly innocent and virtuous. Despite his hard upbringing and destitute circumstances, he has a clear and unwavering sense of right and wrong and a kind, generous disposition. He is so innocent, he doesn't realize that his newfound companions and housemates are criminals until he actually sees them steal something—despite having practiced with them as they pretended to steal from Fagin.

A Virtue of Naiveté

Here's how Dickens describes this moment of Oliver's realization:

> What was Oliver's horror and alarm as he stood a few paces off, looking on with eyelids as wide open as they would possibly go, to see the Dodger plunge his hand into the old gentleman's pocket, and draw from thence a handkerchief! To see him hand the same to Charley Bates; and finally to behold them, both, running away round the corner at full speed!
>
> In an instant, the whole mystery of the handkerchiefs, and the watches, and the jewels, and the Jew [Fagin], rushed upon the boy's mind. He stood, for a moment, with the blood so tingling through all his veins from terror, that he felt as if he were in a burning fire; then, confused and frightened, he took to his heels …

The omniscient narrator assures us that Oliver is inwardly innocent of all wrong, however he may appear to the outside world. Thus, Dickens expects his readers to share his, and Oliver's, uncomplicated moral perspective on petty theft. However much we may like and admire the Artful Dodger, theft is wrong, and good people don't do it.

Because of his moral purity and innocence, Oliver is able to rise above the contrasted social evils at issue in the novel. These are the exploitation and neglect of the poor by the middle and upper classes on one hand and, on the other, theft and burglary committed against the middle and upper classes by a criminal element of the lower class. It's as if Dickens was saying, "These problems will work themselves out if we all just think and behave virtuously like Oliver."

> **Grains of Trivium**
>
> The optimistic outlook known as *meliorism* became popular during the Victorian period. This is the view that social conditions tend to improve and that conscious human efforts to make things better will actually work.

Getting Dark

From the time *Oliver Twist* was published up to the end of the Victorian period, conceptions of novelistic realism shifted. Amid this shift, a general sense of both moral and narrative clarity gradually gave way to uncertainty. A prime example of how far the Victorian novel could go in this direction is Joseph Conrad's *Heart of*

Darkness (1902). This novel raises questions about the relationship between civilization and morality that are difficult to frame clearly, much less resolve.

Dark Hearts, Dark Minds

Heart of Darkness has a good deal in common with *Oliver Twist*. Both Victorian novels were originally published in installments. Each is set in a social "underworld": *Oliver Twist*, London's criminal underworld; *Heart of Darkness*, the imperial underworld of the Belgian Congo. Both address important social issues of their respective days: *Oliver Twist*, crime and the exploitation of the poor; *Heart of Darkness*, "savage" violence and the brutal exploitation of native labor. And if *that* doesn't clinch my point, both novels even make symbolic-realistic use of fog to heighten the sense of drama!

In addition, Marlow, the protagonist of *Heart of Darkness*, undergoes a painful realization that resembles Oliver Twist's when he sees the Artful Dodger steal a handkerchief. To a large degree, Conrad's novel focuses on Marlow's sickening awareness that the supposedly nice people he works for are actually a bunch of bloody thieves!

Canon Fodder
Contrast Conrad's attitude toward imperialism with that of poet, short-story writer, and novelist Rudyard Kipling. Kipling is best known today for *The Jungle Book,* a children's story adapted as an animated feature film by Disney studios. Kipling also wrote the poem "The White Man's Burden," in which he praises British imperialists for taking on the thankless task of bringing civilization to the savage races of the world.

But in Dickens, social problems appear at least potentially outweighed by the goodness (embodied in Oliver and those who are kind to him) and wisdom (transmitted through the narrator) of humanity. No such stuff in Conrad. *Heart of Darkness* casts into serious doubt the ideals of human goodness and wisdom.

Kurtz Rejoinders

Marlow is a riverboat captain who takes a job with a Belgian trading company operating in the Congo. He agrees to sail up the Congo River and return with a shipment of ivory. Upriver, he expects to meet with an agent of the company named Kurtz. Kurtz is reputed to be a talented administrator, and Marlow is eager to meet him.

As the story unfolds, Marlow hears about Kurtz from various different people, including a Belgian journalist, Kurtz's cousin, and, at the end of the novel, Kurtz's fiancée.

These people admire him greatly. Their accounts, however, are completely at odds with Marlow's impression of him when the two eventually meet.

Leading up to their meeting, Marlow discovers that the trading company he works for brutalizes native African laborers. Many of the

Grains of Trivium

Conrad's novel inspired *Apocalypse Now* (1979), a movie by director Francis Coppola set in Vietnam and starring Marlon Brando.

company's European employees seem afraid of Africa and Africans, as it turns out, with good reason. Natives attack the riverboat, shooting arrows and killing the helmsman.

When he arrives at Kurtz's outpost, Marlow learns that Kurtz has established himself as a kind of tribal war chief who leads through intimidation, superstition, and brutality. He has placed severed heads all around the camp, from which he launches raids to get ivory. When Marlow finally meets him, Kurtz is deathly ill and appears to have been driven crazy by his own atrocities. He dies in Marlow's presence, uttering his famous, haunting last words, "The horror! The horror!"

Skip This Section If You Haven't Read the Book

Back in England, Marlow struggles to interpret his experience. In a magnificent final episode, he meets with Kurtz's fiancée, who is grieved by his death and full of admiration for the great man she thinks he was. Annoyed at first that she could be so mistaken about Kurtz, he finally feels pity and lies to her—saying he spoke of her with his last breath to make her feel better when she asks him what Kurtz's last words were. He feels creepy about lying, however, as he realizes that Kurtz's actual last words were authentically truthful. *Horror* acurately describes the circumstances in the Congo.

Kurtz remains an enigma, and his mystery is reinforced by the conflicting perspectives of several different characters. Unlike in *Oliver Twist*, there is no omniscient narrator to sort things out for the reader. Marlow tells his own story from his own limited perspective.

Good Liars

While the Victorian novel explored the limits of perspective, Victorian poetry did, too, in a form known as the *dramatic monologue*. Dramatic monologues are poems

def•i•ni•tion

A **dramatic monologue** is a poem that consists of a speech delivered by a dramatic character.

Grains of Trivium

Browning, like his contemporary Alfred Tennyson, based many of his poems on historical accounts of actual people and events.

in the form of speeches delivered by characters in dramatic situations. These speakers epitomize the "unreliable narrator" whose perspective you can't completely trust but whose account is all you have to go on. Dramatic monologues reflect the personas, thought processes, and biases of their speakers in intriguing ways, often suggesting simultaneously the plausibility and the fallibility of their assertions.

The leading writer of dramatic monologues was Robert Browning (1812–1889), who is sometimes credited with inventing the form. Browning's best-known dramatic monologue is "My Last Duchess" (1842). In this poem, the Duke of Ferrara, a highly polished but phenomenally arrogant seventeenth-century Italian nobleman, displays part of his art collection—and much of his own brilliant but twisted character.

Lady Killer

The poem's title, "My Last Duchess," refers to the duke's former wife, who has died. At the start of the poem, the duke displays her portrait to a visitor (the implied audience of the poem) and proceeds to tell what she was like and what he thought of her. In the process, a number of fascinating aspects of the duke's character emerge.

For one, he's an art connoisseur with a sophisticated appreciation for portraiture. In fact, the duke's interest in his late wife seems oddly overshadowed by his interest in the work of art she posed for when she was alive. He seems so pleased with the painting that her death is a nonissue.

Even so, the painting reveals a crucial, defining aspect of her character. The painter captured a "spot of joy" on the duchess's cheek. While the duke seems to treasure this spot in the painting, he felt it was inappropriate in his wife. She was too happy about too many things:

> She had
> A heart—how shall I say?—too soon made glad,
> Too easily impressed; she liked whate'er
> She looked on, and her looks went everywhere.
>
> …

> ... She thanked men—good! but thanked
> somehow—I know not how—as if she ranked
> My gift of a nine-hundred-years-old name
> With anybody's gift. Who'd stoop to blame
> This sort of trifling?
>
> (21–24, 31–35)

According to the duke, her irksome fault was that she didn't take sufficient pride in being his wife. This was a subtle problem, however, so it wasn't really worth complaining to her about. Nevertheless, it bothered him, so ...

> I gave commands;
> Then all smiles stopped together. There she stands
> As if alive.
>
> (45–47)

Thus, the duke suggests he had her murdered. What's more, he seems to be pleased with himself about the whole thing. He appears proud of his willingness and power to take decisive, drastic measures against a harmless, petty annoyance.

The Mating Game

Our sense of the duke's audacity is further heightened when we learn that he is speaking to an emissary who has come to arrange a marriage between his master's daughter and the duke. Apparently, the duke thinks himself so rich, powerful, and important that he expects his new prospective father-in-law to willingly marry off his daughter to a known wife murderer! In any case, he is impeccably suave, gracious, and polite to his guest throughout the poem.

"My Last Duchess," like many other Victorian dramatic monologues, draws on conventions of Gothic literature (see Chapter 18) to portray the corruption of aristocratic hubris or Catholic hypocrisy to a Protestant middle class. But Browning's duke is not simply corrupt; he is also admirable in many ways. And he is not simply a seventeenth-century Catholic aristocrat. He is, in a different sense, an English Victorian!

> **Canon Fodder**
>
> A number of Victorian dramatic monologues portray Catholics in a negative light, including Browning's "Soliloquy of the Spanish Cloister" and Alfred Tennyson's "Saint Simeon Stylites."

You Better Believe

As mentioned earlier, Victorian novelists generally aimed at realism. Gothic novels (those concerned with supernatural events) didn't disappear, but for a time they lost credibility as serious literature. The gothic novel of the romantic period, with its ghosts and other inexplicable horrors, fell out of literary fashion with the rise of the Victorian era. (See Chapter 18 for more information on the Gothic novel.)

Even so, aspects of the gothic novel made their mark on a number of works of realist Victorian fiction, including *Jane Eyre* (1847) by Charlotte Brontë and *Tess of the D'Urbervilles* (1891) by Thomas Hardy. These works use gothic trappings and ambience in a realistic way to evoke and illustrate the emotional angst of their main characters.

Kudos and Caveats

While British fiction writers tended to avoid supernatural themes in writings from the 1840s through the 1870s, American writer Edgar Allen Poe (1809–1849) became famous for his macabre supernatural tales.

Gasping for Eyre

Jane Eyre is an orphan who becomes a schoolteacher and later a governess at the home of a secretive, mysterious older man named Edward Rochester. They eventually fall in love and agree to marry, despite the fact that there's much about his past and present doings that Jane doesn't understand. But on the day they are to be married, Jane learns Rochester's dark secret: he's already married to a madwoman—a creole who lives hidden in the attic! Although Jane loves him still, she refuses to live with him as his mistress and runs off in the middle of the night.

Canon Fodder

Jean Rhys (1890–1979), a Dominican writer of creole descent, penned a prequel to *Jane Eyre*, told from the point of view of Rochester's creole wife. This novel, *Wide Sargasso Sea* (1966), was recognized by *Time* magazine as one of the 100 best novels written since 1923.

Eventually, Jane is taken in by a vicar (a parish priest) named St. John Rivers. Rivers comes to admire and respect Jane and asks her to marry him so they can work together as missionaries in India. Although Jane admires and respects Rivers in return, she doesn't love him, so she turns him down.

Jane is faced first with a choice to live in sin with a man she loves and, second, to live virtuously with a man she doesn't. Her conflicted feelings for Rochester come through in narrative details that hearken back to the gothic novel of the romantic period. Rochester's mystery and creepiness contrast starkly with the religious virtue associated with Rivers.

Throughout the novel, the prospect of marriage is fraught with emotional angst and flavored with gothic imagery. If *you* were a Victorian orphan, would you marry your biggest fear?

Losing Game

Author Thomas Hardy is known for stories of failure and suffering, and *Tess of the D'Urbervilles* is characteristically bleak in representing a beautiful young woman who is raped (or perhaps seduced) by a man who doesn't care about her and then is later abandoned by her husband on account of her previous sexual encounter. Things go from bad to worse as she tries to work things out, first with one, and then with the other man. Through all the turmoil, gothic overtones add to the dismal proceedings.

In *Jane Eyre*, the gothic represents the challenges and dangers Jane faces in choosing a man. In *Tess*, the gothic underscores the tragic unfolding of forces beyond Tess's control. Whereas Jane is faced with a choice between marrying a piously virtuous suitor and living with a man with a bad reputation as his mistress, Tess must undergo the hardship of being married to a man who rejects her for having been the unwilling mistress of a man who seduced her—the worst of both worlds!

Gothic Revival

For all their gothic trappings, neither *Jane Eyre* nor *Tess* is, strictly speaking, a gothic novel, especially because neither one presents any overtly fantastic, supernatural events. Gothic novels with supernaturalism made a comeback at the very end of the Victorian period with a number of standout titles that resonate with the decadence and decay of the time. How many of these are you familiar with:

- *Dr Jekyll and Mr Hyde* (1886) by Robert Louis Stevenson (1850–1894)
- *The Picture of Dorian Gray* (1891) by Oscar Wilde (1856–1900)
- *The Turn of the Screw* (1898) by Henry James (1843–1916)
- *Dracula* (1897) by Bram Stoker (1847–1912)

Wilde and Earnest

During the final decades of the nineteenth century, a number of writers began to react against the priggishness, prudery, and conformism of Victorian society. They

def•i•ni•tion

Aestheticism is a movement that took place near the end of the nineteenth century that aimed to free art from conventional Victorian morality.

reacted as well against literature that tried to settle important social issues or provide practical guidance on how to live. This reaction is known as *aestheticism*, a movement that aims to separate art from conventional notions of morality.

The aesthetes held that art served no purpose beyond itself. Many went further and affirmed that life itself served no purpose but should be lived as a kind of art form. This "art for art's sake" movement was widely perceived as decadent during the late Victorian period, associated with pleasure seeking and sexual freedom.

A leader of the aesthetic movement was Oscar Wilde (1854–1900), a writer known for his decadent attitudes and his witty, urbane sense of humor, as evident in one of his best-loved works, *The Importance of Being Earnest*. This play is filled with humor derived from conflicts between conventional morality and a sophisticated enjoyment of life. The play's main characters wittily insist that it's good to defy common sense, live in an artificial world, and strive for perfection in frivolous things.

Grains of Trivium

The Importance of Being Earnest was a big hit in the London theater. Its performance run was cut short, however, in the wake of Wilde's trial and conviction on charges of homosexuality— a crime for which he was sentenced to two years' hard labor in prison.

The comedy centers on a character named Jack Worthing, a respectable Hertfordshire landholder who pretends to have a dissolute, irresponsible brother named Ernest, who supposedly lives in London. Whenever Jack wants to get away, he uses his made-up brother's problems as an excuse. Then he goes to London and enjoys himself under his made-up brother's name, Ernest.

In London, he visits a friend, Algernon Moncrieff, a wealthy, pleasure-loving dandy. The two friends take aristocratic pride in their social deceptions, their ignorance of facts, and their expertise in pointless matters. In short, they make a moral virtue of their opposition to middle-class morality.

Jack meets Algernon's cousin, Gwendolyn Fairfax, and falls in love with her. She returns his feelings because of his made-up name—she wants to marry a man named Ernest! Jack seeks permission to marry Gwendolyn from her mother, Lady Bracknell, who refuses because Jack has no family. In fact, as he admits, he was found as an infant in a handbag in Victoria Station.

Jack and Gwendolyn agree to correspond in secret. Meanwhile, he makes plans to have himself rechristened with his assumed name, Ernest. As it turns out, however, a governess reveals that she absentmindedly left Lady Bracknell's baby nephew in a handbag in Victoria Station, so Jack's true parentage is revealed—and his real name isn't Jack. It's Ernest.

So the story has a happy ending, except that Ernest (Jack) is embarrassed to learn he had been telling Gwendolyn the truth about his name all along without meaning to! He says, "Gwendolyn, it is a terrible thing for a man to find out suddenly that all his life he has been speaking nothing but the truth. Can you forgive me?"

The Least You Need to Know

- The Victorian novel emerged as the dominant form of the period and tended to focus on contemporary society in all its aspects.

- Modes of "realism" shift during the period from depictions of a relatively comprehensible world to increasingly problematic representations.

- Dickens's narrators appear in control of the moral challenges his novels present. Narration in Conrad's works underscores moral uncertainty.

- Dramatic monologues, including Browning's "My Last Duchess," have unreliable narrators as speakers.

- Oscar Wilde was a leading figure in the "art for art's sake" movement.

Chapter 20

Modern Methods

In This Chapter

- ◆ Experimenting with Modernism
- ◆ The disillusioned poetry of the Great War
- ◆ T. S. Eliot's search for renewal
- ◆ Virginia Woolf helps pioneer the stream-of-consciousness novel

Modernism is a many-faceted state of affairs. In general, it can be characterized by a sense of disillusionment with a variety of outmoded cultural ideals or dismay over a lack of idealism in the modern world, together with a corresponding array of attempts to create, discover, or distill something new in art and literature. Artists and writers during this time wanted to experiment, both by separating themselves from the past and by connecting to the past in new ways.

The Modern period was a time of prolific experimentation in all the arts, including literature, even as traditional rationales for creative effort came to be seen as exhausted or invalid. Despite widespread disillusionment about such things as God, humanity, society, and the self, Modernism exhibits a hopeful and positive attitude about the arts. People continued to see the arts as relevant to their lives and continued to be interested in what the arts had to say about life, the world, and the times.

You might say Modernism was a sort of "last gasp" for the arts as a widely shared public enterprise, a kind of final fling before fragmenting and dissolving into the instability of postmodernism.

In the Line of Fire

One of the clearest signs that the world was changing in the early decades of the twentieth century was World War I, or the "Great War," as it was known at the time. All of Europe and, later, the United States, was swept up in the conflict that raged on for years in a bloody stalemate. Millions died, thanks not only to the huge scope of the war, but to lethal advances in military technology. Powerful exploding artillery, machine guns, and poison gas were used on both sides by and against forces that hunkered down in trenches they dug in the battlefield.

Entrenched in War

Trench warfare was not like the pitched battles of the nineteenth century, when brightly uniformed cavalries and foot soldiers charged at each other with swords and bayonets. Instead, soldiers fired at each other from trenches in exchanges that were protracted and indecisive as well as deadly.

To many of those who fought in it, the Great War seemed like an absurd, grisly exercise in futility. As they fought, many realized the fighting would drive them crazy if it didn't kill them.

Canon Fodder
A famous Victorian war poem, "The Charge of the Light Brigade" (1854), by Alfred Lord Tennyson, glorifies the noble deaths of British forces heroically annihilated in an ill-conceived attack on waiting Russians in the Crimean War. Despite the useless loss of life, the poem celebrates the "glory" of war. The war poets of World War I, in contrast, objected to the sort of sentiment expressed in Tennyson's poem.

A Tomb of One's Owen

A number of British soldiers wrote poetry inspired by their experiences. These poets produced some of the best—and most harrowing—war poetry written in English. One of the most prominent was Wilfred Owen (1893–1918). Guess why he died so young.

Owen's poetry is full of haunting and horrific images of battle, including the torn bodies of dead and wounded men. It also creates wrenching ironies by contrasting the poetic sentiments of patriotism, love, and beauty with graphically realistic images. The irony is heightened by Owen's verse, which sounds beautiful—it's rhymed, metrical, and lyrical.

One of Owen's many striking poems is *"Dulce et Decorum Est"* (published 1920). The title is taken from an ode by ancient Roman poet Horace (65–8 B.C.E.), part of a famous line, *"Dulce et decorum est pro patria mori"* (It's sweet and decorous to die for your country). Owen uses the allusion ironically in a poem that describes the painful, violent death of a soldier killed by poison gas. Addressing the reader, the speaker says,

> In all my dreams, before my helpless sight,
> He plunges at me, guttering, choking, drowning.
>
> If in some smothering dreams you too could pace
> Behind the wagon that we flung him in,
> And watch the white eyes writhing in his face,
> His hanging face, like a devil's sick of sin;
> If you could hear, at every jolt, the blood
> Come gargling from the froth-corrupted lungs,
> Obscene as cancer, bitter as the cud
> Of vile, incurable sores on innocent tongues,—
> My friend, you would not tell with such high zest
> To children ardent for some desperate glory,
> The old Lie: Dulce et decorum est
> Pro patria mori.
>
> (15–28)

The speaker is haunted by the sight of the agonized death he describes. He looks on with "helpless sight"—unable to help the soldier and unable to look away. It is gruesomely vivid and detailed, yet the poem suggests we would need to see it for ourselves to really feel it the way the speaker does—or dream it in "smothering dreams" that connect the image of the suffocating soldier with vague discomfort we might feel during sleep.

The dying soldier is defiled—his face is like a "devil's," his lungs "corrupted," and his blood "obscene." Yet as the imagery shifts to plural "tongues," they are "innocent." Thus, the poem suggests that soldiers who die in this way are free from guilt. At the same time, "tongues" who talk about war may be "innocent" in the sense of not knowing what they're talking about as they chew over patriotic platitudes. ("Cud" is

Canon Fodder
Other notable war poets are Siegfried Sassoon (1886–1967), David Jones (1895–1974), and Edward Thomas (1878–1917).

the partly digested grass cows regurgitate and chew on.) The image of cud serves as a metaphor both for the choking soldier's vomit and for the evils of war, belied by glorified accounts of war. Thus, "innocent tongues" introduces the notion of telling "the old Lie" to children—a lie that may someday induce them "innocently" to enlist for war.

Showing and Knowing

War poetry heralds the Modern period by evoking an increasingly noticeable gap between language and experience. The things people say don't really resemble the way things are. To deal with this problem, Modernist writers embarked on a variety of experiments with language and form. Some sought new, more authentic ways to represent experience. Others sought new ways to show that representation and experience don't really match up.

Modern Shake-Up

Many people of the time greeted the many modernist innovations in art and literature with surprise and confusion. They had come to expect painting, poetry, and fiction to imitate external reality in clear and obvious ways. To these people, modernist art and literature could seem crazy.

Grains of Trivium
Painting and poetry have been regarded as "sister arts" since the Renaissance.

Modernist paintings distorted traditional subjects in all kinds of ways: through fragmented perspectives (cubism), through strange juxtapositions and mutations of images (surrealism), through attempts to portray the effects of seeing rather than the subject itself (impressionism), and through attempts to convey the inner feelings of the artist (expressionism).

Poets and novelists explored similar innovations. Chief among these were open form, "free verse" poetry that abandoned regular meter and "stream of consciousness" narrative in fiction that represented the protagonist's ongoing inner impressions.

Old and New

The best-known and most successful poet to embrace Modernist innovations was American-born British poet T. S. Eliot (1888–1965). Eliot's poetry is distinctively modernist in its use of irregular meter, odd and often startling juxtapositions of images, and perspectives that seem to shift without notice from one speaker to another. From the beginning, Eliot's poetry confused and challenged his readers. At the same time, it is clearly serious, thoughtful, and well made.

You might think that such an *avant garde* approach as Eliot's would indicate disrespect or impatience with tradition and a desire to tear down outmoded poetic conventions. To the contrary, Eliot was keenly interested in what he saw as Europe's great cultural and literary tradition, and was deeply concerned with keeping it alive amid an increasingly superficial modern society. As a result, Eliot's modern style seems to comment on the disjointedness of the modern world rather than to rebel against the norms of the past.

> **Canon Fodder**
>
> Eliot is one of a number of Americans who left America to become noted literary figures in Europe. Others include poets Ezra Pound and Gertrude Stein and novelist Henry James.

Much of Eliot's poetry has a weighty, classical feel, often punctuated by seemingly banal or frivolous interjections. It's highly allusive, filled with echoes of literature and legends from the past, as well as with scenarios of modern life. In this way, it brings together "timeless" archetypes with the here and now (or the then and there, at any rate). It's also highly symbolic, using traditional images in new ways and in new contexts to evoke and comment on broad themes—humanity, history, and culture.

A Big Waste

One of Eliot's best-known and most important poems is *The Waste Land* (1922), a symbolic portrait of the modern condition that uses echoes of ancient myth and legend to suggest a frustrated search for spiritual and emotional renewal. Here are some lines from Part III, "The Fire Sermon" (this title refers to a sermon Buddha preached in which he characterized desire as a destructive fire):

> At the violet hour, when the eyes and back
> Turn upward from the desk, when the human engine waits
> Like a taxi throbbing waiting,
> I Tiresias, though blind, throbbing between two lives,
> Old man with wrinkled female breasts, can see
> At the violet hour, the evening hour that strives
> Homeward, and brings the sailor home from sea,
> The typist home at teatime, clears her breakfast, lights
> her stove, and lays out food in tins.

Grains of Trivium

Eliot dedicated *The Waste Land* to fellow American expatriate poet Ezra Pound, a leading exponent of the "imagist" movement in poetry. Pound weighed in with revisions for Eliot's poem before publication.

Canon Fodder

According to ancient Greek legend, Tiresias accidentally came upon Athena, goddess of wisdom, while she was bathing. Angry about having her privacy violated, she blinded him by splashing him with water. Then, to make up for his loss of sight, she conferred on him the ability to see into the future.

Out of the window perilously spread
Her drying combinations touched by the sun's last
    rays,
On the divan are piled (at night her bed)
Stockings, slippers, camisoles, and stays.
I Tiresias, old man with wrinkled dugs
Perceived the scene, and foretold the rest—
I too awaited the expected guest.

(215–230)

The poem describes the coming on of evening, "the violet hour" when the typical office worker ("eyes and back / Turn upward from the desk") waits to get off work, as much like a machine as a human being ("the human engine waits / Like a taxi"). This distinctly modern scene is described by Tiresias, a legendary ancient Greek prophet who was said to have been transformed from a man into a woman and back again. He is "throbbing between two lives," man and woman, just as a taxi throbs with its engine running as it waits for a new passenger.

Tiresias is a peculiar figure to be narrating this scenario. He turns up in ancient Greek tragedies such as *Oedipus Rex* and *Antigone* to warn people that something disastrous is about to happen. Is some dire tragedy about to unfold in Eliot's poem? Not exactly. Perhaps Eliot is suggesting that moderns have lost the ability to feel strongly, whether tragically or any other significant way.

Typist as Archetype

Tiresias tells of a "typist" who returns home at teatime like a sailor returning "home from the sea." The comparison seems ironic because the typist's job is confined and mechanical, unlike sailing on the ocean. At the same time, returning home may have common significance for sailors and typists.

The typist's home appears to be a drab efficiency apartment. She dries her laundry on a line outside the window, heats up canned food for dinner, and uses her couch for a bed. Yet Tiresias speaks of these things with grandiose language. The laundry hung on the line are her "drying combinations," "perilously spread" and "touched by the sun's last rays." You'd think the clothes she wears to work were some kind of sacrificial vestment!

The typist—and Tiresias—is awaiting a visitor. The poem goes on to describe him as "a small house agent's clerk" who apparently succeeds in having sex with her, despite her complete indifference to him. She's glad when it's over. His lust and vanity satisfied, he leaves that night, having to grope his way in the dark down unlit stairs.

This sordid and pathetic tryst serves as an emblem for Eliot's view of modern life itself, in which people go through the motions without really understanding the significance—or lack of significance—of what they're doing. Spirituality has been drained from human activities, even though they seem ironically ritualistic. Somehow they *should* feel important, but they don't. Tiresias has been around too long, and he's seen everything already.

> **Canon Fodder**
>
> Eliot took the name of his poem from the wasteland described in medieval grail legends. This was the kingdom of the Fisher King that was placed under a curse and could not bear crops until a virtuous knight on a quest restored fertility to the land.

Stream Lines

Eliot seems to turn ordinary modern existence into something profound and timeless. Other modernist writers tried to convey a sense of modern existence through fleeting, half-formed impressions of the sort that run through people's minds constantly. This is one of the aims of the *stream-of-consciousness* novel, a Modernist form that puts together a story by tracing the thoughts, feelings, and impressions of its characters.

> **def•i•ni•tion**
>
> A **stream-of-consciousness novel** is a modernist form that assembles a story by tracing its characters' thoughts and feelings rather than through the voice of a detached narrator.

What goes on in one's consciousness is often difficult to communicate because the mind doesn't always form clear ideas about everything that passes through it. Authors of stream-of-consciousness novels often try to create a sense of a character's flitting thoughts by using language in peculiar ways. The narrative may veer from topic to topic without explanation or transition. Use of grammar, syntax, and punctuation may seem haphazard, repetitive, or unusual in some other way.

Words Unspoken

One of the preeminent stream-of-consciousness novelists of the Modern period was Virginia Woolf (1882–1941). Her novel *Mrs. Dalloway* (1925) focuses on a woman of the upper-middle class named Clarissa Dalloway who is giving a party for her friends. Although the entire novel takes place on the day of the party, the narrative jumps around in time and from person to person as Woolf traces the thoughts of all the characters.

The technique enables Woolf to suggest psychological states and motivations in subtle ways. One example concerns the relationship between Clarissa and a character named Peter Walsh. Peter had courted Clarissa years before, but she refused him and married Richard Dalloway. Peter shows up at the Dalloways unexpectedly on the morning of Clarissa's party. He had been living in India but returned to England to help arrange a divorce between Daisy, a woman he was in love with, and her husband.

The meeting between Clasissa and Peter is an emotional meeting for them both, evoking a lot of memories that neither talk about, although they come out in the narration through the "thoughts" of the characters. During his visit with Clarissa, Peter's thoughts about Daisy seem to make him feel better about Clarissa turning him down years before. Even so, he senses that Clarissa is more worldly and attractive than Daisy.

Later, after leaving Clarissa's, Peter finds himself attracted to a pretty girl. He imagines asking her out and follows after her. The narrative suggests that Peter's momentary attraction to the pretty girl is brought on by his feelings of longing for Clarissa. He thinks of her last words to him—"Remember my party, remember my party"—the moment he sees that the pretty girl is gone. Thus, his thoughts about the girl disappearing and his frustrated feelings for Clarissa merge in his mind. All this comes across without a lot of clunky statements like *he thought this* and *he thought that*.

Mind in Motion

While, from moment to moment, the narration seems to move in a spontaneous, random, and even disjointed manner, the individual elements of the novel hold together to form a coherent picture of the interconnected lives of the characters. Here, although the novel doesn't explain it directly, it shows how Peter feels about Clarissa by narrating the odd things his mind does to cope with his feelings.

The Least You Need to Know

- ◆ The Modern period was a time of experimentation and innovation in the arts.

- ◆ Poetry of the Great War produces wrenching ironies by contrasting patriotic ideals with the horror and futility of the war.

- ◆ T. S. Eliot's Modernist approach to poetry reflects the disjointedness and uprootedness of modern life.

- ◆ Virginia Woolf, a leading Modern novelist, wrote stream-of-consciousness novels based on the inner thoughts and experiences of her characters.

Chapter 21

This Just In

In This Chapter

- ◆ Keeping current with postmodern literature
- ◆ Late expectations: theater of the absurd and *Waiting for Godot*
- ◆ New tricks: magic realism and *Midnight's Children*
- ◆ Hack writing: cyberpunk and *Neuromancer*

Where are we now? By most accounts, we're living in postmodern times, a period when knowledge and experience are not only increasingly partial and limited, but are defined in ways that are increasingly fuzzy and open to reinterpretation. What's true for some people isn't necessarily true for anyone else—but anyone's ideas can be taken over and reused in different ways.

The literature that is most often pointed to as specially representative of our times is literature that deals with porous borders and fuzzy boundaries, half-truths and coercive fictions, corporate powers and divided selves. This includes two widely influential genres of fiction: magical realism and cyberpunk. In very different ways, these genres are both concerned with struggles to control meaning across permeable boundaries.

Who is "us" and who is "them"? It all depends on representations that anyone can use, imitate, and challenge. It's not that the differences don't matter, but that they have to be controlled by someone and are apt to change at any time.

From Pillar to Post

Many intellectual historians date the beginning of the postmodern period from the end of World War II. Others equate postmodernism less with a particular date than with particular qualities, including a tendency to react against modernism. As a result, the question remains open whether certain works exemplify early postmodernism or late modernism.

Pointless Plays

During the 1940s, 1950s, and 1960s, a new trend in drama emerged in France and spread elsewhere in Europe, including England, and to the United States. It became known as *theater of the absurd* because it tends to depict human experience as irrational or futile while representing the world as intrinsically meaningless. *Absurd* is a term famously used by the French existentialist philosophers Jean-Paul Sartre and Albert Camus to characterize the existentialist view of life: life has no inherent meaning. Things happen for reasons that make no sense, or, if they do make "sense," that sense is delusory.

Kudos and Caveats

The expression *theater of the absurd* is often used metaphorically to refer to political situations that are vexed by corruption, misinformation, futility, and ineptitude.

The theater of the absurd reflects a reality in which people are trapped by their own delusions or struggling to cope with the truth of absurdity. Characters are emotionally isolated, fail to communicate, and are helpless, hopeless, aimless, yet strangely funny. One of the best-known dramas in this vein is Samuel Becket's (1906–1989) *Waiting for Godot*, a bleak yet comic play in which the two main characters spend their lives simply waiting.

Laid Bare

Becket was an Irish novelist and playwright who moved to France, where he developed a close working relationship with James Joyce, who influenced him greatly. *Waiting for Godot* was originally written in French (*En Attendant Godot*) and published in 1952. Becket wrote the English version in 1955.

The play is set on a nearly bare stage. The only scenery is a tree with a few leaves on it and a road next to it. The minimal scenery suggests an encompassing emptiness that resonates with the starkness of the drama. The play provides almost no sense of context. It could be set any time or any place. The almost bare stage and apparent fact that context doesn't matter heightens the sense of spiritual emptiness the play evokes.

Kudos and Caveats

After *Waiting for Godot* debuted in London in 1955, it met with a lukewarm response and was nearly cancelled after the first week. Audiences and critics eventually warmed up to it, however, after they had a chance to think about it!

Arrested Development

Waiting for Godot focuses on two characters, Estragon (Gogo) and Vladimir (Didi). Gogo and Didi could be anybody, but they are dressed like tramps. Their condition is pathetic yet comic. Their dress, speech, and behavior are strongly reminiscent of comic vaudeville characters or the down-and-out protagonists of Charlie Chaplin films. They appear to be simply likable souls, and at times their actions seem like vaudeville shtick. Even so, they are not merely figures out of a low-brow comedy. Throughout the play, they struggle with feelings of anguish, loneliness, restlessness, and uncertainty.

The two-act drama is taken up almost entirely with the actions and dialogue of Gogo and Didi as they wait for a mysterious figure called Godot. Neither one seems to know who he is or what he looks like, when he'll come, or even whether he'll come. Neither do they seem to know what will happen if he does come. Nevertheless, they can't seem to find anything better to do than wait, even though waiting makes them unhappy and, at one point, even suicidal.

Gogo and Didi are capable of positive feelings, but their flickers of warmth die out amid discontentment and confusion. Sometimes they squabble. At other times, they have difficulty understanding each other, and their conversations falter pointlessly and fade into silence.

Grains of Trivium

Critics have suggested that Godot represents God, although Becket has explicitly denied this. The similarity and the difference between *God* and *Godot* are certainly significant, though.

Their hopes of Godot's arrival are repeatedly aroused by the entrance of other characters, including Pozzo and Lucky, who appear to represent a master and his slave. Pozzo holds on to the end of a long rope tied around Lucky's neck. Lucky is unable to speak or, apparently, even think for himself unless bidden by Pozzo—and unless he has his hat on! Absurd though their behavior is, their weird interdependence makes a disturbing comment about class relationships. When Lucky and Pozzo reappear in the second act, Pozzo has gone blind and Lucky has gone mute. Perhaps this suggests that the powerful are unable to "see" what is wrong with the world, while the powerless are unable to make their complaints heard.

The play ends, famously, by seeming never to end. Gogo and Didi eventually realize that Godot will never appear, so they agree to leave. But as the curtain falls they don't move.

Play List

Other notable plays of the absurd include the following:

- Arthur Adamov's (1908–1970) *Le Ping-Pong* (1955)

- Jean Genet's (1910–1986) *The Balcony* (1957)

- Eugene Ionesco's (1909–1994) *Rhinoceros* (1960)

- Harold Pinter's (1930–) *The Dumb Waiter* (1960)

- Tom Stoppard's (1937–) *Rosencrantz and Guildenstern Are Dead* (1967)

Spell-Binders

An important recent development in fiction is a genre known as *magical realism*, which combines familiar novelistic realism with elements of fantasy. This approach to fiction got its start in Latin America, where novelists began to combine realist and "magic" modes to work through the conflicts and complexities of life in a postcolonial setting. When two cultures come together, ideas and values often blend in irrational ways. Magical realism expresses this irrationality by presenting imaginary, magical things as true.

> **Grains of Trivium**
>
> The term *magical realism* was first used to describe a trend in Modern surrealist painting of the 1920s.

Clash of Enchantment

The narrator in a magical realism novel tells the story as if he or she believes that magical, unexplainable things can happen. Often miraculous things that characters in the narrative want to happen actually do happen. This magical outlook helps make crazy, paradoxical sense of the crazy, paradoxical attitudes that shape postcolonial cultures.

Sometimes the magic reflects the persistence of native traditions within a modernized society. At other times, the magic reflects a sense of how bizarre and out of place Western technology and popular culture appear to be within a non-Western culture. Either way, magical realism expresses a point of view that is neither simply native or Western, but attempts to come to terms with both at once.

A Magic State

A novel that is generally regarded as a magical realism narrative is Salman Rushdie's (1948–) *Midnight's Children* (1981), a story told from the point of view of an Indian Muslim named Saleem Sinai who was born at the exact same time India became an independent country: the stroke of midnight on August 15, 1947. According to Saleem, his destiny is mysteriously linked with that of India's.

Yet none of the main characters seem particularly important to India as a nation. They all appear to be caught up in circumstances beyond their control. The magical elements of the novel hold events together that might otherwise seem random and meaningless but are presented as crucial to the growth of the nation.

> **Grains of Trivium**
>
> Many Islamists were outraged by Rushdie's *The Satanic Verses* (1988), claiming it blasphemed against their religion in its irreverant representation of the prophet Muhammad. Ayatollah Ruhollah Khomeini, the leader of Iran, offered a bounty for Rushdie's death. As a result, Rushdie lived in hiding for many years.

Eyes of the Beholders

Much of what seems "magic" about this magical realism novel appears to be all in Saleem's mind. He claims to have an intuitive knowledge of the lives of his parents and grandparents, and be able to read the minds of others born on the first day of Indian independence. He also lends credence to the superstitious fantasies of some of the illiterate characters in the story

 Kudos and Caveats

> *Midnight's Children* easily won the prestigious Booker Prize for literature in 1981 and was unanimously voted to receive a second, commemorative Booker Prize, a "Booker of Bookers" in 1993 as well.

who have important intuitions and insights about the world. Thus, the magic in the novel often provides characters who would otherwise be powerless with a measure of power.

The narrator tells of how his grandmother "eavesdropped on her daughters' dreams" to find out what was going on between them and the men who were interested in them. The dreams themselves are full of mysterious insight into the people involved, their futures, and the future of India. All the dreams and mind-reading helps make sense of things that otherwise seem bizarre or meaningless.

More Charmers

The following are just a few of many other magical realist novels worth checking out:

- Isabel Allende's (1942–) *House of the Spirits* (1985)
- Italo Calvino's (1923–1985) *Mr. Palomar* (1983)
- Peter Carey's (1943–) *Illywhacker* (1985)
- Gabriel García Márquez's (1928–) *One Hundred Years of Solitude* (1967)

Cyber-Fi

Another postmodern literary and cultural phenomenon that's elicited a great deal of attention is *cyberpunk*. The term refers to a combination of cybernetics—the concept of control by means of information flow—and "punk," a countercultural movement that started in Britain's rock music scene during the 1970s. Cyberpunk began as an innovation within science fiction and has gone a long way toward taking over sci fi in the postmodern era.

Don't Call 'Em Geeks

Cybernetics emerged in the late 1940s as a field devoted to explaining organizational systems in living and in nonliving things such as computers. It is especially concerned with the notion of control by means of information flow. Since the 1940s, of course, cybernetic technology has changed the world.

Cyberpunk has literary origins in pulp science fiction and subcultural origins in the jaded youth movement that began in the late 1970s. Punk music and subculture expressed the frustration and disaffection of working-class young people with commercialized, prettified society. Punks were interested in rejecting mainstream rules and norms.

The term *cyberpunk* was first used as the title of a short story by Bruce Bethke that appeared in the pulp serial *Amazing Science Fiction Stories* (1983). The story focuses on the exploits of some young computer hackers. Hacking involves the use of computer technologies in ways not intended by those who put them in place, usually either to cause mischief or to steal protected information. Most hacking is illegal. It can also lead to innovation.

Canon Fodder

Some of the many notable cyberpunk offerings out there include these:

Pat Cadigan's (1953–) *Synners* (1991)

K. W. Jeter's (1950–) *Noir* (1998)

Rudy Rucker's (1946–) *The Ware Tetralogy* (1982–2000)

Bruce Sterling (1954–), editor, *Mirrorshades: The Cyberpunk Anthology* (1986)

Joan D. Vinge's (1948–) *Psion* (1985)

Hackers of the 1980s and 1990s resemble punks of the 1970s in their rejection of mainstream rules and hollow, commercial values. So cyberpunk draws on this punk animosity to suggest that, even as life becomes increasingly dependent on technology, some people can find ways to use it for their own ends, rather than according to protocols set up by corporate capitalism.

Brain Link

Cyberpunk stories tend to be set in the future—usually the near future when corporate control has spread its tentacles everywhere except the hearts and minds of young cyberpunks. These characters are both plugged in and left out. They are technologically connected to the world—or worlds—around them, but are economic and political outsiders, struggling to survive in a high-tech society governed by greed, corporate control, and ruthless power.

They're also struggling to make sense of reality, which is fraught with computer-generated delusions that get plugged into their brains. "Virtual reality"—the notion that three-dimensional existence can be simulated through digital media—looms large in cyberpunk and is often difficult to distinguish from reality, per se. Human minds as well as bodies get taken over by cybernetic technology so brains and computers become interoperational. It's often hard to tell who's the end user!

A Hard Case

A watershed cyberpunk work is William Gibson's novel *Neuromancer* (1984), about a hacker named Case who was formerly employed by racketeers to steal high-security data. When he double-crossed his employers, they took revenge by poisoning him, which left him paralyzed and unable to continue work as a hacker. He is rehabilitated by a new, mysterious employer who has Case's body surgically altered in order to control him more easily. He becomes romantically involved with a bionic assassin and bodyguard named Molly and goes on to unravel a series of intrigues surrounding his new employer.

> **Canon Fodder**
>
> In 1984, William Gibson's *Neuromancer* won the "triple crown" of sci-fi literary awards: the Hugo, the Nebula, and the Philip K. Dick Memorial Award.

Case is a morally ambiguous character whose chief concern is for himself. Yet he lives in a morally ambiguous world where right and wrong seem like irrelevant considerations. Instead, corporate powers compete with one another for control and exert control over everything, right down to Case's bodily functions. Meanwhile, he's temporarily deceived by an encounter with a girlfriend in artificial reality!

Now Is the Future

While cyberpunk got its start as a subgenre of science fiction, it has made its presence known in other media, in youth subculture, and in the academy as well. Its broad interest resonates with the importance of computer technology and corporate power in our lives. It seems quintessentially postmodern in its concern with power, mass technology, the self and otherness, and conflicts over representation and control.

> **Grains of Trivium**
>
> Feminist Donna Haraway wrote an essay called "A Cyborg Manifesto" (1991) that draws on the idea of a cybernetic organism to define and explain her theoretical attitude toward gender. Haraway refutes the notion that gender is an essential biological characteristic.

Cyberpunk stories have been released as hit Hollywood movies. A number of people have embraced cyberpunk as a lifestyle. Cyberpunk scenarios have also been incorporated into video games. Could video game studies emerge on the academic horizon in the near future?

The Least You Need to Know

♦ The postmodern era can be characterized by its partial, limited truths that can be reappropriated by different groups of people.

♦ The theater of the absurd enacts the idea of existential meaninglessness.

♦ Magical realism draws on marvels and miracles to work through the conflicts and complexities of postcolonial existence.

♦ Cyberpunk literature taps into people's anxieties about computer technology and corporate control.

Chapter 22

... And Read All Over

In This Chapter

- Because there's more to life than literature—cultural studies
- Practicing what we preach: cultural theory and the new academy
- And then some: pluralist knowledge
- Fine lines and assembly lines: high culture versus mass culture
- A seller's market: Adorno's critique of the culture industry

While literature has been losing something of its privileged status as a distinctly important body of writing and cultural expression, the techniques of literary study have been proving useful in looking at all kinds of cultural forms—written and otherwise. As a result, approaches to lit study have been widening their focus to include cultural study.

The expanded focus includes popular culture, regional cultures, marginal subcultures, and all the material, media, and ideological forms they produce. Almost anything is fair game; graffiti, corporate décor, microfinance, television, film, music, and cyberspace are all worth examining, interpreting, contextualizing, and deconstructing. And yes, there's a strong theoretical emphasis to most cultural studies.

Cultural theory is closely related to lit theory. It deals with relationships among discourse, power, identities, and subjectivity. At the same time, it's often open to the influence of other academic disciplines, including anthropology, sociology, psychology, history, communications, and economics. It's a whole new academy.

New Theories, Wider Focus

The theoretical approaches to literary study that have developed over the course of the past 50 years or so have radically challenged the privileged position of literature in the academy and in society. The long-standing belief that literature consists of great works of genius that are specially worthy of appreciation and study has been cast into serious doubt. As a result, schools are having to rethink what to teach, and students, what to study.

There's More to Life Than Literature

A widespread, growing awareness that all cultural expressions are political and represent power interests raises a question: *Why study literature as opposed to anything else?* Increasingly, literature appears as only one of many aspects of culture. There are plenty of other interesting things to study. In addition, literature appears to be embedded in power interests that many choose to resist rather than endorse and celebrate.

Kudos and Caveats

Some exponents of cultural studies have claimed that cultural studies and lit studies can flourish together and provide mutual support for one another.

For one thing, dead white guys are not for everybody. Some see traditional lit study as entrenched and overacademic and, therefore, removed from contemporary issues and concerns. It's becoming increasingly difficult to make the case that Shakespeare is relevant in our time—and increasingly easy to make the case that traditional academic disciplines are too narrow to examine culture as a whole.

For another thing, although plenty of new, multicultural literature exists that wasn't written by dead white guys—that is socially, politically, and culturally engaged and that reflects a large variety of cultural backgrounds—many scholars are concerned about this literature, too. Some have argued that this emerging multicultural literature does not represent the authentic alternative voices of marginalized cultures as is commonly supposed.

Instead, it exists to satisfy a market for "marginalized" literature that's generated by the academy and filled by the global publishing industry. It could be that multicultural literature reflects the values of the academicians who choose what to teach and publishers who decide what to sell as much as the values of those who write it. These writers, in turn, are generally well educated and therefore may not actually represent the truly marginalized. If we really want to study marginalized cultures, it may make better sense not to focus on literature, but on other forms of cultural expression instead.

Don't Ask *What*, Ask *How*

For these and other reasons, cultural studies programs have emerged in colleges and universities around the world. They are generally intended for the study of cultural signification in general—not just literature, although lit study is often included. In fact, it's kind of hard to imagine what couldn't be included in a cultural studies program. The field is defined more by its approaches than by its far-flung subject matter.

This approach actually arose largely out of literary study. In fact, the broad theoretical orientation of cultural studies is consistent with poststructuralist theory and political criticism (see Chapters 5 and 6). You could say that cultural studies is a logical extension of literary study in light of poststructuralist thinking. It applies critical approaches developed for literature study beyond the study of literature.

> **Kudos and Caveats** _____
>
> Cultural studies programs often emphasize the fluidity of the field and the potential for change and innovation. What counts as knowledge may be subject to new definitions that the traditional academic disciplines don't necessarily recognize.

Fitting In

Cultural studies may seem like a huge grab bag of subjects and approaches from all over the academic map. In fact, colleges and universities do different things with their cultural studies programs. They may be closely allied with English departments, communications departments, or art history departments. They may fit in with other programs such as black studies, women's studies, or American studies. In some ways, all cultural programs are different. But most have some key features in common.

Act Locally, Think Globally

Cultural studies programs often have a regional character, related in some way to a specific area of the country and arising out of specific intellectual traditions and cultural values. A regional focus may express concern about, and even resistance to, forces of globalization. At the same time, globalization itself is an important issue in cultural studies. How should a global society develop and operate? And what should culture be like in a global society?

def•i•ni•tion

Pluralism is the view that more than one way of thinking and behaving may be acceptable. Relativism is the view that there is no single, overarching set of values or beliefs that is good for everybody, but that different groups are right to embrace their own perspectives.

Instead of suggesting that everyone should do the same things in the same ways as everyone else, cultural studies tend to be *pluralist*—drawing on a number of theoretical orientations and expressing various points of view—as well as *relativist*—recognizing that different groups see things in different ways and that no single way to see things is right for everyone. At the same time, there's often a pervasive concern for social justice.

In fact, a major challenge—both academic and political—is to reconcile cultural pluralism with mutual respect across cultures. Scholars generally recognize a need for power and authority but have yet to agree on the best ways to gain, use, and distribute them. Pluralist and relativist positions often imply that overarching power relations have yet to be worked out.

In addition, cultural studies are often interdisciplinary, drawing on approaches from across the humanities. Cultural studies conferences may include participants from several different fields. A cultural studies program may encourage or even require students to take courses in different subjects.

All Connected

But for all the variety, cultural studies tends to focus on the relationship between cultural signification (what everything means) and political power (who benefits from the ways we do everything). As with lit study, these issues can shed light on how we think and why. But unlike lit study, "we" includes more than readers and writers.

Grains of Trivium

One way of understanding the cultural significance of political power is by means of the term *cultural capital*, proposed by sociologist Pierre Bourdieu. Cultural capital refers to whatever society recognizes as "valuable" because it's either good or persuasive. Anything people want, whether it's a certain tone of voice or the prestige of owning something expensive, can be used as cultural capital.

The theoretical insights of poststructuralist political criticism apply not only to literature, but to culture in general. The point isn't that there's no difference between literature and TV, or literature and graffiti, but that literature, TV, and graffiti all reflect in different ways the workings of power through cultural signification. Thus, it makes sense for political criticism to widen its focus of study to include nonliterary forms.

Writ Large

Despite tendencies toward pluralism and relativism, not all cultural expressions are equal in the world of cultural studies. Cultural scholars recognize and distinguish among different kinds of culture. These distinctions aren't written in stone, but they provide some useful guideposts that have been in place since early in the twentieth century.

Culture: High vs. Mass

Two major areas of concern within cultural studies are *high culture* and *mass culture*. Both kinds of culture represent big power interests that skew the cultural playing field.

High culture refers to the elite, upper-class culture that predominated in Europe from the eighteenth into the twentieth century. It includes such cultural expressions as the fine arts and great literature—poetry, oil paint-

def•i•ni•tion

High culture is elite, bourgeois culture of the affluent and privileged classes. It includes the fine arts and great literature. **Mass culture** is culture that's commodified and mass produced by industry and sold for profit to consumers.

ing, ballet, and the symphony. In contrast, mass culture includes all cultural expressions that are mass produced by industry and marketed as commodities to consumers. These include music recordings, films and videos, books, toys, clothes, and more.

Today there's considerable overlap between "high" and "mass" culture, but in the late nineteenth and early twentieth centuries, they were thought to be in conflict.

What Are We, Barbarians?

The well-educated, affluent, and elite proponents of high culture regarded the rise of mass culture with alarm. To them, mass culture appeared to be crass, tasteless, value-less, stupid, and generally inferior to what they thought was good. In fact, the rise of English literature as a college course of study had a lot to with worries about the narrow and materialistic influence of mass culture. People thought literature might prove to be a good antidote to jazz music and the funny papers.

Since the rise of mass culture, the importance of high culture has faded considerably. At the same time, the high-culture concerns about mass culture have faded as well. Meanwhile, however, a critique of mass culture emerged from a different quarter. This critique stands as one of the foundations of cultural studies and is still debated today.

Industrial Strength

Some of the first academic studies of mass culture were undertaken by Theodor Adorno (1903–1969), a Marxist thinker and member of the famous Frankfurt School in Germany during the 1920s. Adorno proposed influential ideas about what he called the "culture industry." The culture industry is responsible for all the mass-produced elements of culture.

> ### Grains of Trivium
>
> Members of the Frankfurt School conducted a famous study of the "authoritarian personality" to explore the causes of fascism in society. They found that people who are expected to abide by strict standards of personal behavior and who face harsh threats and punishments for disobedience are likely to be highly intolerant of anyone different from themselves. Yikes!

You Are Getting Sleepy ...

Adorno was attempting to understand the failure of the proletarian revolution and the horrors of the Holocaust in the wake of World War II. He believed certain historical and cultural forces prevented people from thinking clearly about their lives and human society. The cultural industry was a particularly important and powerful force, exerting a widespread negative influence on society.

In Adorno's view, mass-produced cultural commodities exert a numbing effect on people's sense of the world and their place in it. In various ways, it makes people less inclined to question their situation, notice problems, and think creatively to find solutions. As a result, consumers allow themselves to be passively manipulated and exploited by the culture industry.

Muddling Along

Because cultural products are mass produced for profit-making purposes, they are standardized, predictable commodities. Pop songs, comic books, and TV shows may seem different from one another, but the differences are superficial. In reality, they are all created from the same predictable formula that prevents artistic innovation.

For example, in Adorno's view, pop music is predictably repetitive, easy to create and produce, and requires little or no thought to understand. People listen to it while doing monotonous, boring jobs because the music serves as a distraction. They don't listen carefully enough to deepen their appreciation or understanding of music—only just enough to divert themselves from their work.

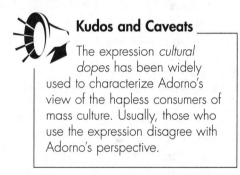

Kudos and Caveats

The expression *cultural dopes* has been widely used to characterize Adorno's view of the hapless consumers of mass culture. Usually, those who use the expression disagree with Adorno's perspective.

This mindless condition helps explain why people accept the status quo, even though they're exploited as workers and manipulated as consumers. Mass-produced culture serves to distract people from the monotony of their lives without stimulating them to change it. It doesn't challenge them to see things in new ways. As a result, they accept their circumstances rather than work to improve them.

Culture R Us

Of course, not everyone accepts Adorno's critique of mass culture. Some say, to the contrary, that people have fun with it and use it in their own ways. In spending money on mass culture, they're making creative choices and responding to products that "speak to them" in special ways. They are also learning from mass culture in an inexpensive and pleasurable way while experiencing the diversity of the marketplace.

In either case, mass culture is a useful concept in cultural studies. Cultural studies may focus on how mass culture is used in unexpected ways or on how local cultural expressions like graffiti or tattoos may either get taken over by mass culture or persist independently. These issues are not simply academic; they have a lot to do with how people actually live their lives. This direct relevance to life today is part of the appeal of the field.

Net Culture

A potentially harmful influence of the culture industry remains a concern in cultural studies. The concern extends to the media industry and its special ability to shape people's thoughts and attitudes. More and more news providers are owned by fewer and fewer corporations. That doesn't exactly bode well for a pluralist society!

This concern remains in place despite shifts in terrain presented by the Internet. Thanks to the Internet, anyone can, in theory, get involved in the culture industry as a producer as well as a consumer. Thus, it has the potential to introduce radical change into the culture industry. It also may change academia.

Lit Lives On

Although cultural studies programs have become firmly established on the academic scene, they do not appear likely to replace English programs anytime soon. For all the problems and debates that go along with it, literature remains a huge, important, and vital field of study. English departments are crucial to academia, and literary scholarship is resilient enough to flourish amid ongoing institutional and intellectual change.

In addition, English programs teach and promote literacy in ways cultural studies programs do not. They may also be better able to focus on the historical aspects of culture than cultural studies programs because historical culture is preserved most clearly and fully in written works. And finally, literature is something people will want to keep reading and discussing.

The Least You Need to Know

- Cultural studies applies theoretical approaches developed in lit study to all aspects of culture.

- Cultural studies tend to stress the relations between signification (meaning) and political power.

- Theodor Adorno's critique of the culture industry argues that mass culture has a harmful influence on society.

- The field of English literature may be old, but it's not obsolete.

Lit Gloss

abstraction   Anything that isn't tangible. In literature, it can be opposed to imagery, the representation of tangible things.

accismus   A pretended, ironic refusal of something you want or denial of something about you that is true. For example: "No, I'm not going to eat that chocolate. I dislike the taste of sugar and cocoa butter."

active reading   Reading to make new discoveries beyond what might be clear and obvious. Active reading includes asking questions about a text and looking for possible answers.

aestheticism   A movement that took place near the end of the nineteenth century that aimed to free art from conventional Victorian morality.

allegory   An extended metaphor used in (or read into) a drama or narrative.

alliteration   The repetition of consonant sounds close to each other.

anacoluthon   A sentence that changes its grammatical structure in the middle, often to suggest disturbance or excitement. For example: "We had almost reached the finished line and then the race had to have been fixed from the beginning."

anadiplosis   Repetition at the start of a sentence of the concluding word or phrase in the previous sentence. For example: "There's only so much exercise you can get on an airplane. An airplane is not the greatest place to work out."

antistrophe   One of three sections of the Greek dramatic chorus and the Pindaric ode, along with the strophe and epode. These forms may be repeated in sequence within a single ode.

aporia   A term used in deconstruction, absence of meaning and multiplicity of possible meanings within a text.

apostrophe   A figure of speech that consists of an address to an absent person, a nonexistent person, an inanimate object, or an abstraction as if that person or thing could hear and understand.

assonance   The repetition of vowel sounds close to each other.

aubade (or dawn song)   A lyric form stemming from the Middle Ages that treats the subject of two lovers waking up together. It may deal with the joy of being together or with the sorrow of having to part.

bad quarto   A published, pirated play reconstructed from memory by someone who acted in it. *Quarto* refers to how a big sheet of paper was folded to yield four pages per sheet in a book (*quarto* means "four").

bard   An Old English minstrel (musician, poet, and storyteller). Years after the Old English period, "the Bard" was used as a popular honorary epithet for William Shakespeare.

bildungsroman   (German for "novel of development") A novel that traces the development of a young person from childhood or adolescence to maturity. It is often written in the form of an autobiography.

blank verse   Unrhymed iambic pentameter poetry, often used in poetic drama and narrative verse.

bombast   Dramatic dialogue that's pompous and grandiose and is associated with Senecan tragedy. The term comes from an old French word used to refer to padding material used in clothing.

caesura   A pause or break in a line of verse. It usually occurs when a grammatical pause, and a comma or period, falls within the line.

canon (of English literature)   An unofficial grouping of works by authors whose importance has become generally recognized by literature scholars.

carpe diem **motif**   Named from a phrase used in an ode by ancient Roman poet Horace (first century B.C.E.) meaning "seize the day." It was widely used by the English cavalier poets.

catharsis   A purging of the emotions that, according to Aristotle, results from attending a tragedy.

cavalier   Type of verse from the seventeenth century that is characterized by smooth elegance, a focus on beautiful things (including women), and an interest in life's pleasures. It took a relaxed stance toward morality.

characterization   The representation of personality in a work of literature. Character may be delineated through all manner of narrative techniques, including behavior, description, imagery, and interaction and contrast with other characters.

chiasmus   A verbal pattern in two parts in which the second part is like a mirror image of the first.

chivalry   The idealized code of the medieval nobility. It stressed honesty and integrity in living up to one's social obligations, courtesy to others, and deference to ladies.

close reading   A careful analysis of a text that discusses specific details within it to shed light on an aspect of the work or the work as a whole.

comedy of manners   A dramatic form concerned with the social conventions of polite society. It may make fun simultaneously of those who abide by these conventions and those who don't.

concrete term   A term for anything tangible; an image. Poetry often makes abstractions vivid by representing them in concrete terms.

condition of England novel   A novel concerned with the negative social and economic impacts of industrialism.

connotation   The secondary significance a word acquires through association that goes beyond its literal meaning. Contrast *denotation*.

cultural difference   A radical discontinuity between cultures that poses a challenge to mutual understanding.

cultural studies   An emerging academic discipline that has grown out of the field of English literature that applies techniques of literary study to any and all areas of culture.

cyberpunk   A subgenre of science fiction that taps into people's anxieties about computer technology and corporate control.

cycle   A collection of works on a common theme such as Charlemagne or the Trojan War. Cycles typically represent the work of several different authors brought together into a group. Cycles are often groups of romance narrative, although mystery plays are dramatic cycles.

deconstruction   The project of discovering the instability of language.

deism   The view that God, the creator of the universe, exists but does not continue to influence the natural order.

denotation   The literal significance of a word. Its dictionary definition considered apart from associations the word may evoke. Contrast *connotation*.

diction   The choice of words used in a text or utterance. A writer's diction may indicate something about his or her values or attitude.

différance   A French term used in deconstruction suggesting that signifiers differ from what they signify and defer their significance to other signifiers. In other words, due to the gap between language and reality, and due to the interconnectedness of signifiers, you can't locate a fixed, stable meaning in any one place.

discourse   A conventional way of thinking, speaking, and writing that defines and limits what can be accepted as meaningful and true. It is shaped by cultural, political, and institutional priorities.

dramatic monologues   Poems in the form of speeches delivered by characters in dramatic situations. These speakers epitomize the "unreliable narrator" whose perspective you can't completely trust but whose account is all you have to go on.

eclogues   Pastoral lyrics—poems that idealize the life of shepherds.

enjambment   The continuation of the grammatical flow from one line of verse to the next.

epic   Heroic poetry with an important subject of crucial national or cultural significance, together with a grand, lofty tone. Many epics tell the story of the founding of a nation or race by means of a battle or journey.

epic simile   An extended comparison that gets developed in considerable detail over the course of several lines of verse.

epistles   Letters, usually formal.

epistolary novel   A novel made up of correspondence between characters.

epithalamium   A poem that treats the subject of a couple's wedding night.

epode   One of three sections of the Greek dramatic chorus and the Pindaric ode, along with the strophe and antistrophe. These forms may be repeated in sequence within a single ode.

essay   A prose form originated by the French Renaissance humanist Michel de Montaigne as an experimental and skeptical approach to writing.

essentialism   When the term is applied to gender, it's the view that differences between men and women are inherent rather than socially constructed.

estate   A medieval term that refers to social status as well as land and other possessions, all of which were passed along from father to son. Medieval Anglos belonged to one of three estates: nobility, clergy, or commons.

eternizing conceit   A convention common in Renaissance lyric poetry that suggests that the poem will confer immortality on its subject and on the poet.

fair copies   Manuscripts of plays professionally prepared by a scribe for a theater company or a publisher. Contrast *foul papers*, the messy manuscripts drafted by a playwright.

fashionable novel   Sometimes called the "silver fork" novel, it focuses on the lives of the rich and elegant.

figurative language   The opposite of literal language. It includes any use of language intended to mean something other than what it literally says. It includes metaphor, simile, metonymy, and irony.

First Folio   The 1623 collection of William Shakespeare's plays published after his death by members of his acting company.

flashback   The narrative devise of switching the timeline backward to a point in the past.

folio   A book made of big sheets folded in two. *Folio* means "fold."

foreshadow   The narrative devise of hinting at events that have yet to unfold.

foul papers   The messy manuscripts drafted by a playwright. During the Renaissance, they sometimes served as the manuscript source for a printed play.

free indirect discourse   The narrative technique of shifting freely between a first-person and an interior third-person point of view.

free verse   Poetry that has no fixed meter, although it has rhythmic lines and line breaks and is therefore presumably composed with rhythmic qualities in mind. It came into vogue during the modern period.

georgics   Poems about farming.

Gothic novels   Novels about gruesome doings and supernatural horrors, usually set far away and long ago. The form emerged during the eighteenth century but gained popularity and respectability in the nineteenth, as the imagination in literature came to be more highly regarded.

hagiography   The study of saints. More specifically, it is a saint's biography.

hamartia   The human failing or "tragic flaw" of the protagonist in a tragedy.

hegemony   Cultural power that works alongside overt force (the police, military, etc.) to control people's thoughts and behavior.

heroic couplets   Rhymed pairs of iambic pentameter lines used in much heroic tragedy of the Renaissance and in Augustan narrative poetry.

high culture   Elite, bourgeois culture of the affluent and privileged classes. It includes the fine arts and great literature.

historical difference   Refers to the radical discontinuity between people who lived in the past and those alive today.

hyperbole   Exaggeration; overstatement. For example: "A flood of tears."

ideology   Made up of the ideas, beliefs, and values shared by members of a society. Ideology is shaped by political interests and serves power interests in ways we might not recognize.

imagery   Any tangible thing named in a language, regardless of whether that thing is literal or figurative.

irony   The use of words to convey the opposite of their literal meaning.

kend heiti   Closely resembles a kenning, except it's literal instead of figurative.

kenning   A figurative stock phrase used to describe something in Old English and Old Norse narrative poetry.

lyrical I   A conventional poetic speaker of much lyric poetry.

magical realism   An attribute of fiction that draws on marvels and miracles to work through the conflicts and complexities of postcolonial existence.

marginalization   The complex social process that pushes certain people outside (to the margins of) mainstream society, usually because they are perceived as a threat to shared values.

mass culture   Culture that's commodified and mass produced by industry and sold for profit to consumers.

metaphor   An image used figuratively to represent something it isn't, as in "love is a rose."

metaphysical poetry   Poetry characterized by elaborate, sometimes bizarre use of metaphor; rough, rugged versification; dramatic speakers; and paradoxical reasoning.

meter   The rhythmic structure of poetry.

metonym   A figure of speech that uses an attribute or portion of a thing to stand for the thing itself, such as "wheels" for a car or "printed page" for books in general.

mimesis   The ancient Greek word for "imitation." Aristotle used it to describe the way drama imitates life.

multiculturalism   On one hand, the fact of diverse cultures within society and, on the other hand, an array of debates over how to understand and respond to this fact.

mystery plays   Plays presented during the Middle Ages by guilds on feast days. They depict important events in Christian history.

mystification   The process of denying or disguising political values by misrepresenting them as natural, universal, or transcendent ideals.

neo-Platonism   A philosophy of the Middle Ages and Renaissance that accommodated the thinking of Plato to Christian theology.

New Criticism   An important critical movement that took hold in the early decades of the twentieth century. It stresses the importance of paying close attention to the literary text as a way to develop critical intelligence.

onomatopoeia   The use of words that sound like the things they mean. The word comes from a Greek word that means "name making." *Poeia*, or "making," is the Greek root for "poetry."

pageant   Originally a platform wagon used for transporting and staging medieval mystery plays, which would be performed in various locations successively on the same day. The term has come to refer to any public procession or a staged celebration of a historical event.

panegyric   A poem praising someone for their achievements, stemming from ancient Greece.

persona   An assumed character such as a character in a play.

personification   The device of presenting abstractions as human characters.

perspective   The position of the narrator in relation to the story. Narratives may be told from a first-person perspective ("I did such and such"), a third-person perspective ("He and she did thus and so"), an omniscient point of view that appears to know everything, or a combination of any or all of them.

plagiarism   The crime of claiming authorship for work written by somebody else.

plot   The pattern of events represented in a narrative. It may be linear or episodic, unfolding in segments.

pluralism   The view that more than one way of thinking and behaving may be acceptable.

political criticism   Concerned with the power of discourse to shape subjects and societies, and includes New Historicism, postcolonialism, feminism, and queer theory.

polyptoton   A construction that brings together different grammatical forms of words that have a common root. For example: "'Tis not through envy of thy happy lot / But being too happy in thine happiness …" (Keats).

poststructuralism   Major, influential thrust of postmodern theory. The term refers to the insight that the structure apparent in language and culture (described by the structuralists) is unstable, both internally and in relation to whatever's outside of it.

presence   A term used in deconstruction for a delusory belief or assumption that stable meaning is located within a text. The idea of presence ignores the fact that meaning depends on what it is not.

prosody (or versification)   Refers to the sound and structure of poetry, including meter, rhyme, assonance, and alliteration.

quarto   A book made of big sheets of paper folded into four pages per sheet (*quarto* means "four").

radical chic   The hip, trendy appropriation by the cultural elite of the style that goes along with a radical political stance. Radical chic makes radical politics more visible as style, but less effective as a means of political change.

realism   In fiction, the concern with representing life as it might actually be lived. The term is problematic, however, as modes of verbal representation keep changing over time together with cultural conceptions of reality.

reception history   The study of the ways events and artifacts are interpreted at different moments in history. Both literary scholars and historians recognize this concept.

relativism   The view that there is no single, overarching set of values or beliefs that is good for everybody, but that different groups are right to embrace their own perspectives.

rhetoric   The art of persuasion, studied in ancient times as applied to oratory. Since then, rhetoric has been used as a way of analyzing other kinds of speech and writing, including both poetry and prose.

rhyme scheme   The pattern of rhymes in a stanza.

satire   A literary work that exposes evil or folly through the use of irony, ridicule, or derision.

secularization   The gradual, historical decline of religion as a controlling social force.

semantics   The branch of linguistics concerned with meaning.

sensation novel   A melodramatic novel devoted to scandalous doings, guilty secrets, and lurid intrigues.

sensibility   Susceptibility to powerful feelings, a literary quality that emerged during the late eighteenth century.

sentiment   The expression of any emotion that aims to suggest the goodness of a character or of people in general.

signifier   A term that refers to something else, a signified. Words are signifiers, but so are other things that express meaning within a culture.

simile   A metaphor in which the figurative comparison is made explicitly, often by use of *like* or *as*.

soliloquy   A speech conventionally understood to convey the private thoughts of the character who delivers it.

speaker   Whoever does the talking in a poem, whether a persona or the poet's actual voice.

stanza   A repeated pattern of lines and rhymes analogous to a verse in a song.

stream-of-consciousness novel   A modernist form that puts a story together by tracing the thoughts and feelings of its characters rather than through the voice of a detached narrator.

strong misreading   A cogent interpretation of a text to mean things its author never intended. The concept has been used by literature critic Harold Bloom in explaining, for example, how early Christians "misread" the Hebrew Bible in writing the gospels.

strophe   One of three sections of the Greek dramatic chorus and the Pindaric ode, along with the antistrophe and epode. These forms may be repeated in sequence within a single ode.

structuralism   A theoretical approach, originally to linguistics and later to anthropology. Structuralists regard their field, whether language or culture, as a structure that's organized internally rather than from without.

subjects   Individuals insofar as they are shaped and delineated by discourse. In this view, we become who we are, for all practical and observable purposes, in response to the cultural influences of discourse.

sublime   A characteristic of art or nature that inspires a feeling of grandeur and mystery. For example: ancient ruins, a storm-swept landscape, or the fall of Satan in Milton's *Paradise Lost*.

syllepsis   The use of a single word in two different senses at once. For example: "I just quit smoking and my job."

tenor (of a metaphor)   The literal term of a metaphorical comparison.

tetralogy   A group of four works.

theater of the absurd   The dramatic genre of the 1950s that enacts the idea of existential meaninglessness.

Theophrastan character   A prose form describing personality types. It was extremely popular during the seventeenth century but has died out since then.

tone   The mood or emotional attitude evoked or reflected in a written work.

trace   In deconstruction, things that are absent from yet suggested by a text. A trace may be the opposite of a written word.

typology   The study of biblical symbolism. Biblical "types" could be found not only in the Old and New Testaments, but in nature and society as well.

vehicle (of a metaphor)   A figurative term of a metaphorical comparison.

verisimilitude   The semblance of truth, a quality that helps distinguish the early novel from fable and romance.

Read On, MacDuff

In this appendix, you'll find some reading to tide you over during your spare time. Included first is a list of many of the greatest hits of English literature: the canon. Of course, it can be (and is) argued as to what belongs in a list like this. Many, many works could be added; some could be removed. What's here represents works and writers most commonly taught in college English courses over the course of the last century. Next comes a big list of American literature. Finally, you'll find a selection of postcolonial literature written in English. And when you've finished with this ….

Early Medieval Period (Fifth to Eleventh Centuries)

Beowulf

Riddles and Charms

Late Medieval Period (Twelfth to Fifteenth Centuries)

Geoffrey Chaucer (1343–1400)

The Canterbury Tales

The Gawain Poet

Sir Gawain and the Green Knight

Drama

Everyman

The Second Shepherd's Play

Thomas Malory (1405–1471)

Le Morte d'Arthur

Margery Kempe (1373–1438)

The Book of Margery Kempe

Renaissance (1540–1670)

Sir Philip Sidney (1554–1586)

Astrophil and Stella

An Apology for Poetry

Christopher Marlowe (1564–1592)

"The Passionate Shepherd to His Love"

Doctor Faustus

Thomas More (1478–1535)

Utopia

Edmund Spenser (1552–1599)

The Fairie Queene

"Epithalamion"

William Shakespeare (1564–1616)

Sonnets

Hamlet

King Lear

Othello

Macbeth

Richard II

Richard III

Henry IV, Part 1

Love's Labour's Lost

Much Ado About Nothing

The Tempest

John Donne (1572–1631)

"The Good-Morrow"

"The Canonization"

"A Valediction: Forbidding Mourning"

"The Sun Rising"

"Air and Angels"

"The Relic"

"Elegy XIX" (To His Mistress Going to Bed)

"Good Friday, 1613, Riding Westward"

"Hymn to God, My God, in My Sickness"

"Sermon XV" (The last enemy that shall be destroyed is death)

Ben Jonson (1572–1637)

"To Penshurst"

"To the Memory of My Beloved Master William Shakespeare"

"To the Memory of Sir Lucius Cary and Sir H. Morison"

Volpone

Bartholomew Fair

Sir Francis Bacon (1561–1626)

Essays

The Advancement of Learning

Robert Herrick (1591–1674)

"Prayer to Ben Jonson"

"His Grange, or Private Wealth"

"Upon Julia's Clothes"

"The Country Life"

Andrew Marvell (1621–1678)

"To His Coy Mistress"

"Upon Appleton House"

"The Garden"

"The Mower Against Gardens"

Robert Burton (1577–1640)

The Anatomy of Melancholy

John Milton (1608–1674)

>*Paradise Lost*

>"Lycidas"

>*Samson Agonistes*

>"L'Allegro"

>"Il Penseroso"

>"Areopagetica"

>"Of Education"

Abraham Cowley (1618–1677)

>*Works*

The Augustan Period (1670–1790)

Samuel Butler (1612–1680)

>*Hudibras*

>*Characters*

John Bunyan (1628–1688)

>*The Pilgrim's Progress*

William Wycherley (1640–1716)

>*The Country Wife*

William Congreve (1670–1729)

>*The Way of the World*

John Dryden (1631–1700)

>"Annus Mirabilis"

>"To the Memory of Anne Killegrew"

"Religio Laici"

"Absalom and Achitophel"

"To My Kinsman, John Driden"

"Essay of Dramatic Poetry"

All for Love

Aphra Behn (1640–1689)

Oroonoko

Joseph Addison (1672–1719) and Richard Steele (1672–1729)

The Spectator

The Tatler

Daniel Defoe (1660–1731)

Robinson Crusoe

Moll Flanders

Alexander Pope (1688–1744)

"Eloisa to Abelard"

"The Rape of the Lock"

"Epistle to Burlington"

"Epistle to a Lady"

"Epistle to Arbuthnot"

Jonathan Swift (1667–1745)

"A Modest Proposal"

Tale of the Tub

Gulliver's Travels

"A Description of a City Shower"

"Verses on the Death of Dr. Swift"

Samuel Richardson (1689–1761)

Pamela

Henry Fielding (1701–1754)

Tom Jones

William Collins (1721–1759)

"Ode to Fear"

"Ode on the Popular Superstitions of the Highlands"

Thomas Gray (1716–1771)

"Eton College Ode"

"Elegy Written in a Country Churchyard"

James Boswell (1740–1795)

The Life of Samuel Johnson

Samuel Johnson (1709–1784)

"The Vanity of Human Wishes"

Rasselas

The Rambler

The Idler

"On the Death of Dr. Levet"

Fanny Burney (1752–1840)

Evelina

Robert Burns (1759–1796)

"To a Mouse"

"Epistle to Lapraik"

"Address to the Unco Guid"

"Holy Willie's Prayer"

The Romantic Period (1790–1840)

William Blake (1757–1827)

"The Marriage of Heaven and Hell"

"London"

"The Sick Rose"

"The Tyger"

"Mock On, Mock On, Voltaire, Rousseau"

William Wordsworth (1770–1850)

"Preface to Lyrical Ballads"

"Tintern Abbey"

"Resolution and Independence"

"Yew Trees"

"Elegiac Stanzas" (Peele Castle)

Sonnet: "Westminster Bridge"

Sonnet: "The World Is Too Much with Us"

The Prelude

Ode: "Intimations of Immortality"

Samuel Taylor Coleridge (1772–1834)

"This Lime-Tree Bower My Prison"

"Rime of the Ancient Mariner"

"Kubla Kahn"

"Frost at Midnight"

"Dejection: An Ode"

Biographia Literaria

George Gordon, Lord Byron (1788–1824)

Childe Harold's Pilgrimage

Don Juan

Percy Bysshe Shelley (1792–1822)

"Hymn to Intellectual Beauty"

"England in 1819"

"Ode to the West Wind"

Adonais

A Defense of Poetry

John Keats (1795–1821)

"On First Looking into Chapman's Homer"

"The Elgin Marbles"

"The Eve of St. Agnes"

"Bright Star"

"Ode on a Grecian Urn"

"To Autumn"

Jane Austen (1775–1817)

Pride and Prejudice

Emma

The Victorian Period (1840–1900)

Charlotte Brontë (1816–1855)

Jane Eyre

Emily Brontë (1818–1848)

Wuthering Heights

Alfred, Lord Tennyson (1809–1892)

"Ulysses"

In Memoriam

Maud

"The Charge of the Light Brigade"

Idylls of the King

Robert Browning (1812–1889)

"Childe Roland to the Dark Tower Came"

"Caliban Upon Setebos"

"The Bishop Orders His Tomb"

"My Last Duchess"

"Fra Lippo Lippi"

"Andrea del Sarto"

Charles Dickens (1812–1870)

Oliver Twist

Our Mutual Friend

Little Dorrit

Bleak House

George Eliot (1819–1880)

Adam Bede

Middlemarch

William Makepeace Thackeray (1811–1863)

Vanity Fair

Wilkie Collins (1824–1889)

Woman in White

Mary Braddon (1837–1915)

Lady Audley's Secret

Thomas Hardy (1840–1928)

The Return of the Native

The Mayor of Casterbridge

Tess of the D'Urbervilles

Jude the Obscure

Matthew Arnold (1822–1888)

"Destiny"

"Dover Beach"

"The Buried Life"

"Stanzas on the Grande Chartreuse"

Culture and Anarchy

Dante Gabriel Rossetti (1828–1882)

"The Blessed Damozel"

The House of Life: Sonnets

Christina Rossetti (1830–1894)

"Goblin Market"

Gerard Manley Hopkins (1844–1889)

"The Windhover"

"Duns Scotus's Oxford"

"Spring and Fall"

Oscar Wilde (1854–1900)

The Importance of Being Earnest

The Picture of Dorian Gray

Joseph Conrad (1857–1924)

Heart of Darkness

Nostromo

The Modern Period (1900–1945)

Wilfred Owen (1893–1918)

"Dulce et Decorum Est"

William Butler Yeats (1865–1939)

"The Rose of the World"

"The Fascination of What's Difficult"

"The Wild Swans at Coole"

"Easter 1916"

"The Second Coming"

"Sailing to Byzantium"

"Leda and the Swan"

"Among School Children"

"Crazy Jane Talks to the Bishop"

"Lapis Lazuli"

"The Circus Animals' Desertion"

Bernard Shaw (1856–1950)

Major Barbara

Saint Joan

Mrs. Warren's Profession

James Joyce (1882–1941)

Dubliners

Ulysses

Finnegan's Wake

D. H. Lawrence (1885–1930)

Women in Love

T. S. Eliot (1888–1965)

"The Love Song of J. Alfred Prufrock"

"The Waste Land"

"Journey of the Magi"

"Four Quartets: Little Gidding"

"Tradition and the Individual Talent"

Saumel Beckett (1906–1989)

Endgame

Waiting for Godot

Virginia Woolf (1882–1941)

Mrs. Dalloway

To the Lighthouse

A Room of One's Own

The Postmodern Period (1945–Present)

In this section, the list is less well established. There are so many works to choose from and not much agreement about which ones are most important.

Stevie Smith (1902–1971)

"Not Waving but Drowning"

"The New Age"

"The Galloping Cat"

George Orwell (1903–1950)

Animal Farm

1984

Louis MacNeice (1907–1963)

"Bagpipe Music"

"Good Dream"

Doris Lessing (1919–)

The Golden Notebook

Harold Pinter (1930–)

The Dumb Waiter

Philip Larkin (1922–1985)

"High Windows"

"Faith Healing"

"Ambulances"

Ted Hughes (1930–1998)

"A Dream of Horses"

"A Disaster"

Crow

Seamus Heaney (1939–)

"Churning Day"

"The Grauballe Man"

American Literature

Here's a big chronological reading list of American literature from pre-colonial times to recent years. You may find a number of works you've never heard of. Even so, there are plenty more deserving works that could be added.

John Smith (1580–1631)

> *Chronology of John Smith and Pocahontas*

Anne Bradstreet (1612–1672)

> "Upon the Burning of Our House by Night When Others Soundly Slept"
>
> "Contemplations"
>
> "A Dialogue Between Old England and New"
>
> "The Flesh and the Spirit"
>
> "The Four Ages of Man"

Benjamin Franklin (1706–1790)

> *Poor Richard's Almanac*
>
> *Autobiography*

Oloudah Equiano (1745–1801)

> *The Interesting Narrative of the Life of Oloudah Equiano, or Gustavus Vassa, the African*

Phillis Wheatley (1753–1784)

> "Liberty and Peace, A Poem"
>
> "A Farewell to America   To Mrs. S. W."
>
> "A Rebus, by Funeral Poem on the Death of C. E. An Infant of Twelve Months"
>
> "Ode to Neptune"
>
> "On Being Brought from Africa to America"
>
> "On Imagination"
>
> "On Recollection"
>
> "On Virtue"

Tecumseh (1768–1813)

> *We All Belong to One Family*

Charles Brockden Brown (1771–1810)

Wieland

Memoirs of Carwin the Biloquist

Washington Irving (1783–1859)

Rip Van Winkle

The Legend of Sleepy Hollow

The Alhambra

The Adventures of Captain Bonneville

James Fenimore Cooper (1789–1851)

The Last of the Mohicans

The Deerslayer

The Pathfinder

William Cullen Bryant (1794–1878)

"To a Waterfowl"

"The Death of Lincoln"

"An Indian at the Burial Place of His Fathers"

"The Death of Slavery"

"To an American Painter Departing for Europe"

Sojourner Truth (1797–1883)

"Ain't I a Woman"

Ralph Waldo Emerson (1803–1882)

"The American Scholar"

"Self-Reliance"

"Nature"

Nathaniel Hawthorne (1804–1864)

The Scarlet Letter

The House of Seven Gables

"Young Goodman Brown"

Henry Wadsworth Longfellow (1807–1882)

"The Song of Hiawatha"

"Evangeline"

"Paul Revere's Ride"

"The Courtship of Miles Standish"

John Greenleaf Whittier (1807–1892)

"The Witch of Wenham"

Snow-Bound: A Winter Idyll

"The Farewell: Of a Virginia Slave Mother to Her Daughters Sold into Southern Bondage"

"Barbara Frietchie"

"The Pumpkin"

Edgar Allan Poe (1809–1849)

"The Fall of the House of Usher"

"A Cask of Amontillado"

"The Tell-Tale Heart"

"The Pit and the Pendulum"

"Ligeia"

"The Murders in the Rue Morgue"

"The Raven"

"The Bells"

Oliver Wendell Holmes (1809–1894)

"The Chambered Nautilus"

"The Autocrat of the Breakfast-Table"

Harriet Beecher Stowe (1811–1896)

Uncle Tom's Cabin

Sojourner Truth, The Libyan Sibyl

Henry David Thoreau (1817–1862)

"Walden; or, Life in the Woods"

"Civil Disobedience"

Frederick Douglass (1817–1882)

Life of an American Slave

James Russell Lowell (1819–1891)

"The Vision of Sir Launfal"

"Under the Old Elm"

A Fable for Critics

Herman Melville (1819–1891)

Moby Dick

"Bartleby the Scrivener"

"The Confidence Man"

"Billy Budd"

Benito Cereno

Walt Whitman (1819–1892)

"I Sing the Body Electric"

"Cavalry Crossing a Ford"

"A Noiseless Patient Spider"

"O Captain! My Captain!"

Emily Dickinson (1830–1886)

> "'Tis little I could care for pearls"
>
> "Hope is a subtle glutton"
>
> "I'll tell you how the sun rose"
>
> "Forbidden fruit a flavor has"
>
> "My life closed twice before its close"
>
> "A narrow fellow in the grass"
>
> "The brain is wider than the sky"
>
> "The mountain sat upon the plain"
>
> "Heart, we will forget him!"
>
> "The bat is dun with wrinkled wings"
>
> "Of bronze and blaze"
>
> "Death is like the insect"
>
> "So Proud she was to die"
>
> "I heard a fly buzz when I died"

Louisa May Alcott (1832–1888)

> *Little Women*
>
> *Behind a Mask: or, A Woman's Power*

Horatio Alger (1832–1899)

> *The Cash Boy*
>
> *Ragged Dick*

Samuel Clemens (Mark Twain) (1835–1910)

> *The Adventures of Huckleberry Finn*
>
> *The Adventures of Tom Sawyer*
>
> *A Connecticut Yankee in King Arthur's Court*
>
> *The Innocents Abroad*
>
> *The Prince and the Pauper*

Bret Harte (1836–1902)

"The Outcasts of Poker Flat"

"The Luck of Roaring Camp"

"Tennessee's Partner"

William Dean Howells (1837–1920)

The Rise of Silas Lapham

The Day of Their Wedding

The Shadow of a Dream

Ambrose Bierce (1842–1914?)

"The Boarded Window"

"An Occurrence at Owl Creek Bridge"

My Favorite Murder

The Devil's Dictionary

Fantastic Fables

Henry James (1843–1916)

The American

The Europeans

The Portrait of a Lady

The Turn of the Screw

George Washington Cable (1844–1925)

"Old Creole Days"

"The Freedman's Case in Equity"

Joel Chandler Harris (1848–1902)

"The Wonderful Tar-Baby Story"

"How Mr. Rabbit Was Too Sharp for Mr. Fox"

"Miss Cow Falls a Victim to Mr. Rabbit"

"Why the Negro Is Black"

"Spirits Seen and Unseen"

Sarah Orne Jewett (1849–1909)

The Country of the Pointed Firs

A Dunnet Shepherdess

The Foreigner

In Dark New England Days

James Whitcomb Riley (1849–1916)

"Afterwhiles"

"Armazindy"

"The Flying Islands of the Night"

Kate Chopin (1851–1904)

"The Awakening"

"The Storm"

"The Story of an Hour"

"Bayou Folk"

Booker T. Washington (1856–1915)

"Up from Slavery"

"The Future of the American Negro"

Charles W. Chesnutt (1858–1932)

Baxter's Procrustes

The Colonel's Dream

The Conjure Woman

The Marrow of Tradition

Hot-Foot Hannibal

Charlotte Perkins Gilman (1860–1935)

    "The Yellow Wallpaper"

    Herland

Hamlin Garland (1860–1940)

    "Prairie Folks"

    "Main-Travelled Roads"

O. Henry (William Sydney Porter) (1862–1910)

    Cabbages and Kings

    The Heart of the West

    Options

    Roads of Destiny

    The Voice of the City

    Whirligigs

Edith Wharton (1862–1937)

    The Age of Innocence

    The House of Mirth

    Ethan Fromme

William Edward Burghardt (W. E. B.) DuBois (1868–1963)

    "The Souls of Black Folk"

Edwin Arlington Robinson (1869–1935)

    "Three Quatrains"

    "Richard Cory"

    Merlin

    The Town Down the River

Booth Tarkington (1869–1946)

>*Alice Adams*
>
>*The Conquest of Canaan*
>
>*The Flirt*
>
>*Penrod*
>
>*Seventeen*

Edgar Lee Masters (1869–1950)

>"The Hill"
>
>"Lucinda Matlock"
>
>"Knowlt Hoheimer"
>
>"Fiddler Jones"
>
>"Race Suicide"
>
>"Hail! Master Death!"

Frank Norris (1870–1902)

>*The Octopus*
>
>*McTeague*
>
>*Blix*
>
>*The Pit: A Story of Chicago*

Stephen Crane (1871–1900)

>*The Red Badge of Courage*
>
>*Maggie: A Girl of the Streets*

Theodore Dreiser (1871–1845)

>*An American Tragedy*
>
>*Sister Carrie*

Willa Cather (1873–1947)

Alexander's Bridge

My Antonia

Death Comes to the Archbishop

O Pioneers!

The Professor's House

The Song of the Lark

Amy Lowell (1874–1925)

"Before the Altar"

"Azure and Gold"

"Venetian Glass"

"Fatigue"

"Roads"

"Teatro Bambino"

"Frankincense and Myrrh"

Robert Frost (1874–1963)

"Stars"

"Mending Wall"

"The Death of the Hired Man"

"Home Burial"

"The Wood-pile"

"The Road Not Taken"

"Birches"

"Fire and Ice"

"Stopping by Woods on a Snowy Evening"

Gertrude Stein (1874–1946)

Tender Buttons

Three Lives

The Making of Americans

The Autobiography of Alice B. Toklas

Portraits and Prayers

Owen Davis (1874–1956)

The Detour

Icebound

I'd Like to Do It Again

Nellie: The Beautiful Cloak Model

Edgar Rice Burroughs (1875–1950)

Tarzan of the Apes

The Gods of Mars

The Land That Time Forgot

The Warlord of Mars

Jack London (1876–1916)

"To Build a Fire"

The Call of the Wild

"The Inevitable White Man"

Sherwood Anderson (1876–1941)

Winesburg, Ohio

Upton Sinclair (1878–1968)

The Jungle

The Profits of Religion

Vachel Lindsay (1879–1931)

    "The Flower-Fed Buffaloes"

    "Abraham Lincoln Walks at Midnight"

    "The Leaden-Eyed"

    "The North Star Whispers to the Blacksmith's Son"

    "The Congo"

    "General William Booth Enters into Heaven"

Wallace Stevens (1878–1955)

    "Disillusionment of Ten O'Clock"

    "The Snow Man"

    "Sunday Morning"

    "The Emperor of Ice Cream"

    "Thirteen Ways of Looking at a Blackbird"

    "Anecdote of the Jar"

    "The Idea of Order at Key West"

James Branch Cabell (1879–1958)

    The Certain Hour

    The Eagle's Shadow

    The Cream of the Jest

    Jurgen

    First Gentleman of America

Carl Sandburg (1878–1967)

    "Prairie Waters by Night"

    "Adelaide Crapsey"

    "Portrait of a Motor Car"

    "Leather Leggings"

"Always the Mob"

"Near Keokuk"

"In Tall Grass"

"Chicago"

"Mill-Doors"

"Skyscraper"

"Murmurings in a Field Hospital"

William Carlos Williams (1883–1963)

"Berket and the Stars"

"April"

"This Is Just to Say"

"Spring and All"

"The Red Wheelbarrow"

"A Sort of Song"

"The Use of Force"

Sara Teasdale (1884–1933)

"The Long Hill"

"Barter"

"Peace"

"Dooryard Roses"

"Water Lilies"

"Night Wind at Amalfi"

Flame and Shadow

Rivers to the Sea

Ring Lardner (1885–1933)

"Haircut"

Sinclair Lewis (1885–1951)

Main Street

Babbitt

Dodsworth

Arrowsmith

Ezra Pound (1885–1972)

"In a Station of the Metro"

"Sestina: Altaforte"

"Ballad of the Goodley Fere"

H. D. (Hilda Doolittle) (1886–1961)

Sea Garden

Robinson Jeffers (1887–1962)

Poems

Marianne Moore (1887–1972)

"Silence"

"Poetry"

"The Paper Nautilus"

"Baseball and Writing"

Eugene O'Neill (1888–1953)

Beyond the Horizon

Long Day's Journey into Night

Mourning Becomes Electra

The Iceman Cometh

Desire Under the Elms

The Hairy Ape

Maxwell Anderson (1888–1959)

"Winterset"

"Key Largo"

Raymond Chandler (1888–1959)

The Big Sleep

Farewell, My Lovely

The Long Goodbye

John Crowe Ransom (1888–1974)

"Emily Hardcastle, Spinster"

"Survey of Literature"

"Captain Carpenter"

"The Tall Girl"

"Antique Harvesters"

"Painted Head"

Conrad Aiken (1889–1973)

"Bread and Music"

"Rimbaud and Verlaine"

"The Walk in the Garden"

Hervey Allen (1889–1949)

Anthony Adverse

The City in the Dawn

The Forest and the Fort

Toward the Morning

Fannie Hurst (1889–1968)

>*Just Around the Corner*
>
>*We Are Ten*
>
>*Gaslight Sonatas*

Conrad Richter (1890–1968)

>*The Trees*
>
>*The Fields*
>
>*The Sea of Grass*
>
>*The Town*
>
>*The Light in the Forest*

Henry Miller (1891–1980)

>*Tropic of Cancer*
>
>*Tropic of Capricorn*

Edna St. Vincent Millay (1892–1950)

>"Renascence"
>
>"Tavern"
>
>"Ashes of Life"
>
>"Sorrowful Dreams"
>
>"Once More into My Arid Days"
>
>"Night Is My Sister"
>
>"The Cameo"
>
>"Bluebeard"

Robert P. Tristram Coffin (1892–1955)

>"Foxes and Graves"
>
>"This Is My Country"
>
>"The Cupola"

Archibald MacLeish (1892–1982)

"Voyage West"

"Ars Poetica"

J.B.

Pearl S. Buck (1892–1973)

The Good Earth

The Proud Heart

Command the Morning

The Living Reed

Dashiell Hammett (1894–1962)

Red Harvest

The Maltese Falcon

The Glass Key

The Thin Man

e. e. cummings (1894–1962)

"anyone lived in a pretty how town"

"Buffalo Bill's"

"in Just-"

"maggie and millie and molly and may"

"somewhere i have never travelled, gladly beyond"

"Spring is like a perhaps hand"

"what if a much of a which of a wind"

"the Cambridge Ladies Who Live in Furnished Souls"

"r-p-o-p-h-e-s-s-a-g-r"

"why must itself up every of a park"

Jean Toomer (1894–1967)

> "Becky"
>
> "Seventh Street"
>
> "Bona and Paul"
>
> "Her Lips Are Copper Wire"
>
> "The Lost Dancer"

Katherine Anne Porter (1894–1980)

> *Ship of Fools*
>
> *Noon Wine*
>
> *Pale Horse, Pale Rider*
>
> "The Jilting of Granny Weatherall"
>
> "Flowering Judas"

F. Scott Fitzgerald (1896–1940)

> *The Great Gatsby*
>
> *Tender Is the Night*

Robert Sherwood (1896–1955)

> *Abe Lincoln in Illinois*
>
> *The Petrified Forest*
>
> *Idiot's Delight*
>
> *The Love Nest*
>
> *There Shall Be No Night*
>
> *Roosevelt and Hopkins*

John Dos Passos (1896–1970)

> *U.S.A.*
>
> *Manhattan Transfer*

William Faulkner (1897–1962)

The Sound and the Fury

As I Lay Dying

"A Rose for Emily"

Louise Bogan (1897–1970)

Dark Summer

The Sleeping Fury

Collected Poems

Thornton Wilder (1897–1975)

Our Town

The Bridge of San Luis Rey

Stephen Vincent Benet (1898–1943)

"The Drug-Shop; or, Endymion in Edmonstoun"

"Rain After a Vaudeville Show"

"Dinner in a Quick Lunch Room"

"The Fiddling Wood"

John Brown's Body

The Devil and Daniel Webster

Malcolm Cowley (1898–1989)

A Dry Season

The Literary Situation

Hart Crane (1899–1932)

"To a Brooklyn Bridge"

"The Broken Tower"

"The Hurricane"

Ernest Hemingway (1899–1961)

    "A Clean, Well-Lighted Place"

    The Sun Also Rises

    A Farewell to Arms

    The Old Man and the Sea

Allen Tate (1899–1979)

    "Ode to the Confederate Dead"

    "The Mediterranean"

Thomas Wolfe (1900–1938)

    Look Homeward, Angel

    You Can't Go Home Again

Margaret Mitchell (1900–1949)

    Gone with the Wind

Oliver LaFarge (1901–1963)

    Laughing Boy

    Tribes and Temples

    The Enemy Gods

Langston Hughes (1902–1967)

    "The Weary Blues"

    "Harlem"

    "Song for a Dark Girl"

John Steinbeck (1902–1968)

    The Grapes of Wrath

    Of Mice and Men

    Tortilla Flat

The Red Pony

Cannery Row

Ogden Nash (1902–1971)

"The Sniffle"

"A Watched Example Never Boils"

"The Clean Platter"

"The Party"

"A Lady Thinks She Is Thirty"

"Riding on a Railroad Train"

"Shorts"

Countee Cullen (1903–1946)

"Heritage"

"The Wise"

"That Bright Chimeric Beast"

"Incident"

"Saturday's Child"

"Fruit of the Flower"

"The Loss of Love"

"From the Dark Tower"

Zora Neale Hurston (1903–1960)

Their Eyes Were Watching God

"Sweat"

James Gould Cozzens (1903–1978)

Michael Scarlett

The Last Adam

Guard of Honor

By Love Possessed

Erskine Caldwell (1903–1987)

Tobacco Road

God's Little Acre

Clare Booth Luce (1903–1987)

The Women

Kiss the Boys Goodbye

Margin for Error

John O'Hara (1905–1970)

Appointment in Samarra

Butterfield 8

Robert Penn Warren (1905–1989)

All the King's Men

Stanley Kunitz (1905–2006)

"The Science of the Night"

"Robin Redbreast"

"The Round"

"Touch Me"

"The Testing-Tree"

"The Portrait"

Clifford Odets (1906–1963)

Waiting for Lefty

Golden Boy

Awake and Sing

The Big Knife

The Country Girl

Sidney Kingsley (1906–1975)

Men in White

Dead End

Detective Story

Darkness at Noon

W. H. Auden (1907–1973)

"This Lunar Beauty"

"As I Walked Out One Evening"

"Musée des Beaux Arts"

"The Unknown Citizen"

"In Praise of Limestone"

Richard Wright (1908–1960)

Native Son

Black Boy

Theodore Roethke (1908–1963)

"Elegy for Jane"

"I Knew a Woman"

"My Papa's Waltz"

"In a Dark Time"

"The Waking"

William Saroyan (1908–1981)

The Human Comedy

James Agee (1909–1955)

A Death in the Family

Let Us Now Praise Famous Men

Eudora Welty (1909–2001)

The Ponder Heart

A Curtain of Green

"A Worn Path"

"A Still Moment"

Elizabeth Bishop (1911–1979)

"Filling Station"

"The Bight"

"Lullaby for the Cat"

"The Shampoo"

"In the Waiting Room"

"One Art"

"The Moose"

Tennessee Williams (1911–1983)

The Glass Menagerie

A Streetcar Named Desire

Cat on a Hot Tin Roof

The Rose Tattoo

Suddenly Last Summer

The Night of the Iguana

John Cheever (1912–1982)

"The Death of Justina"

"The Fourth Alarm"

Bullet Park

The Wapshot Chronicle

Robert Hayden (1913–1980)

"Those Winter Sundays"

"Full Moon"

"Middle Passage"

"The Whipping"

Karl Shapiro (1913–2000)

"The First Time"

"You Lay Above Me"

Randall Jarrell (1914–1965)

"Next Day"

John Berryman (1914–1972)

"The Ball Poem"

"Dream Song 1"

"Dream Song 4"

"Dream Song 13"

"Dream Song 29"

Bernard Malamud (1914–1986)

The Assistant

The Fixer

The Magic Barrel

John Hersey (1914–1993)

A Bell for Adano

Hiroshima

The War Lover

White Lotus

William Burroughs (1914–1997)

Naked Lunch

Ralph Ellison (1914–1994)

Invisible Man

Saul Bellow (1915–2005)

The Adventures of Augie March

Herzog

Mr. Sammler's Planet

Arthur Miller (1915–2005)

All My Sons

Death of a Salesman

The Crucible

After the Fall

A View from the Bridge

The Price

Herman Wouk (1915–)

The Caine Mutiny

Marjorie Morningstar

Youngblood Hawke

Don't Stop the Carnival

Walker Percy (1916–1990)

The Moviegoer

Horton Foote (1916–)

The Trip to Bountiful

The Young Man from Atlanta

Robert Lowell (1917–1977)

"Father's Bedroom"

"A Quaker Graveyard in Nantucket"

Carson McCullers (1917–1967)

Reflections in a Golden Eye

The Heart Is a Lonely Hunter

Member of the Wedding

The Ballad of the Sad Cafe

Gwendolyn Brooks (1917–2000)

"The Bean Eaters"

"We Real Cool"

"Sadie and Maud"

"Kitchenette Building"

J. D. Salinger (1919–)

Catcher in the Rye

Lawrence Ferlinghetti (1919–)

"Pictures of the Gone World"

"A Coney Island of the Mind"

"Short Story on a Painting of Gustav Klimt"

"Sometime During Eternity"

"Baseball Canto"

"Dog"

Howard Nemerov (1920–1991)

"Because You Asked About the Line Between Prose and Poetry"

"Definition"

"Trees"

"Learning by Doing"

"The Great Gull"

Ray Bradbury (1920–)

The Martian Chronicles

Fahrenheit 451

James Jones (1921–1977)

From Here to Eternity

Some Came Running

The Pistol

The Thin Red Line

Richard Wilbur (1921–)

"In the Smoking Car"

"Bone Key"

"Compulsions"

"Boy at the Window"

Jack Kerouac (1922–1969)

On the Road

About On the Road

The Subterraneans

Kurt Vonnegut (1922–)

Slaughterhouse-Five

Breakfast of Champions

Anthony Hecht (1923–2004)

"Chorus from Oedipus at Colonos"

"The Transparent Man"

Joseph Heller (1923–1999)

Catch-22

Denise Levertov (1923–1997)

"The Secret"

"Variation and Reflection on a Theme by Rilke"

"The Ache of Marriage"

"People at Night"

"Remembering"

Norman Mailer (1923–)

The Naked and the Dead

The Armies of the Night

Truman Capote (1924–1984)

Other Voices, Other Rooms

In Cold Blood

Breakfast at Tiffany's

James Baldwin (1924–1987)

Go Tell It on the Mountain

Notes of a Native Son

The Fire Next Time

Flannery O'Connor (1925–1964)

Wise Blood

"The Geranium"

"The Artificial Nigger"

"A Good Man Is Hard to Find"

Maxine Kumin (1925–)

"In the Park"

"Woodchucks"

Gore Vidal (1925–)

Williwaw

The City and the Pillar

A Search for the King

The Judgment of Paris

Visit to a Small Planet

The Best Man

William Styron (1925–2006)

The Confessions of Nat Turner

Lie Down in Darkness

Alan Ginsberg (1926–1997)

"Howl"

"Kaddish"

"Sunflower Sutra"

Robert Creeley (1926–2005)

"Four Days in Vermont"

"Nothing New"

"Goodbye"

"Ballad of the Despairing Husband"

"The Conspiracy"

Donald Justice (1926–2004)

"The Assassination"

Harper Lee (1926–)

To Kill a Mockingbird

James Merrill (1926–1995)

"Lost in Translation"

"The Changing Light at Sandover"

W. D. Snodgrass (1926–)

"April Inventory"

"Heart's Needle"

John Ashbery (1927–)

"Some Trees"

"Faust"

"Forties Flick"

"For John Clare"

James Wright (1927–1980)

"Autumn Begins in Martin's Ferry, Ohio"

"Beginning"

W. S. Merwin (1927–)

"Yesterday"

"My Friends"

"Beggars and Kings"

"For the Anniversary of My Death"

"Some Last Questions"

Anne Sexton (1928–1974)

> "Her Kind"
>
> "My Friend, My Friend"

Edward Albee (1928–)

> *The Zoo Story*
>
> *Who's Afraid of Virginia Woolf?*
>
> *A Delicate Balance*
>
> *Tiny Alice*
>
> *Seascape*
>
> *Three Tall Women*

Maya Angelou (1928–)

> "Phenomenal Women"
>
> "When You Come to Me"
>
> "Poor Girl"
>
> "Woman Work"
>
> "Where We Belong, A Duet"
>
> "Come, and Be My Baby"
>
> "Still I Rise"
>
> "The Lie"

William Kennedy (1928–)

> *Ironweed*

Philip Levine (1928–)

> "Animals Are Passing from Our Lives"
>
> "They Feed They Lion"
>
> "Salts and Oils"

"Gin"

"What Work Is"

Ursula LeGuin (1929–)

The Lathe of Heaven

Dancing at the Edge of the World

The Dispossessed

Adrienne Rich (1929–)

"Miracle Ice Cream"

"In Those Years"

"For the Dead"

"From a Survivor"

"From Two Songs"

Lorraine Hansberry (1930–1965)

A Raisin in the Sun

John Barth (1930–)

The Sot-Weed Factor

Giles Goat-Boy

Lost in the Funhouse

Donald Barthelme (1931–1989)

"The Piano Player"

"Some of Us Had Been Threatening Our Friend Colby"

E. L. Doctorow (1931–)

The Book of Daniel

Ragtime

Billy Bathgate

Loon Lake

Waterworks

Toni Morrison (1931–)

Beloved

The Bluest Eye

Song of Solomon

Tom Wolfe (1931–)

The Electric Kool-Aid Acid Test

The Right Stuff

Sylvia Plath (1932–1963)

The Bell Jar

"Daddy"

"Two Sisters of Persephone"

"Lady Lazarus"

"Metaphors"

"Mad Girl's Love Song"

"Mushrooms"

"The Colossus"

"Paralytic"

"Virgin in a Tree"

John Updike (1932–)

Rabbit Run

Rabbit Redux

The Centaur

Cormac McCarthy (1933–)

>*The Orchard Keeper*
>
>*Outer Dark*
>
>*Child of God*
>
>*Blood Meridian; or, the Evening Redness in the West*
>
>*All the Pretty Horses*

Philip Roth (1933–)

>*Portnoy's Complaint*
>
>*Goodbye, Columbus*
>
>*American Pastoral*

Imamu Amiri Baraka (LeRoi Jones) (1934–)

>*Dutchman*

Natachee Scott Momaday (1934–)

>*House Made of Dawn*

Carol Shields (1935–)

>*The Stone Diaries*

Annie Proulx (1935–)

>*The Shipping News*
>
>*Bedrock*

John Kennedy Toole (1937–1969)

>*A Confederacy of Dunces*

Claude Brown (1937–)

>*Manchild in the Promised Land*

Arthur Kopit (1937–)

Oh Dad, Poor Dad, Mamma's Hung You in the Closet and I'm Feelin' So Sad

Indians

The Day the Whores Came Out to Play Tennis

Thomas Pynchon (1937–)

The Crying of Lot 49

Gravity's Rainbow

Lanford Wilson (1937–)

Lemon Sky

Raymond Carver (1938–1988)

Short Stories

Joyce Carol Oates (1938–)

Them

"Where Are You Going, Where Have You Been?"

Charles Simic (1938–)

"The Wooden Toy"

"Everything's Forseeable"

"Against Winter"

"In the Fourth Year"

"He Held the Beast"

"I Was Stolen"

"Miracle Glass Co."

Anne Tyler (1941–)

Breathing Lessons

Nikki Giovanni (1943–)

"That Day"

"Communication"

Louise Gluck (1943–)

"The Silver Lily"

"Circe's Power"

"Confession"

"Celestial Music"

James Tate (1943–)

"More Later, Less the Same"

"The Wrong Way Home"

"Happy As the Day Is Long"

"The Definition of Gardening"

"The New Ergonomics"

"Days of Pie and Coffee"

"Restless Leg Syndrome"

Richard Ford (1944–)

Independence Day

Alice Walker (1944–)

The Color Purple

August Wilson (1945–)

The Piano Lesson

Fences

Robert Olen Butler (1945–)

> "Love"
>
> "Fairy Tale"
>
> "Missing"
>
> "Salem"

David Mamet (1947–)

> *Glengarry Glen Ross*
>
> *Speed the Plow*

Jane Smiley (1949–)

> *A Thousand Acres*
>
> *Moo*

Jorie Graham (1951–)

> "The Surface"
>
> "Le Manteau de Pascal"
>
> "Manteau Three"

Rita Dove (1952–)

> "My Mother Enters the Work Force"
>
> "Lady Freedom Among Us"
>
> "The Slave's Critique of Practical Reason"
>
> "Flirtation"
>
> "The Yellow House on the Corner"
>
> "Adolescence I"
>
> "Hade's Pitch"
>
> "The Fish in the Stone"
>
> "Used"

"History"

"Afield"

Tony Kushner (1956–)

Angels in America

Postcolonial Literature in English

Finally, here's a reading list of works written in English in countries other than England and America. This list is highly selective, including only some of the best-known writers. This is all the more the case since new writers keep emerging all the time!

Africa

Nadine Gordimer (1923–)

July's People

Amos Tutuola (1920–1997)

The Palm Wine Drunkard

Chinua Achebe (1930–)

Things Fall Apart

Flora Nwapa (1931–)

Efuru

Wole Soyinka (1934–)

Death and the King's Horseman

Ngugi Wa Thiong'o (1938–)

Devil on the Cross

J. M. Coetzee (1940–)

Waiting for the Barbarians

Ama Ata Aidoo (1942–)

Our Sister Killjoy

Buchi Emecheta (1944–)

The Joys of Motherhood

Ben Okri (1959–)

The Famished Road

Australia

David Malouf (1934)

Remembering Babylon

Peter Carey (1943–)

The Unusual Life of Tristan Smith

The Caribbean

Jean Rhys (1890–1979)

Wide Sargasso Sea

George Lamming (1927–)

In the Castle of My Skin

Derek Walcott (1930–)

Another Life

Omeros

V. S. Naipaul (1932–)

The Mimic Men

A Bend in the River

Michelle Cliff (1946–)

No Telephone to Heaven

Jamaica Kincaid (1947–)

Annie John

Lucy

Edwidge Danticat (1969-)

Breath, Eyes, Memory

The Farming of Bones

South Asia

R. K. Narayan (1906–2001)

Man-Eater of Malgudi

Raja Rao (1908–2006)

Kanthapura

Kamala Markandaya (1924–2004)

Nectar in a Sieve

Ruth Jhabvala (1927–)

Heat and Dust

Michael Ondaatje (1943–)

The English Patient

Salman Rushdie (1947–)

The Satanic Verses

Midnight's Children

Rohinton Mistry (1952–)

A Fine Balance

Arundhati Roy (1961–)

The God of Small Things

Index

C

E

O

Check Out These
Best-Sellers

Grammar and Style SECOND EDITION
978-1-59257-115-4
$16.95

Buying & Selling a Home FIFTH EDITION
978-1-59257-458-2
$19.95

Being a Groom THIRD EDITION
978-1-59257-451-3
$9.95

Learning Spanish FOURTH EDITION
978-1-59257-485-8
$24.95

Investing THIRD EDITION
978-1-59257-480-3
$19.95

Baby Sign Language
978-1-59257-469-8
$14.95

Total Nutrition FOURTH EDITION
978-1-59257-439-1
$18.95

Positive Dog Training SECOND EDITION
978-1-59257-483-4
$14.95

The Bible THIRD EDITION
978-1-59257-389-9
$18.95

Calculus SECOND EDITION
978-1-59257-471-1
$18.95

Music Theory SECOND EDITION
978-1-59257-437-7
$19.95

The Perfect Resume FOURTH EDITION
978-1-59257-463-6
$14.95

Playing the Guitar SECOND EDITION
978-0-02864244-4
$21.95

Manga Illustrated
978-1-59257-335-6
$19.95

Knitting & Crocheting Illustrated THIRD EDITION
978-1-59257-491-9
$19.95

More than *450 titles* available at booksellers and online retailers everywhere

www.idiotsguides.com

ALPHA